Last Doctor
out of Biafra

The War Zone Journal

of Dr Ann Jackson

edited by

JOANNA & WILLIAM STORRAR

British Library Cataloguing in Publication Data:

a catalogue record for this publication

is available from the British Library

ISBN   978-1-912052-47-9

© Handsel Press 2019

Typeset in 11.5pt Minion Pro
at Haddington, Scotland

Printed by Bell and Bain, Glasgow

The photograph on the front cover shows Ann Jackson fleeing from the
advancing Nigerian army to Uli for her rescue flight out of the country on
January 10th 1970, half an hour before the President of Biafra flew into exile
from the same airstrip.

Contents

For all those who stood by their missionary doctor in a war zone,
especially the Jackson family and Ann's friends in Carluke and Biafra

Acknowledgements

Without the literary and editing skills of Will and Joanna, their commitment and their knowledge of the publishing world this manuscript may never have gone to press. I do appreciate all the hard work they have done, in spite of their own busy schedules and I do thank them for their kindness and care for me during this traumatic time going back through the events in the journal.

Dr Ann W Jackson MRCOG

When Dr Ann Jackson asked if we could help to publish her journal, she did more than entrust us with these precious pages of her life in Biafra. She opened her heart to us, bravely re-living what remains a traumatic memory of harrowing times. Yet she also told us an inspiring story of God's presence with her as she walked through this valley of the shadow of death. Our prayer is that these leaves from her journal will be for the healing of the nations from Nigeria to Scotland and a witness to Christ, which is Ann's own prayer for her book.

The publication of Ann's journal would not have happened without the encouragement of her friend Joy Fraser. We are deeply indebted to Joy and to Liz Barthram for carefully scanning the journal's pages for our transcription and editing. And we are grateful to our graphic designer Debra Trisler and publisher Jock Stein of the Handsel Press for turning the journal into this book with its accompanying maps and illustrations.

With Ann's agreement, we have made minor edits to the original text of her journal for publication purposes. We have kept Ann's spelling of 'Ibo', the name of the majority ethnic group in Biafra typically used at the time, but followed the contemporary convention of spelling it 'Igbo' in our commentary.

We commend Ann's journal to a wider readership with love for its author and thanksgiving for her ministry of healing. Dr Ann Jackson surely meets the theologian David Cairns' definition of a saint – someone who makes it easier to believe in God.

Joanna and William Storrar, Editors

THE HOLY SPIRIT IS FORGIVENESS.
—WILLIAM BLAKE

Sunday, 27th. August 1967.

"Create in me a clean heart, O God; and renew a right spirit within me."

Sunday, a new day, first day of the week and first day in a new chapter of my life. Why today? Because I don't want to drift anymore — I want to go forward gripped by the love of God and fired with zeal and power. I want to be used by God and to be used I must give my whole self to Him. To lose my self-centredness, my laziness, my lack of concern and be filled with Christ and a passion for souls.

Why do we drift, why do we let go Christ's hand, why do we try to "go it alone" when we know all the time that "He alone can satisfy", when we know that He is the One who brings joy and love into our lives.

Why do we play on God's mercy, His love and forgiveness — He is so patient and loving and He watches over us so carefully. Yet we continue to drift, knowing that He is there, that He loves us, that He is waiting for us.

There can be no excuse for us to drift!

"God forgive me for drifting, for not yielding my whole self to Thee, for not clasping Christ's hand tightly. I thank Thee, O God, for keeping

The first entry in the journal Ann kept as a missionary doctor in Biafra, 1967-1970

2

Foreword

Introducing Dr Ann Jackson and her Biafran Journal

On the evening of the 10th of January 1970, the President of Biafra flew into exile from his shrinking country's only airstrip at Uli. No more than a short stretch of road, it was his last avenue of escape from the advancing Federal army and the collapsing republic that he had led since 1967 as a breakaway state from the rest of Nigeria. Just half an hour before the Biafran airliner departed with its defeated leader, a smaller plane had flown out of the same airstrip. On board were the last medical missionaries airlifted out of Biafra by the World Council of Churches. Among them was a Scottish doctor called Ann Jackson.

This is Ann's story. She tells it here in her own words in the journal she kept in the war zone that was Biafra. She was there to the end. It is not a heroic tale of triumph. Ann left Biafra in poor health and feeling a failure as a missionary. This conviction haunted her in the years that followed, first as a missionary doctor again with the Church of Scotland in Malawi and then as a senior partner in the local medical practice in her native Carluke in Lanarkshire. It was my privilege to get to know Ann there. She was a much-loved GP in the community and a deeply respected Elder in St John's Carluke, where I was parish minister.

At first, I knew nothing of Ann's years as a young missionary doctor in wartime Biafra. Our collaboration started through her life of prayer for healing which she exercised alongside her work as a medical doctor. Within weeks of my induction as minister of St John's, Ann asked if she could start a healing service in the church. I agreed and we began a monthly service of prayers for healing in the mid-1980s. Ann has now run it continuously in St John's for over thirty years, with the support of all my successors as ministers of this amazing congregation.

One evening after we began these healing services, I called at Ann's home on a routine pastoral visit. It turned out to be anything but routine. She told me how moved she had been by a hymn tune we had sung in church the previous Sunday. It was the tune *Finlandia* by the composer Sibelius. It was also the tune to which we sang the national anthem of Biafra, she said, before showing me a well-worn notebook. It was the journal she had kept during her time as a medical missionary in that war-torn country. Biafra became a byword in those years for mass starvation amid the atrocities of civil war. For the first time, the nightly television news showed horrifying film coverage of skeletal infants and children with swollen bellies, dying of hunger in their thousands. Ann had been there from almost the beginning to the very end of Biafra's short life as an independent state, caring for these innocent and suffering victims of war as a missionary doctor. Hearing *Finlandia* in church brought back too many painful memories for her. Ann was going to burn the journal, she told me, if I hadn't happened to call that evening. I sat and listened as Ann quietly and modestly told me her story of living through one of the worst wars in postcolonial Africa.

Nigeria had declared its independence from Britain in 1960. It was a federal state whose arbitrary borders had been drawn by the colonial occupiers. The majority Muslim North had been stuck together with the predominantly Christian South of this large West African country. Nigeria's early history as an independent nation was marred by a military coup in January 1966, led mainly by Southern army officers, and a second, counter coup in July of that year, led by Northern army officers. These two coups in swift succession exacerbated existing inter-ethnic and North-South tensions in Nigeria. A series of massacres of Igbos living in the Northern Region in May, July, and September 1966 culminated in a mass exodus of terrified Igbos to their own Eastern Region. This was matched on a smaller scale by the massacre and flight of Hausa and other tribal Northerners living at the time in the East of the country. Within the Eastern region itself, the other ethnic groups such as the Efik and Ibibios were just as wary of the locally dominant Igbo people. Faced with this political crisis and these cross-cutting ethnic tensions, Colonel Ojukwu, the Governor of the Eastern Region, declared its independence from the rest of Nigeria on the 30th of May 1967. It was hoped the Republic of Biafra would provide a safe haven from ethnic slaughter, win international recognition as a sovereign state, and negotiate peace with its Nigerian neighbour. It was not to be.

From July 1967 to January 1970 the well-equipped Nigerian forces attacked Biafra by land, sea, and air. They captured Biafra's capital Enugu and seaport of Calabar by October of 1967. The Federal Military Government under General Gowan assumed its victory over the rebel state would be swift and soon. Again, it was not to be. Subject to aerial bombing, lacking in military hardware and trained armed forces, quickly losing its rich oilfields, and facing mass starvation through an effective blockade, somehow the fledgling republic fought on to defend its shrinking landmass through two more years of spirited resistance and night-time airlifts of food and arms. Then, with Ojukwu's own night flight as head of state and his successor's surrender the following day, Biafra ceased to be on the 11th of January 1970. The final toll of the conflict is staggering, with conservative estimates of a million deaths from starvation and disease alone. And through it all, Ann Jackson chose to stay and serve as a doctor in the ever diminishing Biafran state from September 1967 to its very last days in January 1970. Listening to Ann's story on that evening in her home in Carluke, I learned why.

Told at high school she should aim to be a nurse, not the doctor she felt God calling her to be, this devout daughter of a close and loving family in a small Lanarkshire town was having none of it. God was calling her to be a missionary and would open a way for her. Ann went on to study medicine at Glasgow University and then applied to be a missionary with the Church of Scotland. Still a young woman in her twenties, she was accepted and sent to Nigeria as a medical missionary in the spring of 1966. The Scottish Presbyterian churches had carried out missionary work in this part of West Africa since the 19th century. Ann's first weeks in her new life were spent at the Mary Slessor Hospital at Itu in Eastern Nigeria. Founded in 1905, the hospital was named after another young Scottish woman in her twenties who heard God's call to spread the Gospel. As a girl in Carluke, Ann had read all about Mary Slessor's life in Africa. The seed planted then was now bearing fruit.

The young Dr Jackson hoped her work as a doctor in caring for the sick would also be a witness for Christ. As the first entries in her journal show, Ann had been nurtured in a warm evangelical faith and was supported by a prayerful circle of family and friends in Carluke, especially Sarah Watson and Frances Cadzow. She was therefore expecting a similarly close fellowship with her missionary colleagues. As Ann records in her journal, she was mentored in her work and inspired in her faith by many dedicated Christian doctors, nurses, administrators and church workers, including May Russell, a missionary deaconess from Carluke. But Ann also learned that a missionary community of diverse personalities could be as fraught with friction as any group of people working together under pressure. Almost from the start, she was caught up in the relentless round of her medical duties, with little time for prayer and Bible study. Within months of her arrival in Nigeria in 1966, Ann was on the frontline of human suffering in the country. She treated the fleeing Igbo victims of violence in the North who made their way to the Queen Elizabeth Hospital in the town of Umuahia where she had been posted. She witnessed at first hand the fear gripping the people of the Eastern Region. It was not the mission field she had imagined. It was to change her life.

When that Eastern Region declared its independence on the 30th of May 1967, Ann was home on leave, recovering from illness and exhaustion after working with little rest as a hospital doctor treating traumatized Igbo refugees fleeing the North. While the Church of Scotland pulled its mission staff with families out of Nigeria as the country descended into civil war in the summer of 1967, many missionaries and doctors chose to stay and served the sick and starving with compassion. Among them were the Holy Ghost priests and Holy Rosary nuns from Ireland, the French doctors who founded *Médicins Sans Frontières*, and Joint Church Aid, nicknamed Jesus Christ Airways due to its blockade-busting relief flights with much-needed food and medicines. Ann was clear in her own mind what she must do. Having cared for the refugees from the North, she was persuaded of the justice of their cause. She chose to return to what was by then Biafra because she supported the newly independent state and wanted to serve its people. While history will remember Winnie Ewing as the young lawyer who changed the face of Scottish politics in 1967, the social history of women in that era is incomplete without the equally remarkable story of the young doctor from Lanarkshire who stood by another small country, a continent away – at the risk of her life, the cost of her health, and the testing of her faith.

The journal you are about to read is Ann's own account of these years. It was written in moments snatched from her ceaseless rounds as an overworked doctor in overcrowded hospitals. It was written when she was all but overwhelmed by the scale of the suffering and the lack of medicines and food supplies to meet it. It was written under shellfire and during bombing raids, as she ran clinics near the warfront and ran for cover in slit trenches in the bush. It was written with a novelist's eye for the comic and the absurd that are also part of war, making this forgotten story of Biafra come alive, fifty years on. And then there were the letters she wrote home to her beloved Mum and Dad and family. We have included some letters here to fill in the missing days and months in the story when Ann had no respite to write in her journal. They were often brief and to the point: "Bombing raid today. But don't worry, Mum, I'm safe." Safe! "My poor mother, what was I thinking," Ann laughs now.

It is important that we hear Ann's laughter as well as her tears in these pages. She made lifelong African friends in the crucible of their ordeal together in hospitals and clinics in a war zone. They love her for saving countless Biafran lives. Her own life has been blessed in turn by their friendship, especially with Victoria Igbokwe and her family. Once, when Ann was sharing her sense of failure with an African friend from those Biafra days, the woman replied, "The important thing Ann was – you were there. You stayed. That was what was important. You stayed with us." As we learn in these pages, so did her Lord.

Ann recounts a clinic at the height of the blockade of Biafra by Nigerian forces in 1968, when thousands of children were dying for lack of food and medicine. A mother asked for her dead child to be tied on her back to look alive so that she could get back to her village. Ann felt she could not go on in the face of such horrors. Yet in that moment of utter despair, she felt somebody beside her. She knew, if she just turned around, she would see Jesus.

When Ann celebrated her 80th birthday with the same loving circle of family and friends in Carluke that stood by her during her years in Biafra, praying, fundraising and sending aid, she knew it was time to publish her journal. It is a testimony not to her failure but to her skill as a doctor, her witness as a missionary, and her gift as a writer. It is a testimony to the Scottish town that stuck by its native daughter in a war zone. It is above all a testimony to Christ's presence with a suffering nation through disciples like Ann Jackson. She was there to the end, the last doctor out of Biafra as its half of a yellow sun set forever.

William Storrar, Easter 2019

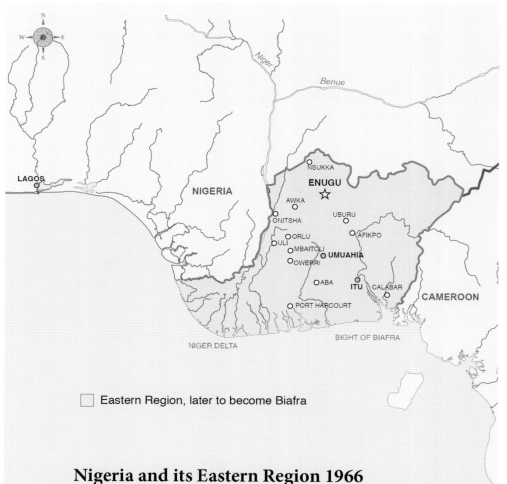

Eastern Region, later to become Biafra

Nigeria and its Eastern Region 1966

After arriving by ship at Lagos, Ann first worked as a
medical missionary in the Eastern Region of Nigeria from
May 1966. She was posted briefly to the Mary Slessor
Hospital at Itu near Calabar and then to the Queen Elizabeth
Hospital in Umuahia, which received the wounded Igbo
refugees fleeing ethnic massacre in the Northern Region.

Timeline
Nigeria and its Eastern Region 1966

1960 –1965	Key Events
1 October 1960	Nigeria declares independence
March 1965	Ann's Dedication Service as a medical missionary in her home congregation, the OS (Original Secession) Church, Carluke
1966	
January	First Military Coup in Nigeria
April	Ann sails from Liverpool to Lagos on ship *Accra*
May	Ann starts work at Mary Slessor Hospital, Itu, Eastern Region, Nigeria
July	Ann moves from Itu to Queen Elizabeth Hospital, Umuahia Second Military Coup in Nigeria
September – October	Massacre of Igbos living in the Northern Region Igbo refugees flee home to the Eastern Region Ann treats wounded refugees fleeing massacre

The journal Ann kept in Biafra, recording her close collaboration
with African colleagues like Caroline, her interpreter with Igbo patients

The Journal 1967

Welcome, True Biafran

"Mr Eme, the Synod Clerk was very pleased to see me and greeted me with, 'Welcome, true Biafran!' I am the first woman missionary to return to the Presbyterian Church."

One of Ann's first journal entries in Biafra, October 1967

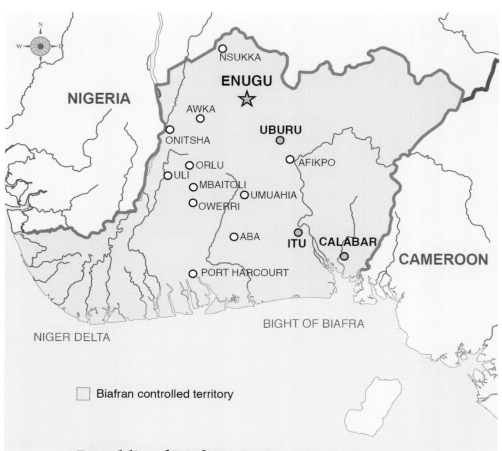

NSUKKA

ENUGU
☆

NIGERIA

AWKA

ONITSHA

UBURU

ORLU
ULI
MBAITOLI
OWERRI
UMUAHIA

AFIKPO

ABA
ITU **CALABAR**

PORT HARCOURT

CAMEROON

BIGHT OF BIAFRA

NIGER DELTA

Biafran controlled territory

Republic of Biafra, 1967

The Eastern Region declared its independence from the rest
of Nigeria in May 1967, while Ann was home on furlough.
The invading Nigerian Federal government forces moved into the
new state's territory in July 1967, and by October, its capital of
Enugu and seaport of Calabar had fallen. Ann returned secretly
to what was by then the Republic of Biafra, arriving in Calabar
from neighbouring Cameroon in late September 1967. She
worked first at the Mary Slessor Hospital in Itu; in November,
she moved to the Presbyterian Joint Hospital in Uburu.

Timeline

Republic of Biafra 1967

1967	Key Events
April	Ann home on furlough, ill and exhausted after her first term working as a missionary doctor in Nigeria's Eastern Region, but planning to return
30th May	Republic of Biafra declares independence from Nigeria
July - August	Nigerian Military Government forces attack Biafra, which resists the invasion with its own poorly equipped army and later counter attack into Nigeria's Mid-Western Region, temporarily capturing Benin City
September	Church of Scotland tells Ann she can return incognito to Biafra Ann travels via London and Paris to Cameroon and overland to Biafra
October	Ann works at Mary Slessor Hospital, Itu, near Calabar Enugu, capital of Biafra, and Calabar captured by Nigerian forces
November	Ann moves to Presbyterian Joint Hospital, Uburu

The Republic of Biafra declared its independence from the rest of Nigeria on the 30th of May 1967. The civil war broke out in July 1967, as Nigerian Federal forces attacked the breakaway state. Ann was on leave in Scotland at the time. She had been recovering at home in Carluke from her first exhausting period as a medical missionary in Nigeria, beginning in May 1966 at the Mary Slessor Hospital at Itu and then moving to the Queen Elizabeth Hospital at Umuahia in the Eastern Region.

Ann had arrived in Nigeria at a time of political instability and ethnic violence. There were two military coups in January and July of that year. By October 1966 she was treating the wounded among the thousands who had fled east after murderous attacks against them as ethnic Igbos living in the Northern Region. These two factors of political crisis and ethnic violence prompted the Governor of the Eastern Region and Igbo homeland, Colonel Ojukwu, to declare independence. Other Eastern ethnic groups were more ambivalent about the new Igbo-led state.

Ann's journal begins in August 1967 when she was at home in Carluke. These first journal entries give us a sense of her spiritual life as a Christian, her life of prayer for healing, and her calling as a missionary. In September 1967 the Church of Scotland told Ann she could return to what had once been the Eastern Region of Nigeria but only incognito. With two colleagues, she flew via Paris to Cameroon in West Africa and then travelled by land in a clandestine journey over the border into Biafra. Apart from periods of sick leave in Scotland, Ann was there to the end.

August 1967

Sunday 27th August

"Create in me a clean heart, O God; and renew a right spirit within me."

Sunday, a new day, first day of the week and first day in a new chapter of my life.

Why today? Because I don't want to drift anymore – I want to go forward gripped by the love of God and fired with zeal and power. I want to be used by God and to be used I must give my whole self to Him. To lose my self-centeredness, my laziness, my lack of concern and be filled with Christ and a passion for souls.

Why do we drift, why do we let go Christ's hand, why do we try to 'go it alone' when we know all the time that "He alone can satisfy", when we know that He is the One who brings joy and love into our lives.

Why do we play on God's mercy, his love and forgiveness – He is so patient and loving and He watches over us so carefully. Yet we continue to drift, knowing that He is there, that He loves us, that he is waiting for us.

There can be no excuse for us to drift! God forgive me for drifting, for not yielding my whole self to Thee, for not clasping Christ's hand tightly. *I thank Thee, O God, for keeping thine own hand firmly on me and for the love of Christ. "O love that wilt not let me go."*

Today I attended the evening service in St George's Tron Parish Church in Glasgow with Sylvia Forrest and her friend Cathie. A tremendous service and I was thrilled to be one of that large congregation – the church was packed to capacity. We could hardly find a seat and there were no Visitors Hymnbooks left! A truly wonderful experience to see so many people crowding in on a Sunday evening to hear the Word of God. An almost unheard of thing in this day and age – what an awful admission! What has happened in our other churches?

We are not preaching Christ – we are not proclaiming the Gospel message. The ministers don't preach it from the pulpit and we hesitate to proclaim it in our words and lives. I remember admitting this many years ago and here I am still pleading guilty to my share yet seemingly no further forward! The sermon tonight struck home.

We were asked to consider Paul and why he spoke and did so much – what was the driving force? Why did he speak with power? Why did he make such an impact on the early church? Paul, himself, gives us the answer. II Corinthians 5, verses 14-21 "For the love of Christ constrains us . . ." I will try to summarize. We were asked to consider –

What Christ did <u>for</u> us

What Christ does <u>through</u> us

1. Christ died for all – left his glory –> became man –> became the servant-man –> became sin itself for us. God himself – who hates sin – takes all this upon Himself. The agony & human suffering is awful yet we were given this new picture of what it must have been for the sinless Christ to have all this sin, degradation and shame thrust upon Him. (Can we ever really grasp this love of Christ? It is so beyond our ken – yet not beyond us!)

2. We became ambassadors for Christ. But only by living henceforth <u>not</u> unto ourselves, but unto Him who died and rose again.

– A new creature – reconciled to God and called to preach the gospel of reconciliation.

And all because of the love of Christ for us – Paul had been gripped by this wonderful love. He yielded to Christ. We were given a picture of the great Yangtse River in China which flows on and passes through between two great banks. It is constrained or hemmed in – 1– it is given depth, no shallowness; 2 – it is given force, i.e. energy and power that can be harnessed and 3 – it is given direction and nothing can make it deviate or go off course.

May the love of Christ constrain me and give me concern for a sick and troubled world. For Christ's sake. Amen

Monday 28th August

John 3, 27: "A man can receive nothing, except it be given him from heaven."

Last night sleep evaded me – I tossed and turned, my head filled with thoughts and strange ideas. I tried to sift them but could not. I felt compelled to rise and go down on my knees before God.

God seemed to say "NOW" – no delay, no excuses, no doubt, no refusal – a new task must begin NOW. I felt compelled to write to dear Sylvia from Aden and I did so remembering Sarah had said that I had not to miss the opportunity to serve God in every way. Allow God to work great things through us although we are afraid of our own weakness, unsure of ourselves – but sure of God.

Do our thoughts and ideas come from God? Sometimes they are too big for us. Thoughts can be so persistent, insistent – nag, nag, nagging until suddenly we cannot push them back, we cannot deny that God is insisting that we act on them – NOW – and we can only yield to His Will. I stayed on my knees last night for almost an hour, and I read JOHN, chapter 3, and verse 27 held me. "A man can receive nothing, except it be given him from heaven."

I then followed a reference to James chapter 1, verse 17: "All good giving and every perfect gift comes from above, from the Father of the lights of heaven." New English Bible

This morning I also read in this first chapter, "Only be sure that you act on the message and do not merely listen; for that would be to mislead yourselves."

And this was God's message to me last night and still is today. I must have the faith and courage to take God at his word, to receive His gifts with open hands and to act in Christ's name – to heal through the power of prayer, to continue Christ's ministry of healing. It involves so much – yet Christ was involved. And I cannot deny that God is calling me to some special task.

O God, forgive my frailty, my hesitant and weak attitude, my doubts and fears – which seem only to be for myself. Constrain me, harness the love that is in me, fill me with the love of Christ and send me forth ready, willing and able to do only Thy Will –'THY GRACE IS SUFFICIENT' – in Christ's name I ask this and may all be done for His glory. May Jesus Christ be praised. Amen

Monday 28th August (continued)

John 15: 1-8 "I am the true vine…"

A very happy day – full of the unexpected, full of joy and good tidings – and God was at work in a more real sense to me. Visited Margaret Dean at Hamilton – joy –>3/12 pregnant. Babysitting with Liam in the evening at Crossford. Sarah, Frances & I met for the first time for Bible Study and prayer – true fellowship in Christ. Asked God to make us whole and guide us. So many folk need Christ and we hope to give Him to others but first we must let him permeate our whole selves. Enjoyed reading Sarah's talk on John 15: 1-8. Just right!

Please God cleanse us, accept us and use us. In Jesus' name. Amen

Tuesday 29th August

A quiet day. Read through Mark's Gospel and now must study it with 'The New Bible commentary'. My thoughts have been turned more and more to God and His Presence has become so real. Felt very close to Sarah & Frances tonight and our new Prayer Fellowship at 10 pm.

Wednesday 30th August

Visited Flora in Edinburgh and enjoyed her company. On my way home alone in the car I did feel so close to God, so aware of His Will for us and sure that He will use us in this special way. At 10:30 pm this evening I passed Sarah's lighted window and was thrilled to know that at this very minute she too is in communion with God. We are truly blessed to have this opportunity of working so closely together with God. May we be worthy of His trust in us.

Thursday 31st August

Read J. Cameron Peddie's book 'The Forgotten Talent' [on healing] and really felt that God was, as always, in earnest. I must spend more time in prayer and meditation. Frances & Sarah came this evening but we were not separate or alone, too many interruptions. We had a short Bible Reading and prayer led by dear Sarah who is so close to God and who loves our Lord Jesus so dearly. I feel that Frances must experience God's healing power first – she too has deep faith in our Lord Jesus. May God bless each one of us.

September 1967

Friday 1st September

Today I have been strangely content to be on my own reading quietly. Strange to admit this – when I used to spend so much time in quietness, in reading, in meditation – but for a year or so I have only had spells of wanting to be alone. I was too restless, too keen to be thinking and working things out for myself or, at times, too tired or lazy to think. Now, thanks be to God, I am waiting on Him. My way is committed to Him, once more He has brought me to the foot of the Cross, and the sweet love of the crucified Christ has enveloped me and lifted me. "What a friend we have in Jesus" indeed! "Dear Lord and Father of mankind, forgive our foolish ways; Reclothe us in our rightful minds; in purer lives Thy service find, in deeper reverence, praise." Hymn 245.

Dear Lord Jesus Christ, I do thank Thee this night for Thy love and patience, for bringing me into communion with God, our Father, for bringing me the peace that is beyond understanding and beyond price. Forgive me for so long running from Thee, for not committing my whole self to Thee. Take me now and make me truly Thy disciple, may my witness be ever pleasing to Thee. May God be glorified and Thy dear Self, Christ my Savior, praised. Amen

Saturday 2nd September

Joshua 14:12 "If so be the Lord will be with me, then I shall be able to drive them out . . ."

Hebrews 13: 5&6 "He hath said, I will never leave thee, nor forsake thee . . ."

We are so truly creatures of habit and of moods – up yesterday down today!

In these past few days I have been having quiet times of self examination and prayer, times when God was close and real, times when I was so sure of His Will. He does lead us and makes His Will known to us – through Scripture, through prayer and thoughts, and through people. I believe He has led me to this point. He has made His way known to me – the task is great but so wonderful and I do feel privileged. God has patiently and lovingly guided me. God does indeed choose the weak to make obvious His power and strength. I accepted His call, I committed my way to Him, I gave myself to Him yet from time to time I try to keep a wee bit of myself back. He demands my all yet I give it so reluctantly, that's probably why he needs to demand! He knows me too well! And the wonder of it all is that he still wants me.

Today I received a letter from 121 re Nigeria. It seems that a move will be made soon to send missionaries back to Biafra.

I don't know if I will be one of the ones to go or not. Everything is so uncertain and I must admit I am a wee bit afraid of all the responsibility and work involved in Nigeria at the moment. "My grace is sufficient for thee, for my strength is made perfect in weakness."

Tomorrow is such a big day for Frances, Sarah and I – we are going to take God at His Word – we are going to ask for Christ's gift of healing. Frances will be made whole; no more weakness, no more fears, no more doubts, no more pain. Jesus Christ will make her whole and He will bless and use her even more. Her whole life is dedicated to His service and she will bring many others to Him.

I feel so sure about this tonight yet this afternoon I was so unsure of myself again. There is no doubt about it, I am weak and sinful, ready for the least excuse to hide or lay down the banner. Afraid of myself or afraid for myself? Afraid to take the step forward in complete trust. Afraid to be involved, to stand up in the midst of a few or a crowd for Jesus! God forgive me!!

Sarah and I arranged to meet tonight. We went for a short run to Tinto, a cold blustery night, too cold even for the walk we had planned. So we talked as we drove back to Lanark and to Carluke. Sarah and I have become very close in these past 5 months, she is a very lovely person and has been a real source of joy and strength to me. I thank God for her friendship and the fellowship we have shared. Love of Christ brought us together and I pray that we, and the strength of our friendship, fellowship and love for one another, we will go forward to give a better witness for Christ, our Redeemer and friend. Tonight Sarah gave me an envelope with a considerable sum of money in it for the work of Christ in Nigeria. Sarah, herself, is already fully committed to Christ and His Cause. I do thank God for her witness and for the encouragement and help she has given me in these past few months.

Dear God, our Father in heaven,

Please bless and guide dear Sarah; keep her ever close to our dear Lord Jesus. May she know joy and peace through Him, may the love of Christ enfold her, warming her, strengthening her and may Christ be seen in and working through her. I commit her and her loved ones to Thy tender care and keeping. In Jesus' name I ask it.

Dear Lord, this night I would ask for a special blessing on dear Frances. Prepare her, O God, for a new day tomorrow. She, too is already committed to Thee and Thy Cause and she is now willing to take this act of Faith. Heal her in Thy great mercy, stretch forth Thy healing hand and restore her, make her whole, and grant her Thy blessing and favour. God Thou art a great God and great King, Thy thoughts are far above our thoughts, and Thy ways beyond us yet O God we seek Thee because Thou didst first seek us. In the name of Jesus Christ, Thy Son who has redeemed us and made us Sons of God, we ask Thee, humbly and trustingly, to grant us the power to heal in Jesus' name. Bless each one of us this night and always. Amen.

Sunday 3rd September

<u>Malachi 3:17</u> "And they shall be mine, saith the Lord of Hosts, in that day when I make up my jewels…"

This is indeed the Lord's Day! All praise and glory and honour be His as is His due and right! All praise to Christ the Son! All praise to his Holy Spirit! Oh, what a Saviour!!! This has been a very special day and one I wish to record. Frances, Sarah and I have been led by God to this day. For me it has been building up over a long period. Thanks be to God for His patience, His Love, His guiding presence and His Word.

We, three, in love and faith attended the service in St. George's Tron tonight where the Rev. George B. Duncan was preaching. His text was Malachi 3:17, and we were asked to consider the individual and his worth to God – a precious gem. 1) Worth seeking 2) Worth shaping and 3) Worth showing. He said God wanted us there in Church tonight and I really did feel the message was just for us, very much for me. "God may be seeking you for a special task, I don't know," said Mr Duncan, "but God has his eye on you." God will shape us to fit the task, to bring out the best in us, to make us perfect and Christ-like. Then he said that God wants to show us, to place us in full view of men so that they will want to turn to God, to give him praise and honour. And God spoke to me tonight. As Mr Duncan announced the last hymn, as we started to sing it I was very much aware of the presence of God. I was tingling all over as we sang the first verse and I was so close to God. I really felt that only God and I were in that Church as we sang that hymn. Strange but wonderfully true! And to God be the glory!

Frances, Sarah and I then went to Miller Street and Frances' home. We had arranged a holy tryst with Jesus there. He kept his Word.

Hymn 245 "Dear Lord & Father of Mankind" said together in prayer.

Reading – Psalm 27. Prayer.

Frances then related her illness, her fears and doubts.

Read Psalm 28, verses 7– 9.

Read sayings of Jesus and felt His very Presence with us in the room.

The Lord Jesus did heal Frances, make her whole tonight in that wee living room and Sarah and I were truly blessed to be present and involved in that act of healing.

May Jesus Christ be praised and may we go forward, fully committed and strengthened with the love of Christ in our hearts, love which will constrain us and use us to reach others, to bring them to the Cross, to the redeeming and healing work of Christ. And may all be done and said and thought to the Glory of God and of His Son Jesus Christ our Lord and Saviour. Amen.

Friday 8th September

Visited Sister Catherine at St. Mary's Hospital in Lanark and was made very welcome. Had a long talk with Sister Catherine and Sister Rosalie and was asked if I had known to come specially on that day, a special feast day and a day of special joy and blessing for the St. Vincent de Paul Sisters of Charity.

Needless to say S. Catherine had to explain to me. Today – 8th September – has been set aside by the Catholic Church as the birthday of the Virgin Mary, Mother of Jesus. There was a special service at 5 pm when special blessings were given. Sister Catherine asked me to stay and I did so, with some apprehension.

It was a simple service, prayers in English were said by the priest and I was pleased to be part of it. Sister Catherine knelt beside me in the beautiful wee chapel and I felt this was right. We had talked together much, we had shared experiences and it was good to be at prayer before God together.

I pray that God will continue to bless Sister Catherine and our fellowship together. He brought us together and we are at one through our dear Lord and Saviour Jesus Christ.

May his name be ever praised!

Wednesday 13th September

Heard today that I can go to Biafra and am very very pleased. This is God's doing and I believe He wants me in Nigeria now. May my witness for Christ be strong & good at home here and in Africa.

Sunday 17th September

Visited St Colm's College yesterday. This is the Reunion and Retreat long weekend and it was great to be at the table, at prayers and in fellowship with former students, especially our own Sylvia, Cathie and Grace. Catherine was with us too and we were wishing we had arranged to stay parts of the weekend.

Today I attended St. John's Church with Sarah then went round to the Sunday School to hear Lexa Boyle's talk to the children. Had lunch with Frances, her mother and Lexa and thoroughly enjoyed the afternoon talking about our work and experiences.

Mr Haddow preached at the evening service and he was very good. At Mrs Rule's house in the evening with the missionary group to hear Lexa and see slides. Happy to say that Sarah was with us.

I have been worried about speaking so freely about going to Nigeria. Mr Auchinachie seems to think it should be kept very quiet but I have already talked freely. I am so pleased and happy that God has opened up this way for us. Nigeria needs us. Nigeria needs Christ.

Wednesday 20th September

God is good, patient, loving and ever merciful and He fulfills all His promises to us.

Sarah's birthday and a truly wonderful day for me!

Yesterday was the African Area Committee meeting and I was pleased to hear first hand news but very worried about how secret they expect us to be over the news of our departure to Nigeria. Mrs Leitch had already phoned the Hamilton Advertiser, I have already written to my partners and all Carluke must surely know.

Last night I was very depressed, worried and could not sleep. Did not even say my prayers properly.

Today. Wakened today with no feeling of depression or worry and feel most assuredly that God is taking care of things for me. It is now out of my hands and in God's hands. William asked me to go to Motherwell with him in the car and I know he wanted to talk. He and I have always been very close and we have talked freely many times together. We talked for about 1 ½ hrs and I was so pleased and thankful. My prayers have been answered and today William and I said a short prayer of committal in the car – Jesus Christ is first in his life and I pray that God will richly bless him and use him in Christ's work. May Jesus Christ be ever near him and strengthen and encourage him to higher service.

Thanks be to God for his love and patience and for answering the prayers of his unworthy disciples. "With God all things are possible."

Sylvia arrived today, it was great to see her and we had a long talk this afternoon. She has been thinking, reading and praying about Cathie in these past few days and feels we should do something about her. I told her the whole wonderful story about Frances, Sarah & I, and Sylvia felt we should go and see Cathie today. We went by car to Lugton – 1 ¼ hrs away – after we had spent a short time in prayer. Cathie came in later and Sylvia explained our mission, I suppose it was all very unexpected but Cathie said she had been praying for healing only in the past few days. She wants us to go down on Friday. Meantime we must pray for God's guidance and blessing.

Frances & Sarah came in the evening and we had a wonderful time of fellowship together. Sylvia is very much involved in this with us too. God be with & bless each one of us.

Cathie Chapman was in Pakistan for short term service as a nurse with the Church of Scotland, is engaged to an Anglican pastor, was injured in a car crash just before she came home. Has been off work for months with an injured right knee – badly limps, has much aching and pain. Does God want her to be healed? I believe so!

Oh God, our dear Father in Heaven, we thank Thee for revealing Thyself to us through our Lord and Saviour Jesus Christ, Thy Son. We pray O Lord that Thou will cleanse us, forgive us and use us as Thine instrument of healing.

Thursday 21st September

Went to Margaret's house for tea. Enjoyed the evening very much. Margaret, her mother & father and I talked about the things that mattered and I was pleased to be able to speak confidently about Christ and the Faith and doubly pleased that they were all interested to talk so.

I feel they are hungry for fellowship & the Word. Dear Margaret seems still to be unsure and not fully committed to Jesus. I told them about William and how it was all in answer to constant prayers for him. I must continue to pray for Margaret and her family too. May they soon walk hand in hand with the Lord Jesus and feel His power & strength and be happy. Told Margaret about the healing. She seems unsure.

Friday 22nd September

Margaret came to lunch so we could continue our discussion on healing and I let her read the beginning of this journal. There is not much to discuss

– I can only state facts and they are so simple and so wonderful. Margaret, I feel, must first realize and accept that Jesus Christ died for her sins, that He had the power to rise from the grave, that He has still the power to heal and to save.

O God, I commit Margaret and her loved ones to Thy tender care and keeping. May Thy Holy Spirit convict her of sin and convince her of the power of Christ to forgive all our sins. May she come to love and trust Christ as her Saviour & Lord and go on to witness for Him. In His Love, Amen.

2.30 pm Collect Sylvia from Motherwell and we set off for Lugton – it was a lovely sunny day and I enjoyed the run and the company. Cathie was expecting us, and her folks made us very welcome. We later went upstairs and talked about Jesus and His power now to heal. "Jesus Christ the same yesterday, today and forever." Cathie said that she would pray and expect healing for someone else but found it difficult to accept it for herself. I can understand that. She was expecting her leg to get better gradually and has only recently been praying for healing instead of patience & strength as before. I asked, – "If Jesus Christ walked in that door just now what would you say to him?" Cathie replied, "I would ask him to heal my knee." For me this was all we needed. We had only to ask Him and as He had willed us to this point so He would be willing to make Cathie whole. She also said, on questioning, that she was worried about finding work for the months before her wedding. I was very pleased when she said that she did not just want to fill in the time. She wanted to serve God and do a worthwhile job. We had a lovely meal with her folks then Cathie asked us to continue our discussion. She was indeed ready. We had a short healing service and we had a wonderful sense of the Presence of Christ, fellowship and oneness together in Him. Sylvia and I had a nice run home, talking and singing praises to our wonderful Saviour and powerful Lord.

Tuesday 26th September

8 am. Jean Jardine came to set my hair and cut it shorter.

9 am. Collected Morene and we set out for Edinburgh. Met with Neil Bernard, Gordon Auchinachie and Miss Stewart [from the Church of Scotland overseas council] to go over last minute details for the journey. Mr Bernard gave us another chance to withdraw and stay at home but we were both keen to go on.

We are now all set and looking forward to working in Biafra. Neil Bernard & "121" [Church of Scotland offices in Edinburgh] have certainly had a great deal of work and worry these past few months. They do a great job and we really do not fully appreciate their hard work and concern for us.

I spent a quiet evening with Mum & dad, Walter & Diane and wee Walter. Then Mrs Leitch and Tolu Ibiam[1] came to see me. I have so much to be thankful for – family and friends and work & Christ. Sarah and I [visited a friend to pray for healing] then left and I took her to Douglashall – my last evening – but many a happy hour I spent with Sarah and her mother there. My own family this evening were in good spirits and God must have given us all strength for this hour.

Wednesday 27th September

<u>D-DAY</u>

Psalm 23:1 "The Lord is my shepherd; I shall not want . . ."

"O Lord our God, in whose hand is the issue of all things . . ."

A very busy morning visiting Morag, Jenny, Aunty Ness and Aunt Nancy was visited yesterday. Annie Mac came to see me & Aunty Mary.

Went & collected Sarah at lunchtime and we went to Douglashall. I was sorry to upset her wee mother who has been so good & kind to me. I have enjoyed their company so often and so very much. Sarah is so faithful and full of the strength and love of God – she has been an inspiration and blessing to me on this my first furlough. Said "goodbye" to Alex, Hazel & the children, also William, Isobel and Liam. May God bless and care for my brothers and their children and may they, each one, come to love and trust the Lord Jesus.

Mum, dad & Aunt Ina took me to Abbotsinch. I had to try to find a watch strap and dad bought me a beautiful gold bracelet, also a Scottish stone bracelet. I am well-off indeed! We were all quite quiet and composed at the airport but parting is so hard and I do hate to cause my loved ones pain and sorrow. I can only commit all my loved ones to God and His keeping! Thanks be to God for His Word and His promises to us!

---

1 Tolu Ibiam and her sister stayed in Carluke with Dorothy Leitch for their schooling. They were the daughters of Dr Akanu Ibiam, a distinguished medical missionary and statesman from Nigeria's Eastern Region who supported Ann during her time in Biafra.

5.10 pm. Left Abbotsinch for London. Met Gordon Auchinachie with his wee travelling bag and could hardly contain myself with laughter. I was so heavily burdened with my hand luggage – tartan shoulder bag, textbook, radio and handbag so he took the radio, the lightest thing I had to help me. He walked on swinging his wee bag and I struggled behind him trying to look as if my load was nothing. I was certainly smiling, and almost laughing out loud, at the situation. We arrived Paris and met Ron McGraw, had dinner at the airport then caught the 11 pm flight to Douala. Poor Ron almost did not get a seat on the plane because the airline people in Dublin had failed to confirm his booking. This caused us all a wee bit worry as it was imperative that we stayed together for our journey to Biafra.

5:30 am, Thursday 28th September

Arrived at Douala in the Cameroon. We sat there until 8.15 am waiting to be collected but we had no word from, and could not contact, the Paris mission. Ron McGraw wanted to take a taxi to Mamfe, alone or together and Gordon tried to impress on him Mr Bernard's instruction that we should all stay together. I said nothing but was not at all impressed with Ron's attitude or ideas. He is very much an individual, headstrong and selfish in his motives – he could be quite a troublemaker I'm sure. Everything sorted itself out and we chartered a private plane to Mamfe. It was a wee 5-seater affair and I was a wee bit apprehensive. However it was a good flight. We had a wonderful view of the area – forests, rivers and very few roads. Exciting country!

9:30 am Arrived Mamfe. The small airport was full of soldiers and police and there was an American couple waiting for their plane to arrive. Dr & Mrs Linden from Onitsha Eye Clinic had been working in Nigeria for 9 years but now felt obliged to go home. Mrs Linden seemed very discouraged and tired. I think they must have had a rough time on the way from Calabar.

Mr & Mrs Van der Veld and Raphael were very nice and friendly and they gave us a warm welcome to the Basel Mission House which is just across the road from the airport. They are doing great work in these difficult times – giving hospitality and shelter to those passing to and from Biafra, sorting out letters to and from Biafra and this involves a lot of extra work for them. We had our first bite to eat at 2pm – about 17 hrs after our dinner in Paris. We should, of course, have told our hosts.

5.30 pm. A car load of missionaries arrived with David Craig from Calabar. They looked wearied and tired and wet but in good spirits and very pleased that we were returning to our posts. Agnes Gollan, Margaret Mitchell, Halstead, Ledge, Wragg and a Biafran student. Poor souls had been made to open their cases to be searched in the pouring rain, some had experienced quite a bit of anti-British feeling at their place of work. All expressed their hope of returning to Biafra. Agnes stayed at the Mission House with me while the others went to the local Rest House. We had a long talk and I was so pleased to meet with her.

Friday 29th September

LUKE 12: 35 – 48

Comments from International Bible Reading Association notes, "The only anxiety which is legitimate for Christian disciples should be that which keeps them on the alert for the Lord's coming."

A PRAYER OF TRUST: *O Lord Jesus Christ, who hast created me and redeemed me, and hast brought me hither where I am; Thou knowest what Thou wouldest do with me; do with me according to Thy Will, with mercy.* (King Henry VI).

1.30 pm. We, Ron, Gordon, David Craig and myself, left Mamfe to begin our journey to Calabar. What a journey! Ron gets sick in the car so I had to sit in the back seat! We had been thoroughly but politely searched at the airport on our arrival and we were searched again before we left the Cameroon. There were lots of armed soldiers around and someone had reported seeing tanks and many soldiers near the border – a show of strength to discourage Federal forces from entering Cameroon to get into Biafra by the back door. The road was quiet but very rough and muddy. Deep ruts and puddles all the way and the rain started to come down heavily. We were pretty badly shaken up but survived. David Craig had a paper from Francis Ibiam[2] saying that he was working for the Presbyterian Church and should be treated as a friend. This saved us much palaver and we had safe conduct in our journey. We arrived Calabar at 8.15 pm. One incident is worth noting.

We had really left too late in the day and we had to complete our journey in the dark, darkness fell about 6:15 pm. It was raining heavily, we were tired and sore with all the bumps and shaking up. Instead of going by ferry we took a private road through a limestone quarry. What a road! Steep winding down hill tracks, thick mud and limestone, (almost 1 foot deep in places and only

2   Sir Francis Ibiam, Presbyterian doctor and Nigerian statesman who renounced his UK knighthood and English first name, calling himself Dr Akanu Ibiam in protest at British military support for the Nigerian forces blockading and invading his country, Biafra.

a land rover could tackle this way). I was glad in a way that we could not see much of the road before us or the steep declines I was told were on either side of us. It was a dangerous road to go in the dark but we made it safely thanks to David Craig's skillful driving and God's presence with us. It was eerie, too with the lights being reflected on the white limestone giving an appearance of snow.

About 5 miles from Calabar we crossed a long bridge – a car-load of Europeans, full headlights on, coming out of the dark wet night. There was an army patrol at the other end of the bridge and we must have startled them. Boy, were they excited! They shouted at us to put our lights off and descend, then we had to approach them slowly one by one with our hands up. Their guns with bayonets attached were pointed menacingly at us and they sure meant business. I think we all got quite a fright!! This is just the time when accidents happen when people are excited and startled. However, after standing in the pouring rain for about 15 – 20 minutes, questioned individually with our hands up in a wee shack by torchlight (and torch in our face), the men had to empty their pockets, we were surrounded by soldiers but eventually allowed to drive on. Quite an experience but really our own fault for being so foolish to drive at night in these war times over a road that was seldom used.

Saturday 30th September

Luke 12, 49 – 59

Prayer of Ignatius Loyola: *"Teach us, good Lord to serve Thee as Thou servest; to give and not to count the cost; to fight and not to heed the wounds; to toil and not to seek for rest; to labour and not ask for any reward, save thought of knowing that we do Thy will." In Jesus name we pray this. Amen.*

Stayed overnight in Calabar then caught 12.30 pm launch to Oron. Strange exciting Africa with all its noise and bustle. I was the only European woman in Calabar and one man came on to the launch, otherwise Biafrans with all their black, shiny laughing faces. Everyone was friendly and the searching soldiers courteous and polite.

At Oron the place was teaming with soldiers and people with their children and loads waiting impatiently to board the launch – a very colorful busy African scene. In the midst of all this I spotted May Russell and I was so happy to see this well-kent Carluke face. She was looking well, the same cheery talkative May and she was pleased to see me. We had a picnic on the way and she brought me up to date with the news and people. Everything seems much as usual apart from the frequent road checks.

We stopped for food stores on the way – things have changed very much in this sphere – no milk, no butter, no sugar & no flour. I did manage to get a few tins of meat etc. but this is quite a problem for me arriving in the midst of a food shortage. No doubt things will sort themselves out for me.

I received a very warm welcome from Eme, Effiong, and Edet at Ekot Obong – May's three wee boys. Life goes on much the same as usual there with the water tanks, the lamps and the warning about the rats. May always seems to cope with everything but it certainly is a 'bush' station. I spent a happy two nights there.

October 1967

Sunday 1st October

Aunt Ina's birthday! I hope everyone at home is well and not too concerned about me.

9 am. Service in the Itu Leper Colony Church and I was made very welcome. It was good to see everyone – McDonalds looking tired and drawn a wee bit. I think it's time they went home and had a really good rest. Margaret and Murray Philip are also looking tired but all are well. The Duncans are their usual cheery selves.

We had coffee at the Duncans & lunch with the Philip family. It was good to be at the Colony service, to worship together, to sing with the band and hear the Lord's Prayer sung so reverently and meaningfully.

At Ekot Obong in the evening Mary Louise and Janet came specially to welcome me. It was very nice of them. May & I had to go to Ibiaku Secondary School in the afternoon so I could deliver 2 letters to Ruth Hannah, a young Methodist teacher. Poor Ruth's father had died and I had to convey the news to her. We waited around until Miss Cameron and Miss McLaren were there as I did not want to spring the news on the girl, also I was a stranger to her. Ruth arrived on scene as we were talking so we did not mention the news but I must say I felt uncomfortable and deceitful in keeping quiet. However,

I'm sure I did the right thing. It was kinder for her older colleagues to break the news to her gently and quietly when she was on her own.

May the God of peace and comfort be with Ruth and may our Lord Jesus be with her to strengthen and guide her. In His name we ask this. Amen.

In all her years of missionary service in Nigeria and then Biafra from 1966 to 1970, Ann was proud to work for the Presbyterian Church of these countries. This denomination has its roots in the mid-19th century Scottish missionary work of the United Presbyterian Church (UP) in Calabar and in the Presbytery of Biafra, established in 1858. The UP Church's Foreign Mission Board sent Mary Slessor to serve as a missionary in that eastern region from 1876. She was there until her death in 1915.

The Presbyterian Church was responsible for the three hospitals where Ann worked before and during the Biafran war: Mary Slessor Hospital at Itu; Queen Elizabeth Hospital at Umuahia; and Presbyterian Joint Hospital, Uburu. It was this Church which welcomed Ann back to Biafra as its first returning woman missionary with the words, "Welcome, true Biafran!"

Monday 2nd October

Set off at 8:30 am with Murray Philip for the special Medical Board meeting at Umuahia. Murray Cochrane gave me news of Sjouka and said he was expected back later this month. Mr Oji and Mr Eme, the Synod Clerk were very pleased to see me and greeted me with, "Welcome, true Biafran!" I am the first woman missionary to return to the Presbyterian Church and the second to Biafra (a Mrs Garrett arrived before me).

The meeting was short and it was decided that I should go to Itu with Dr Philip until 10th Nov. then go to Uburu for 3 wks to relieve Kees for a spell. I was happy with this decision.

I travelled with Ken Meechison and Mr Eme to Uburu to collect my loads and received a warm welcome from Alicia and Charlotte who were not expecting me at this time.

Enjoyed very much my stay at Uburu and feel much happier at going there to work next month. It has always been strange ground for me – I have only paid two quick visits there before. Visited the Ante Natal Clinic and Infant

No. G 716564

The bearer, whose Name is

(DR) ANN W. JACKSON

and whose Photograph appears opposite, is an accredited Church Worker with the Presbyterian Church in Biafra. ~~He~~ She is allowed free movement within the Republic of Biafra.

Akanu Ibiam

(Dr. Akanu Ibiam)
Adviser to the Military Governor

& *Head of State*

Holder's Signature

Ann W. Jackson

Ann proudly worked for the
Presbyterian Church in Biafra,
with its history of missionary leaders—
Akanu Ibiam & Mary Slessor

THE
HILL OF
HEALING

**MARY
SLESSOR
HOSPITAL**
ITU

DIAMOND JUBILEE
1905—1965

Welfare clinics with Alicia and it was great fun. There is a good attendance and they start singing choruses and dancing – Alicia, of course, has plenty of energy and "go" in her and the women obviously were enjoying themselves.

Mr MacDonald told me that when he first visited Uburu about 30 years ago it was a famine area for part of the year. The people lived only on yam and were small, wizened and starved looking. They are certainly a healthy lively group now thanks to Uncle John Paterson who has helped them to cultivate rice. He was there at Uburu doing some work of his own while I was there. I really enjoyed being with the women and joining in the rhythm and clapping. One woman thrust a wee laughing boy into my arms and he clung to me for the rest of the time – just with his wee shirt on and wee bare bum. Two happy days at Uburu. I had a long talk with Charlotte who is missing letters from home but otherwise is in good spirits. I told her all about healing and the work I was doing at home and she was very interested and asked me to make her part of our group at 10 pm. Alicia, Charlotte & I spent Thursday evening together talking quietly and then we had short family prayers at the end of the evening. It was good to be together, to have the company and the fellowship.

Bill Cluness was good enough to allow me into their foodstore to collect some things. I was very pleased and grateful because it really is impossible at present to get sugar or margarine and he gave me tinned cheese, meat and beans.

Wednesday 4th October

Left Uburu and travelled to Umuahia for lunch with the Ritchies. We had no trouble with the checkpoints but the road is crawling with soldiers. Enugu is being shelled and the women and children have been advised to leave. Queen Elizabeth was packed with vehicles of all kinds, soldiers, Red Cross workers. It seems that 101 casualties had arrived from Enugu General Hospital and they were expecting 2 teams of surgeons and auxiliary staff within the next few days. 100 beds were going into the Recreation Hall and another 100 into the wards. It will take some organising to get all these people integrated & working together.

Thursday 5th October

Spent my first night at the Mary Slessor Hospital, Itu and really feel as if I have come home. I'm staying in Lewis Fraser's house meantime and have Ma Mary, the Church Sister assigned to the hospital as my neighbour. Mr &

Mrs Archibong, Sister and Business Manager are across the road, then Janet Brown (Matron) and another Sister are up the road from them.

Wakened this morning at 6 am with a noisy cock crowing and the folk next door removing their shutters. This really is Africa. Light came streaming in at 6.30 am and I heard Ma Mary and her family singing hymns and having their morning devotions together.

This hospital has never had a Church Sister working here before and Ma Mary has only been here since June. She takes the services at the clinics and visits the patients in the wards and takes the nurses' Bible study. Janet says she has left everything to her and says this is her job now and not ours. However, I do not agree. I hope to work with Ma Mary and I certainly have no intention of doing my bare medical work – evangelism is a definite part of my work and I hope to witness more this tour with my words, my work and my life. I do hope that I will grasp the opportunities when they arise and I pray that God will guide and lead me in the way of His truth.

I pray that soon we will have an effective team here at the Mary Slessor Hospital witnessing for Christ. May God bless all our doings and guide us and may all be done for the glory and praise of God, the Father.

Friday 6th October

Have done some more unpacking and felt terribly depressed and very homesick on Thursday after sorting out my things. Suddenly I just wanted to go home. I'm sorry to say I had to go to bed and lie down, had a good cry, then wrote to the family, Sarah and Winnie and felt a wee bit better. Strange this homesickness!

Went to the clinic at Okopedi and saw about 25 patients and did not get back until about 2.15 pm. I hope we can encourage more people to attend. Rita was there, the assistant nurse who was so friendly and helpful to me the last time. Everyone was pleased to have me back and I know I am going to enjoy my work here. I visited Bob & Jean MacDonald at tea time and enjoyed talking to them. They have a nice house with a lovely view of the Cross River and I like it very much. Jean & Bob hope to leave with all their loads next week to go to Tiko to get a boat to London. They have served this country faithfully for 38 yrs and deserve a good rest and happy days at home together.

May God bless them, strengthen and restore them, give them a quiet mind and the peace that passes understanding. I pray that God will guide them safely and easily back home and that everything here and at home will work out for their good. I like the MacDonalds very much and I like their house so I have decided to live there myself. There is a spare separate room so I can have guests and there is so much to offer them.

As we sat chatting a canoe passed by, filled with men and women who were singing and playing drums as they paddled down river. I am going to enjoy living in that lovely house and I pray God that all who come to stay with me will find rest and peace and contentment. I pray that they will go from my house refreshed in body, mind and spirit, happy in their work for Christ and joyful in the fellowship of His Church. May God give His blessing to all who live in my house and may He guide me to give more of myself to others, to be caring and loving for Christ's sake.

Evening prayers at the hospital are as I remember them, joyful and with the swinging rhythm of the drums. "What a friend we have in Jesus" is surely my favourite.

Saturday 7th October

A very quiet day. I have reorganized my loads but not wholly unpacked because I will definitely be moving up to the MacDonalds' house.

From Monday I will be in charge of Female, Maternity and Children's wards and do most of the outside clinics. Edet was at the market yesterday; prices are quite fantastic (fish 7/- for a piece, onions 3/- for two wee wizened things, no salt, no potatoes, no flour, no sugar, no margarine, no fresh meat). I have no marmalade either so had toast with margarine for my breakfast. Bread is sometimes available at increased prices. Had spaghetti and then fresh fruit salad for my lunch and enjoyed that very much.

I think I will make a real effort at slimming now that so much has become short anyway. Jean Mac has a good recipe for oatcakes so must get Edet to bake these instead of biscuits. It has been raining heavily on & off all day. A very quiet day!

Sunday 8th October

9 am. Service at Itu Leper Colony Church with Rev. Bob MacDonald preaching and he was very good. He arrived in Calabar in 1929 and this would probably be the last sermon he will preach in Biafra; he hopes to leave for home next month. He made reference to the first sermon he preached at Calabar. Jesus said, "Give ye them to eat." And how the disciples protested that they had nothing to give but our Lord said "bring what you have to me." And the

multitudes were fed. His reading was Rev. 1, 4-11 and Rev. 2 verse 29 "He that hath an ear, let him hear what the Spirit saith unto the churches."

We must be listening intently to hear what the Holy Spirit is saying to our church today, saying to each one of us today. We must take what talents we have been given and present them to Christ and He will use them and us. "Give ye them to eat." Speaks volumes and is again the message for me. May God guide me and strengthen me for the task He has in store for me.

Had coffee with the Philips & MacDonalds & Duncans, Mr Gordon and Miss Mac. May Russell came in the evening for a special Women's Work Service at 5 pm, and she & Janet stayed for dinner. A very enjoyable evening and I hope we can arrange a Christmas Drama or Act of Worship for the nurses. Edet gave me a cookery lesson this afternoon and I now know how to make yam cakes. What a lad!

Tuesday 10th October

4.30 am. Had to get up to leave with May Russell and Alison Duncan to go to Port Harcourt. I did not prepare my Aladdin lamp the evening before so had to fumble in the dark to get dressed, only had my tiny torch so it wasn't really much use to me. Fortunately I had organized my handbag and shopping bag the night before – my usual rush in the morning so had to leave with no breakfast, clothes thrown on and my legs swathed in bandages. I must have looked a pretty sight! The mosquitoes & sandflies have been having a good tuck-in on me, they seem to like fresh blood, so I had to soak bandages in TCP and put on my legs and ankles at night. My legs were very sore, itchy and covered in bites but are much improved today.

8 am. We reached Port Harcourt and came through many roadblocks but with no real trouble. We had a note or pass from the District Officer so we were allowed through with little or no searching. Kingway Store did not open until 10 am so we had to wait a wee while; there were very few Europeans. In fact we only saw 9 – 2 women, 2 sisters and 5 men and this is so unusual for Port Harcourt. They had a lot of canned meats and fish but no flour, sugar, margarine, butter or salt. I spent £25 but did not seem to get all that much to show for it. I now feel happier with my stores though and flour is really the only thing I am low on.

The sun shone all day until about 5 pm then started to pour down heavily. It became a real African tropical stormy evening with lightning and rain lashing down non-stop on to the road. Visibility was very very poor. We did not leave Port Harcourt until 5 pm and did not get home until about 8.30-9 pm. May stayed and had supper with me. We had had a good, profitable but tiring day.

Wednesday 11th October

Did ward rounds this morning then went to Okopedi Clinic and came for my lunch at 2 pm. We seem to be having more children with malnutrition and protein deficiency diseases but I suppose this is unavoidable in view of the conditions of war. There is no bread, meat, fish or milk for these wee mites and they are just starving.

We have 5 ill children just now and they are on the last of the American milk & wheat. I have decided to use the money given to me from the various Sunday Schools to buy eggs to supplement the diet of these children. Some have hospital diet but some are fed by the mothers (yam & gari – yam & gari etc.) so I think we will give them a raw egg each day, mixed with milk and sugar. We would need about 3 dozen eggs so I hope we can get the fresh ones from the Leper Colony Farm Settlement at 3/6 – 10/6 per week.

Received news over the radio today that all British personnel have been advised to go home. The Federal Army is planning to march to Port Harcourt from Enugu. Margaret Philip and Alison Duncan and the children are hoping to go to Calabar & Mamfe sometime soon. I think the Uburu folk will come down to Itu. I would be happier if they came down very soon. I fear for their safety at Uburu – there was too much unrest, ill feeling and suspicion in that area. We can only commit ourselves to our dear Lord.

Friday 13th October

9 am. Rev. R. M. M. & Mrs MacDonald arranged to leave this morning by canoe – large canoe with an engine. Work more or less stopped at the Colony. Janet, Mr & Mrs Archibong, Edet the driver, and one or two others from Mary Slessor Hospital came to see them off. The boat was of course late.

Eventually we all trekked to the Colony Beach – the road was impassable by car – a long file of expatriates and Biafrans winding on our way along the bush path chattering and laughing though we were all very much aware of this great couple's departure. And everyone was sorry to see them go at this time but they needed the rest. I was sorry I did not have a longer time and more opportunity to be with Jean & Bob and get to know them. I certainly liked them and was especially drawn to Mrs MacDonald.

I think we were all reminded of the old days when Mary Slessor tramped these pathways with all her bearers. At the beach there was a great crowd standing waiting, some murmuring, some talking, many in tears and the Brass Band was playing sad sentimental tunes. "God be with you till we meet again." "Auld lang syne."

The launch arrived & was loaded up with the trunks and suitcases. The river was high and flowing very fast and in no time at all it carried the boat and Mr & Mrs MacDonald from our sight.

May God bless & guide them on their way home. Grant them a restful journey and a new awareness of God's peace.

Saturday 14th October

News is not very good these days and worse still, is not reliable. Margaret Philip, Rosemary, David, Susan and Alison Duncan have decided to go home. I think this is a wise decision. There are so many uncertainties these days, so much hardship and scarcity of things and no school – no place for the children.

May Russell, Janet, Mrs Ema and I had to go to the Immigration Authorities in Uyo today. We had an uneventful trip, thanks to the District Officer's letter and were treated politely but coldly at Uyo.

Today I decided to move into the MacDonald's house so had my trunks moved before I left for Uyo. It really is a very lovely house with a truly magnificent view of the Cross River with the wee dwellings across the water and the canoes quietly passing by. I like my new house very much. Unpacking is a humbug (as May Russell would say)! This is my weekend on call so I hope it will stay quiet. Our wards are half empty these days – people are not coming to the hospital, ?ourselves ? lack of money ? war situation. We have stopped doing routine 'cold' surgery because of our drug shortage and the government have asked us to economise and be prepared to deal with casualties. We cannot afford to do routine hernias etc. – catgut, thread, local anaesthetic, and general anaesthetics are in short supply. Needless to say this means that the money is not coming in and the general running costs become higher. We cannot get drugs these days – no therapeutic Anti Tetanus Serum, no anti-rabies at all in the hospital.

Sunday 15th October

Attended the Leper Colony Service in the morning then had coffee with the Philip family who are in the midst of making preparations for home. It must be quite a thought to have the family separated.

We talked for a long time about missionaries, here and at home and I was enlightened in many ways and shocked. "For a man with a family it really is a sacrifice financially and materially to come to the Mission Field." With the higher cost of living these past few months Margaret says they will be in debt with 121. They have no money saved at home, they will go to a furlough house and sometimes they are not in good condition or furnished very well. The Duncans are also very worried. They have recently bought a new house and have rented it out. David has still one year of his tour to do, so this means they will lose this rent income. They can hardly afford to keep two homes going at this time. They were stating facts yet not complaining and I do sympathise with them. Women's Guild Branches and Youth Groups could help missionary families to set up home, to help more in the furnishing and comfort of furlough houses, help to supply TV, radio, washing machine etc. Second hand things can be found if folk are ready to scout around. I would like to see a furlough house in Carluke, where the people would welcome and care for the missionary and his family.

Monday 16th October

This has been my first weekend on call and my re-introduction to surgery. I had to do a laparotomy on a young girl who turned out to have peritonitis but could find no primary cause. Appendix & tubes were normal. Murray agreed to assist me because I was a wee bit apprehensive about tackling the surgery on my own. I suppose I have been away from it for too long – 6/12 and my confidence is not all that good. During the night – 12.30 am I had to take another woman to theatre – she had stab wounds to abdomen and gut was pushed outside and had been covered with leaves and mud. She was quite a mess! She was also 9/12 pregnant and went into labour when she was on the table, anaesthetized. I cleaned and repaired the 3 perforations in small bowel made by the knife, and then had to go on and do a Caesarean Section. A live female child was born with little difficulty I am happy to say. Mother & child are well.

There was a great palaver with the police who were sure that they had a murder case on their hands. The relatives had said there was no hope for the woman and the news was all round Okopedi this morning. The hospital had several visits from the police and one even came to the clinic to tell me my patient had died. They were surprised to find her sitting up answering their questions clearly. Dr Philip says that my name is now made with the police. I can only say that the woman must have had a strong constitution and that God had a hand in it.

Thursday 19th October

So much has happened in these past few days. On Monday morning I asked Ben, the lab man, if I could take morning prayers in his stead. I really felt I had to speak out, make my own position clear. I did not want to jog along with the others.

Our clinics are poor, wards half-empty, patients seem to be reluctant to come to us. I know money is scarce, I know people do not want to be in hospital at this time of uncertainty and war. Our witness here is poor, I have heard complaints of the nurses' pride and carelessness towards patients. They seem to forget that they are the privileged ones who are allowed to nurse the sick, that they have a hand in God's healing ways because He wills it, they forget that they must present a good witness, show forth Christ's love for all men.

Few nurses attend evening prayers, many come late. Bible Study on Friday evenings is conducted in Efik and very few attend. I chose I Cor. 13, Philips' translation and used this as a basis for my talk. I said, and I mean it with all my heart, that if our witness for Christ is not good then we should not be here. I pray that God will look mercifully upon us all here at Mary Slessor Hospital and reform and perfect any work we do in Christ's name. May Jesus Christ indeed be praised in our work, our words and our lives!

On Tuesday Margaret Philip, Rosemary and David, Alison Duncan and Susan quietly left Itu from Queens Beach in the District Officer's canoe. David and Murray went with them in their 2 hr journey across & upriver to Ikot Oporo. Unfortunately David Craig did not meet them and they were given a very frightening reception from the soldiers stationed there. They were forced to march with their hands up in single file while soldiers stood all around them with guns cocked at the ready and bayonets gleaming in the sun. The poor children must have been very frightened but David said they behaved well. Once the launch had been recognized and the D.O.'s letter read everything was all right and they were well received but the harm had been done. We have since had a phone call to say that they had an uneventful further journey to Calabar. They have since given us much thought and anxiety.

On Wednesday evening Calabar was taken by the Federal army. All night long we heard gun fire and there is no way of communication. We can only hope and pray that they managed to escape to Mamfe in time.

Today Thursday. I did my first theatre list – bilateral inguinal hernias, a very large lumbar hernia that proved to be very difficult & took me 2 hrs to do, cleaning & resuturing a wound, redressing a burns wound and I was overjoyed to see that the skin graft I did had taken, also examination under anaesthesia. Quite a good first list and everything went smoothly. In the afternoon I had to do an emergency laparotomy on a child – obstruction due to fibrous bands.

Friday 20th October

On Mondays, Wednesday and Fridays I do ward rounds in the Children's, Female and Maternity wards at approx. 8 am. I seem to finish quickly today. There is a girl of 10 yrs in the Children's ward and she is much in my thoughts. The right side of her wee face is all swollen and distorted with a tumour – Burkitt's tumour – and there is nothing we can do about it surgically or medically. At 10.45 am I went down to the clinic at Okopedi and was pleased to see more people than last week. I think there would be about 22 or so.

I re-read a book – Rachel Cade in the afternoon and enjoyed it though I feel I must spend my time doing Bible Study and improving my knowledge. I should also be reading some Medicine. Next week I hope to rise at 6 am and spend ½-1 hr in Bible Study, prayer and meditation. It only needs a start. Prayers are at 7 am so I could have ½ hr before and I don't need to go to the wards until 8 am so I could have my breakfast and another ½ hr study. My intentions are good. This evening I went up to Chapel for Bible Study at 8 pm but all was in darkness and only Ma Mary the Church Sister was waiting. We have started taking blackout precautions, and all the hospital is now in darkness, and the nurses were too frightened to venture from their rooms. We did not pursue the matter but will have Bible Study next week in the Nurses Sitting Room and we can adhere to the blackout regulations more easily. War is always frightening.

Sunday 22nd October

Yesterday I did not go to the hospital until 10.30 am but rose at 7 am – an hour's longer lie. I re-sorted my Medical Bag and I think it is a good First Aid

Kit with everything I would need in an emergency. Murray & I will need to meet sometime soon to think out First Aid measures, as he is the organiser for the district.

I saw the few who came to the clinic and then had to do a Caesarian Section for placenta praevia – all went well and the child is doing well though she was slow to respond. In the afternoon Janet, Mrs Ema & her son & I all went to Okopedi market. What a place! May Russell keeps telling me what an evil place it is and I believe her. There is quite a mixture of people, Ibos, Ibibios and Rivers and it is really crowded. The streets and stalls are dirty and foul smelling. There are many dingy wee beer parlours, mangy dogs foraging around and people pressing and shoving together. We were greeted on all sides – Beke, Makara, Doctor, Sister and at times just glared at. The women are almost always friendly but the men are sometimes insolent in their looks. I'm afraid the men get a cold stare back but I do love the women and especially the children. They smile shyly, laugh and wave to us, and look so pathetic in their wee vests or dirty shirts, many skinny and half starved, many showing the early and chronic signs of the deficiency diseases. My heart bleeds for these wee ones who are the innocent victims of this war and all the extra hardship and suffering it brings with it.

<u>Sunday</u> – a very quiet and restful day. I went to the service in the Colony Church this morning. Then came home and wrote to Alicia and Charlotte at Uburu, also to Dr Kees Reijnierse. Medical Board which was to have been held at Abiriba, near Uburu, has been cancelled because of the present situation but I think I am still duty bound to go to Uburu on the 10th November. I am facing this with mixed feelings – I am happily settled here at Itu, Murray is having things much easier and needs this respite, Uburu is so near Enugu and when I last visited there was unrest and suspicion. Here we are among friends but at Uburu there have been too many frictions and ill feeling in the past. I would love to see Charlotte and Alicia again and I do feel they need or would be pleased to have my company. Alicia is certainly working very hard at the Rural clinics and I'm sure Kees is too. My help would be appreciated and I would ease their burden for a wee while.

However, I will need to wait and see. The Federals are well established in Calabar and have moved 30 miles – I think towards Mamfe and Ikot Oporo so the Mamfe road and mail run has been closed. We were happy to receive two confirmed reports that the Duncan and Philip families did leave Calabar safely on Wednesday morning so they should now be safe at home. We are all very much relieved and thankful to God. I suppose the Federals must sooner, or later, come up river or from across river to take Itu. We can only wait and pray. May God protect the ordinary people from themselves & from the army.

Monday 23rd October

My mother's birthday – I hope she has a very happy day, that there is nothing happening at home to worry and that she is not worried unduly about me. May God bless this day and give my mother His blessing and peace.

What a day! Rumours, rumours and more rumours! The people here are very frightened and the tragic thing is that they fear each other. The Ibos fear the Ibibios and the Efiks and vice versa – there is talk of plans to attack each other, families are fleeing from Okopedi and from the Colony here. Murray had to arrange to have a guard at all the entrances to the Colony last night. There is a mixture of Ibos & Ibibios and Efiks here. The Ibo staff nurses want leave to go home yet we are depending on them in our First Aid plans. I think that when fighting starts everyone will take flight and flee but we can only wait and see and hope for the best. There is certainly much fear & distrust in the air especially these last few days. What a truly tragic thing war is!

It is very dark tonight, very few electric lights are on and I've had to take the bulbs out my outside lights. There have been flashes of lightning and thunder but these days it is difficult to know if it is indeed thunder or gunfire. The Federal troops must certainly be quite near us.

We had prayers in the nurses' sitting room this evening and I enjoyed it – fellowship was good in the light of the bush lamps – our electricity was cut off. I hope we can praise God & end our day like this every night.

Tuesday 24th October

Theatre day but I only had a bilateral hernia on my list. People are scared to come into hospital these days in case the storm breaks and they are not at home with their own family. A strangely quiet day!

7am prayers were held in Chapel & not in the Wards as is usual on a Tuesday. Dr Philip took the service and asked everyone to be ready to stay at their posts. The hospital must be ready and staffed to cope with any emergency, we are the vital link in the First Aid organisation. There have been so many rumours, and some nurses seemed to want the hospital to close and allow the staff to go to their various homes. This idea was quenched this morning but who will stand when the fighting starts? We will need to wait and see. "Who is on the Lord's side?" indeed! An appropriate hymn we sang this morning. Reading Ephesians 6 verse 10.

Murray had to do a postmortem on a policeman who was shot by a soldier in a scuffle last night. No wonder people are afraid. We heard that at Calabar all the police and senior army officers ran away, they were the first on the Ikot Oporo ferry and that civilians were roughly treated & beaten up by the soldiers at the ferry. Meanwhile the Federal army captured Calabar! A truly sorry state of affairs and quite quite tragic!

There has been gunfire this evening but it is difficult to guess how near or far. There is now a curfew on 6 pm-6 am so we will have few patients in the night. The soldiers are young, excitable and gun happy. I would not like to venture far at night these days.

Friday 27th October

Wakened this morning to find several soldiers just outside my sitting room. It seems that a number have come from the fighting at Enugu and will be guarding Itu and the hospital. I was a wee bit startled to have them so close and told Edet I was not very keen to have them here. The bold lad seemingly told them that I was afraid and did not want them near the house. Since this morning I have had 3 visits – 2 from the Cadet Sergeant and one from the Lieutenant in charge to reassure me that there is no need for me to worry. It was very good of them to come but I'm a wee bit annoyed that Edet gave them the impression that I'm frightened.

8.15 pm. The Sergeant arrived, introduced his men who would be guarding me and who would be placed outside my bedroom where they got a good view of the river. It's a wee bit disconcerting but I can't honestly say I'm scared. They have all been very polite & courteous. And so they should be, of course – I treated 35 of them at the clinic this morning – fever & cough, fever & cough – let's hope that none of the ones with a bad cough are outside my room tonight!!

We decided to have evening prayers instead of Bible Study tonight – the men who come to Bible Study are not allowed to go out because of the Curfew at 6 pm and they come from the bottom of the hill. Ben the lab man seems very keen, also Oji the dispenser. Keenness can so easily be blunted! I hope mine does not, nor theirs!

Memories of home & loved ones are sweet and it is good to remember.

Saturday 28th October

Today I felt I wanted to write a letter, to communicate with those dear to me in far off Scotland. I wrote a long letter to Sarah but alas, I have no way to send it. Anyway I shared my thoughts and ideas and I feel much more content and I will be able to post it sometime. Things are quiet here today and my thoughts have indeed been straying homewards. It is such a joy and blessing to know that I do have many at home – friends and my own dear family – who love me and who are loved by me. God has indeed blessed me throughout my life – I have many treasured memories of my childhood and youth. We had so many happy times together as a family. As I travelled along life's road I have made many good true friends, and I do value their friendship and their love and their prayers. God has given them to me, and I pray that I will always be loving and faithful to each one.

God has given me work to do and what wonderful and enriching work it is – His work and I can only pray that it will always be His Will that I do. I love my work, I love the people especially the children and God has given me a Saviour and a Friend who is above all others. One who loves me, Who makes my work & love for others possible and Who binds all those I love to Himself.

God is indeed good. He is gracious and He is merciful and loving. Thanks be to God for our Lord Jesus Christ and for all His many gracious benefits!

Sunday 29th October

Philippians 4:4-7 _ "Rejoice in the Lord always, again, I will say, Rejoice…" Thanks be to God for His Word & Truth!

This is my weekend on duty but so far has been very quiet. Patients are afraid to come to the hospital these days, in case there is fighting in the area and also lack of money prevents them. There has been no more talk of fighting among the smaller tribal groups Efiks, Ibibio and Ibos. This is Efik/Ibibio country and already many Ibo traders have fled to their own home villages. The people are afraid of one another and also of a Nigerian attack from the River.

Market day continues to be every 4th day but very little trade is done, too few items are available, prices are fantastic for most things, many Ibo stalls have closed and money is tight. Also the army have moved in, and the traders must supply them so they take away a lot of yam & fruit etc. We can still buy small pieces of fish and fruit, but no meat and even yams were scarce yesterday. Salt costs 4 shillings for one cup, a cigarette tin full. Sugar costs 1 penny for a cube. One onion cost 5 shillings. Batteries which used to cost 7 pence now cost 3 shillings to 3 shillings and six pence.

Money is indeed tight. Our own money is now cut off from Calabar, where there is reputed to be fierce fighting. All our missionaries except Dave Craig are reported safe and in other parts of Biafra. Our hospital staff are now on half salary, the Presbyterian ministers in Biafra are now in 2 months arrears with salary and teachers have no income at all these days. The situation becomes increasingly difficult.

We continue to see militia and army personnel at our clinics in numbers from 12 to 35. So far we have had no trouble, they are civil and friendly, but they insist on carrying their heavy rifles with them at all times and are very reluctant to put it down when I want to examine them. We did have some trouble at first with one or two who were supposed to be on duty at the hospital but we discovered that they relax and sit in the Maternity Ward. We cannot have this at all – for the patients' sake and also we do not want to encourage their association with our nurses. We have reported the matter to the officer in charge.

Today about 4 or 5 pm two soldiers appeared at Dr Philip's house threatening to shoot down the Colony notice board which states in bold letters "The Presbyterian Church of Nigeria" instead of Biafra. They were half dressed and very drunk and disorderly and very threatening. We were afraid of them running amok in the Colony, menacing or threatening patients with their loaded rifles. Eventually they went away and the matter was reported.

The Colony service today was taken by Dr Murray Philip. I invited David Duncan, Murray, Alistair Gordon from Etam Secondary School, May Russell and a Celonese family, the Mulsinchings, for coffee. Janet was on duty.

It is difficult these days to extend hospitality and provide eatables so I did not ask the Archibongs or Mrs Ema. Also I only have 6 cups & saucers because I have packed my own china. We talked of the situation and exchanged news. May Russell has at last decided that it is unwise and unsafe to continue living by herself at Ekot Ebong so she will move to Ibiaku to join Misses Cameron and McLaren. I think it is a good idea as the compound is very isolated and there are many soldiers in the area and also one or two nearby who seem to bear May a grudge over some old dispute.

Mr & Mrs Mulsinching, two sons and a daughter, are a Trinidad family who lived at Calabar, where the husband taught at Hope Waddell Training

College. They were given many opportunities to leave Calabar but decided to stay although the school is closed & has been for some months. Suddenly last Wednesday morning Calabar was attacked by Nigerian forces, and Calabar was shelled. They were quite unprepared and had to flee by car – very little money, no food and only the clothes they were wearing. They arrived on our doorstep on Friday and have since been put into the Colony Sisters house. They are very fortunate to be alive and this has been a frightening experience for them yet they are very foolish. They have three small children to think of, and they did have the opportunity to escape. Dr Philip and David Duncan sent their own family home so that in emergency only single people had to be considered, and now they have this family under their care. It's a bit uncharitable to think this way, and the poor souls are well and truly stuck here, and probably have now lost most of their possessions and food store. Many houses have been destroyed at Calabar, and there is no hope of returning in the very near future.

Listening to everyone talking of their own individual plans and preparations I realize that I must finish packing my own trunks and be prepared. It's true we do not know if and when an attack will come from down river or we may experience the shelling. Also when the Nigerian Federal army comes we do not know how we will be received. We may be classed as collaborators and I certainly came back to help Biafra after independence had been declared; we may all be put together – Europeans – for the sake of keeping us safe during the subsequent fighting; we may be deported; or we may be allowed to carry on our work here at the hospital. I hope & pray this will be so.

I am still waiting for word to go to Uburu, so should leave all my belongings locked in the trunks just in case anything happens while I'm away, and looting is the common practice.

What a long tragic tale of war this has turned out to be. *May God forgive us for our sins and deliver us from all evil and continue to bless us with His Presence. Amen.*

Monday 30th October

We had a fairly big clinic this morning I am happy to say. The children's ward is still my favourite haunt though we only have about 9 or 10 patients at the moment. Mainly malnutrition and anaemia, wee Enok with terrible ulcers on the dorsum of both feet showing all the extension tendons. The ulcers are improving with olive oil soaks. Sister Ema & I have been reading and trying to find an ointment to aid this healing process, and it is only in the past week that there has been this definite improvement. Mr Archibong told me that there is a fund available in the hospital – government source – to supply extra nutrients for the children. So we buy eggs, bananas, ground-nuts and ovaltine for them. I do not give the Sunday School money but will keep it until later and use it for Church work. I will need to wait anyway because I cannot at present cash my travellers cheques.

We also have a boy of 10 years, Michael, who has a fractured femur and has developed a deep infected pressure ulcer of his heel. His young sister age about 6 or 7 years is his attendant doing his cooking etc. When we were taking off the first plaster several weeks ago he was bravely telling her not to cry, while she stood weeping and sighing for him. She has since proved a very faithful attendant, a friendly wee soul in a long grey/black & white jumper which goes down to her knees. It's difficult to tell whether she's a wee boy or a wee girl.

Anyway this shirt or jumper became more & more dirty and it seemed that she had no other clothes. Matron looked out a wee dress to fit her and we had a fashion parade. There were actually 4 dresses which fitted her so she was allowed to choose one and it was a red one with white lace. She looked very nice and the nurses made quite a show of her. She was very pleased with herself and we had then to give her soap from the Children's ward so she could wash her other jumper or shirt (whatever it was).

This afternoon and this evening I have packed away most of my belongings and locked the trunks. I have also packed my blue rucksack as an emergency bag with a change of clothes (dress & underwear), nightdress, toilet bag & essentials, medical kit, candles, a few tins of beans & sausages, tea, coffee, sugar & milk in small tupperware containers, a mosquito net, waterproof and knife, fork and spoon, and torch. Everything in fact that I think I would need if I had to leave here suddenly for another place or the bush. It seems, maybe, an unnecessary step to take but I feel it is wise and necessary. We just do not know what to expect and I would hate to be caught like the Mulsinchings totally unprepared. I must admit I feel happier in my own mind now that I have all my belongings gathered together again and in some kind of order.

Let's hope all this organisation will <u>not</u> be necessary and we can safely unpack in a few days or weeks. There is no news at all on the Radio these days of Nigeria or Biafra. What is happening at Calabar?

Tuesday 31st October

No operations today and very few patients in fact now in the hospital. There can be very little money drawn in from the hospital or clinics these days.

The Sergeant in charge of the Militia in this area called in at the clinic yesterday to see Dr Philip and myself. Dr Philip had phoned the District Officer after the trouble with the drunk soldiers and he had advised him to have a word with the Brigadier who was in charge of the whole of Uyo province and who happened to be visiting Itu on Sunday. He was very understanding and promised to speak to his men so we were expecting the Sergeant to be helpful and cooperative. Imagine our horror when he arrived at midday and was quite quite drunk himself. He is certainly no good as an example to his men and this really makes us a bit uneasy about the whole situation. However, he was civil enough and told us to report any soldier who gave us any trouble. He also warned us that there would be a strict curfew from 6 pm to 6 am and that if any of our staff were caught disobeying they would be put in detention. We have since been given a number of passes for those of us who will be outside at night. I even need one, & Dr Philip, to travel from my house to the hospital. Needless to say we have had few night calls because patients are afraid to venture out into the night. We hardly ever see May Russell these days either because she is afraid to leave her wee boys alone in the compound.

November 1967

Thursday 2nd November

Things have quietened down quite a bit here at the hospital and in the Colony. Soldiers now do guard duty at the Colony Beach and are not stationed at my house. They have not been at the hospital either at night so we are very much relieved. For the past 3 nights, 4 or 5 policemen (armed) have been on guard duty & patrol in the Hospital Grounds and we are much happier with this arrangement. These men are older, local, and they are experienced, also they know us & the hospital and they are responsible to the District Officer. He is very friendly and cooperative, Ibo, and has spent some time in Scotland. His wife is there at present doing her midwifery training and she trained at

Law Hospital, Carluke. He has been very good to us and I'm sure he will give us every assistance if trouble does come.

Today I went down to the Colony at 8 am and saw the routine of giving out medicines to working patients (x2 per week) then did a ward round with Dr Philip. What poor souls some of these patients are and they have such horrible deformities and ulcers. I went to theatre in the afternoon to see metatarsal heads being removed and deep ulcers scraped to encourage healing. I hope to spend more time at the Colony and I have 3 books to read on leprosy.

It's about time I stopped reading Agatha Christie novels anyway. There is so little work here at present and I am beginning to get restless with having no definite work to do. Queen Elizabeth was certainly never like this – probably the other extreme and I seem to remember moaning then too. There is no pleasing some people!!!

Friday 10th November

Edet and I travelled from Itu to Umuahia where Bill Cluness was waiting to collect us and take us on to Uburu. It was great to see everyone at Umuahia again – Sjouka had only arrived a few days before – weary and footsore. He had gone by air to the Cameroons, met an English doctor there, was taken by Colin McDonald to the border, was met by Biafran Military who conveyed them part of the way. The Nigerians had taken the main Mamfe/Calabar road so they had to walk by a small bush path, escorted by soldiers through heavy brush, which the soldiers cut away. A bridge of two trees had to be made to cross the River and they proceeded this way for 20 miles. Poor Sjouka had blisters on both feet and was quite exhausted – he had to have 10 days to recover. Quite an adventure but a grueling experience.

Diane North was her usual bouncing self and she promises to visit us here at Uburu. Everyone else was well and gave me a good welcome. Murray Cochrane laid on a very nice meal and gave me a warm invitation to go to Umuahia for a meal when passing or for a weekend. Had a fairly good journey with Bill to Uburu though the last 10 miles of road is atrocious. Alicia, Harry, Charlotte, Hillie & Kees were all pleased to see me. They must be at the stage when any new face is welcome. Everything is quiet here and Edet seems happy to have come with me – there is no evidence of any Ibo/Efik conflict or tension.

Presbyterian Joint Hospital Uburu

1913 – 1988

Ann worked not only in Presbyterian hospitals like this one in Uburu but also with the World Council of Churches in its extensive relief work in Biafra

1/69

STATISTICS OF SICKBAYS

NAME OF WCC PROVINCE: OWERRI   PERIOD UNDER REVIEW: FROM 24TH OCTOBER TO 31ST OCTOBER, 1969.

NO.	ADDRESS	AGENCIES SUPPLYING	NO. OF ADULTS	NO. OF CHILDREN	TOTAL	NO. ADMITTED IN ABOVE PERIOD	NO. DISCHARGED IN ABOVE PERIOD	DEATHS IF ABOVE PERIOD
	AHIARA SUBSTORE							
1.	St. James, Ihiteafoukwu	WCC	-	30	30	+ 45 eaters	+ 100 milk drinkers	
2.	Okwu, Nguru	× CARITAS/ WCC	30	71	101			-
3.	Aguneze	ICRC/WCC	6	70	76			2
	ATTA SUBSTORE							
4.	St. Matthew's, Atta	WCC	6	24	30			
5.	Urudim, Atta	"	-	30	30 15			
	AVU SUBSTORE							
6.	Umuguma, Umuoma	"	-	30	30 35			
7.	Avu, Uzuhiete	"	-	42	42 50	20		
	IFE SUBSTORE							
8.	Ife Community, Ezinihitte	"	-	30	30	7		
	EZFU SUBSTORE							
9.	Emii	"	-	45	45 30	+ 45	+ 100	
10.	Awaka	"	-	40	40	-		
	IHIAGWA SUBSTORE							
11.	Baptist, Ihiagwa	"	-	58	58 60	-		
	INYISHI SUBSTORE							
12.	Baptist, Amaimo	"	5	25	30 40	-	5	-
	MBIERI SUBSTORE							
13.	Mbieri, Ubakuru	"	5	31	36 50	-	3	3
	OGWA SUBSTORE							
14.	Community, Ogwa	"	6	39	45 60	-	-	-
			70 58	762 565	832 653	27	34 8	5

December 1967

Letters to and from home were a lifeline for Ann. She was a regular correspondent with her parents and close friends like Sarah Watson in Carluke, when the erratic wartime postal service allowed for the delivery of international mail. Ann also wrote prayers letters back to Scotland for her prayer partners in local congregations, keeping them up to date with developments in Biafra.

Monday 4ᵗʰ December

A Prayer Letter Home to Scotland

"Christ is coming! Let creation   Presbyterian Joint Hospital
From her groans and travail cease;   Uburu
Let the glorious proclamation   Via Afikpo
Hope restore and faith increase   Biafra
Christ is coming!
Come, Thou blessèd Prince of Peace."

My dear friends,

Greetings to you all from Biafra!

Christmas is a time when we should all make a special effort to contact friends and relatives, a time to renew friendships, a time to share news, a time to bind closer existing bonds of love and friendship, a time to remember what God has done for us through Christ, His Son. I like this time, and I am very pleased indeed to have the opportunity to send you some news and warm greetings.

Only last week we were told that the Biafran Government had arranged overseas postal services and, needless to say, we were all delighted. I enjoy writing letters and, like everyone else, I love to receive them. I received my last letter six weeks ago but some of our missionaries have had no news from home for six or seven months. God is good and it's amazing how He gives us the grace to accept every situation. No letters – but we know that this does not mean no communication – our thoughts, our prayers and our love for Christ and His service keep us united, keep us near to one another. This Christmas let us think of the many ways in which God has upheld us in recent months, strengthened us and drawn us closer to Himself. Let us give God special thanks for Christ whose Grace is all sufficient for each one of us.

4/12/67

"Christ is coming! let creation
From her groans and travail cease;
let the glorious proclammation
Hope restore and faith increase:
Christ is coming!
Come, Thou blessed Prince of Peace."

Presbyterian Joint Hospital
Uburu
via Afikpo
Biafra
4th Dec. 1967.

My dear friends,

Greetings to you all from Biafra! Christmas is a time when we should all make a special effort to contact friends and relatives, a time to renew friendships, a time to share news, a time to bind closer existing bonds of love and friendship, a time to remember what God has done for us through Christ, His Son. I like this time, and I am very pleased indeed to have the opportunity to send you some news and warm greetings.

Only last week we were told that the Biafran Government had arranged overseas postal [...] war for independence and are, at present, under siege. War always brings hardship and suffering

Letters to and from home were a lifeline for Ann

53

Most of you will be aware, to a certain extent, of the situation here in Biafra. We are involved in a war for independence and are, at present, under siege. War always brings hardship and suffering and, in some areas, the people are very much aware of this. Fortunately here at Uburu we are off the main road and all is quiet. The hospital is very busy though many drugs are in short supply. This is the beginning of the harvest and there is plenty of rice and yam in this area. Salt is also produced here from the local lake so the people are very busy making salt – and making money. Salt is very scarce and costly these days. For us it means that the local people have the money to pay for medicine and hospital fees.

The situation at Itu was quite different when I left three weeks ago. There is very little trading being done, no money circulating and the people are short of rice and yam. The Ibos are the main traders in that area and recently there has been some tension so trading has decreased. Itu is, of course, nearer to Calabar, where fighting is still going on and people are unwilling to be admitted to hospital at this time. The Mary Slessor Hospital was very quiet even for inpatients and I was sent to Uburu to relieve Dr Reijnierse who is in charge of the General Hospital, River Health work and Leprosy. Usually two doctors are required for the work here but for the past few months only one has been available. For the past 3 weeks I have been in charge of the General Hospital and outpatient clinics while Dr R visited Leprosy Clinics in outlying areas. The hospital has approximately 110 beds and a 90% bed occupancy so we are kept fairly busy. I enjoy the work and so far, have been able to cope. My lesson in hard work & experience in Queen Elizabeth Hospital last year is standing me in good stead.

Friday 15th December

I have neglected to keep this journal up to date. A sign that I have neglected many other things – no Bible Study, scanty prayers, too much time wasted playing Canasta and learning to play Bridge. It is good to have company but at times it is good to be alone – alone to think, to pray, to reconsider one's life and witness. A sober time because usually if one has to stop to do this then one is doing all the wrong things.

I have been here at Uburu for 1 month now. Edet has gone back to Itu to see his people and he assured me that he would come back in 2 weeks but I doubt it. There are very few Efik boys in this area and there has been talk of trouble starting again down Itu, Uyo way so I think Edet's people will advise him to stay near his own home, among his own people. Obasi is looking after me these days but he is Mr Cluness' boy and I am not too happy or at ease with him. I will need to make arrangements sometime soon to find another boy.

I have started doing the clinics on Tuesdays and Thursdays and enjoy these very much. It has been very hot and very tiring, very noisy and frustrating at times but it is good to see all the mothers and babies and to be welcomed by them.

I am now in charge of the female and children's ward and I like this very much. We certainly see some poor wee mites.

At the moment we have Esther and Eke in the ward. They have been there for 2 weeks now. Eke is about 2 years old and is a severe kwashiorkor, very thin, pot belly, hair scanty, straight and fair, very light skinned, cannot walk because of his weak general condition. Esther is his sister, age 7 yrs, pretty lively wee thing who is his attendant, cooks his food and takes care of him. She is always around carrying him on her back or front and he is much too heavy for her. The mother comes once or twice in the week to bring food to them, the husband has left them so she has to go home to work the farm to make some money to feed them. They are very friendly, lovable and only in the past four days Eke has started to smile. This is always a good sign and I take great encouragement from it. I have been giving them eggs now & again and fruit. No child can improve on their diet of rice & yam with a little soup. We give milk, casilan, multivite, yeast and iron tablets. The patients here are fed by the relatives but fortunately the hospital has a supply of milk & wheat which we can give to supplement the children's diet.

I have my meals with Bill Cluness here in my house, his boy Obasi does the cooking, Alicia & Charlotte come in the evenings to eat with us then Harry Smith comes and we usually play Canasta.

Last night Hillie invited us all to her house to have coffee and discuss Christmas. We talked of Christmas, having a family meal and quiet evening together but our behaviour and attitude to one another made a mockery of Christmas, of Christ's teaching & life, of the family. We seem to be in a rut and it's about time we shook ourselves out of it. Because of this realisation over last night I have decided to start doing Bible Study again, keep this journal up to date, spend more time on my own, more time with God, and more time doing God's work. I have not been going to Bible Study with the nurses (I thought previously that it was all done in Ibo) and I have been lazy about going to prayers in the morning, having a lie-in sometimes.

I must be prepared for Christmas and I must encourage the others to be prepared also. It means so much to us but it is the same old story – we are so easily led astray, so ready to take the easy way out.

God forgive me for all my sins of omission and commission in these past weeks. Strengthen me and help me to be a true and earnest disciple, give me a heart like Christ's, willing and obedient and ready to do only God's will. Amen.

Thursday 21ˢᵗ December

Christmas Party at the General Hospital. The chapel was cleared and the tables nicely decorated with flowers. I enjoyed the hot rice and goat this time though it was "a bit" (+++) peppery. We had a very nice social evening with a play, film strip, singing, and then dancing started at 10.30 pm. At first it had been decided that there would be no music or merry-making because we were at war and living in difficult times. The labourers and nursing staff joined together for this meal and party for the first time. Finance was the main argument for it. The dance went well and I enjoyed it very much. Alicia, Harry, Bill & I stayed until 1.30 am. I did not have the nerve to try the "high-life" though I enjoyed watching the others.

Saturday 23ʳᵈ December

Today I went with Bill Cluness and Harry Smith to visit the Aitkens at Abakaliki, the Hutchisons at Iquo and Eva Liisa Karpinen at Norcap. A very busy tiring but enjoyable day.

We set out at 8.15 am and travelled the tar road to Abakaliki - miles. We had to cross the pontoon – a raft big enough to carry one car and a few people. Faith, Bill and the children Jean, Marion, Robin, & Sally were pleased to see us. We had to go through about 5 or 6 road checks to see them. They are in the Presbyterian Secondary School, and Bill is the Principal. At present the school is invaded with military police, militia and soldiers and is very very noisy and full of activity. In Abakaliki the wives & children of most of the Biafrans have gone home so it is strange to go along the street and meet no children. We heard the latest news then stayed for lunch. I was pleased to hear that Miss Eva Liisa Karpinen from Norcap was arriving for lunch also.

We went on to visit the Hutchisons who are struggling away near the war front, hearing gunfire every day, living wholly on Biafran chop. However, the four girls seem healthy enough and they are all in good spirits. We spent a very short time at Norcap, collected 2 turkeys then went on to deliver turkeys at Itigidi. A very tiring but enjoyable day and one I would wish to repeat.

I have neglected my things in this past month. I think I will now jot down a few things worth noting – for interest, for a reminder and for encouragement to change.

Sunday 24ᵗʰ December

May Russell arrived on 23ʳᵈ for 2 weeks rest. What a shock we got to see her. She had moved to Ibiaku Secondary School to be with Miss McLaren and Miss Cameron and the school compound had been bombed three times. May had a very narrow escape, sitting in her car only a few yards from where the bomb fell. For a week there had been daily bombing raids and the missionaries and their few staff (boys) have been running out & into the bush trying to take cover. May developed a sore back, and is very badly shaken up and nervous. She talks of the bombs all the time and is very nervous and edgy. It has certainly been a nerve-wracking experience for them all at Itu and district.

The nurses did a Nativity play instead of the usual Sunday evening service. The Chapel was filled to overflowing with nurses, friends, patients and other outsiders. They were original in many ways and did well – the children almost fled from the chapel when the angel Gabriel suddenly and unexpectedly appeared. I think everyone got a fright with this white ghost-like apparition. I laughed outright I'm afraid, when the shepherds appeared, there were no sheep, but the noise they made was terrific and very realistic!

After that service we all went to the Colony service at 9 pm and it was well done. There were actually sheep in this one but they did not 'baa' at all. Nativity plays tell the same old story. "Tell me the old old story of Jesus & His love." It is always good to hear and to let the full meaning of Christmas sink in. These two plays brought it home once more to me. Christmas has come, Christ has come with all His love & promises. Thanks be to God!

Christmas Day, Monday 25th December

Today I went to a service in the Leper Colony Church. Dr K. Reijnierse was preaching, and he was very good. He explained that the disciples & Jews were expecting a King with power, a King who would deliver them from their oppression and hard times. God sent His Son as a tiny newborn baby. Was He strong enough to deliver them? This was not what they expected. Then he asked if we thought Christ, the newborn babe was <u>not</u> what we expected or wanted to deliver us from our hardship, our war. Christ has still the power and we must put our trust in Him and thank God for His most precious gift.

At the end of the service there was a discharge service. All these lepers who had been healed received a certificate to state that they were free from leprosy. Before the names were called Kees said that most of these patients were <u>not</u> getting what they may have expected or wanted. They were being given a certificate but they could not be given new limbs or new features – they must still bear the marks of the leper. Life would not be easy because many people outside would still not accept them into the community. Christ must be their leader, their guide and their strength in the difficult days that lay ahead.

About 20 names were read out. I always find this discharge service very moving, truly humbling and thankful to God for my many mercies. These poor souls did indeed bear the marks of leprosy – a young man with a below-knee amputation, a young man with no foot, a man with the unmistakeable leonine features, a woman walked forward on knee pads, she had below knee stumps only. They were so happy, they shook hands so warmly, started singing and it was a joy to see their thankfulness yet oh so pathetic and heartbreaking. Only Christ could give them the strength & courage to face life and the outside world.

I have sent and received no Christmas cards this year.

O God, grant to all my friends and loved ones a very blessèd Christmas. May Christ be real to each one. May He guide and protect them in the coming year and may the peace of God stay in their hearts. Once more I commit my family and all my friends to the love and tender care of God & His Holy Spirit. Amen.

Friday 29th December

Alicia, May Russell, and I set out early this morning in the Peugeot to spend the day on the sandbank at Itigidi. We had coffee with Cor Middlekoop, waited for one of the Dutch sisters, Brechta, then set out by canoe for the sandbank about 12.30 pm.

We were carrying a collapsible chair for May because of her bad back, and the men in the 'cane-u' set it upright. May seated herself in the middle of the 'cane-u', sunglasses, straw hat and all – Mary Slessor herself! (Alicia said). She really looked the part. We laughed & laughed! Brechta, Alicia and I lazed around and sunbathed and swam in the river. May sat in her chair, hat, sunglasses and umbrella for shade – comfortable and relaxed. Brechta called her Mary Slessor all day. The Middlekoop family arrived later, also the other Dutch sister. We really enjoyed ourselves and stayed until 6.30 pm.

Sunday 31st December

On Hogmanay Bill, Harry, Uncle John and I agreed to go to Hillie's at 9.30pm for coffee and spend the evening together to wait for the New Year. I was so pleased to have made ginger wine from essence I brought with me from Carluke and I had a tin of Crawford's shortbread. We waited about half an hour then separated. I went to bed at 1.15am.

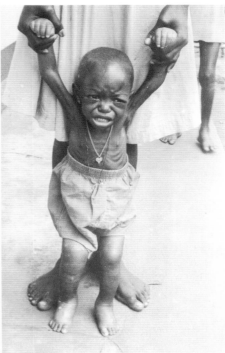

Kwashierkor.
Protein deficiency.
1. Oedema (swelling of
legs, hands, feet
+abdomen)
2. Skin discolouration
& depigmentation. Hair
changes.
3. Anaemia (straight+ discol.)
4. Usually goes on to sores
on legs. Breakdown of skin
5. Miserable appearance.
6. Pitiful wailing cry.

June 1968

At the height of the blockade of Biafra
in 1968, thousands of children died
from malnutrition and diseases like
kwashiorkor, as Ann's handwritten
medical note from that time records

The Journal 1968

Hail Biafra!

"His Excellency, Lt. Col. Ojukwu visited Queen Elizabeth Hospital, Umuahia on this day. He took the salute in the hospital grounds . . . It was a very moving occasion . . . HAIL BIAFRA!"

Ann's journal entry for May 30th 1968, first anniversary of Biafran independence, already marred by famine

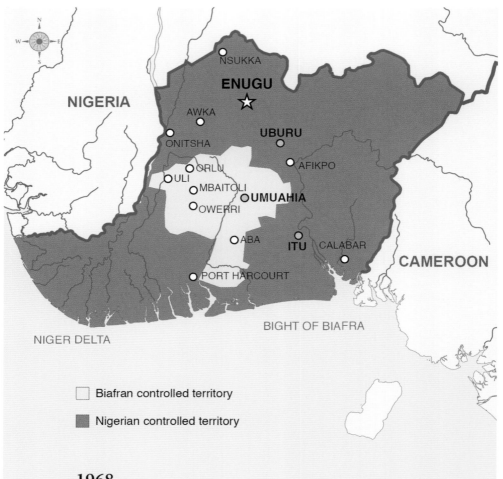

1968

Ann had to move from hospital to hospital as the war front
shifted in the course of this year and throughout the war.
Ann started 1968 working briefly in the Mary Slessor Hospital
at Itu. Throughout the rest of the year, she moved between the
Presbyterian Joint Hospital at Uburu and the Queen Elizabeth
Hospital at Umuahia—conducting evacuations as the Nigerian
forces advanced and the hospitals were bombed by their
military planes.

Timeline 1968

1968	Key Events
January	Ann returns briefly to Mary Slessor Hospital, Itu, then goes back to Presbyterian Joint Hospital, Uburu Mary Slessor Hospital, Itu, bombed
March	Heavy fighting at Itu – Mary Slessor Hospital evacuated Ann moves to Queen Elizabeth Hospital, Umuahia; start of her refugee work, providing clinics in refugee camps Mass starvation due to the blockade of Biafra by the Nigerian military government forces
April	Afikpo falls to Nigerian forces Presbyterian Joint Hospital, Uburu, evacuated with Nigerian advance
June	Thousands of children dying of malnutrition due to the Nigerian blockade of Biafra Ann uses money sent by Carluke churches to pay medical fees for sick children
July	Ann moves back to Presbyterian Joint Hospital, Uburu, after town is recaptured by Biafran forces in a shifting war front
August	Mass starvation and deaths escalate under Nigerian blockade Hospital medical fees being paid in salt due to lack of currency
September	Uburu evacuated again; Ann narrowly escapes capture and returns to Queen Elizabeth Hospital, Umuahia Daily air raids and bombings of hospital Murder of two elderly Anglican missionaries and Red Cross workers by Nigerian forces
October	Ann suffers asthmatic attacks and health worsens Memorial service for Anglican missionaries at Queen Elizabeth Hospital Chapel
November and December	Ann on furlough in Carluke due to serious illness Ann reports to the Church of Scotland the massive scale of infant deaths from starvation that she has recorded as a doctor. She is not believed.

As the Nigerian government forces continue their attack on Biafra, an effective food and medicine blockade of its shrinking borders leads to mass starvation and death from related diseases.

The crisis reaches its height by May and June 1968, with appalling suffering, before church bodies and international aid agencies are able to break the blockade with emergency night time airlifts of desperately needed food and medical supplies into Biafra from offshore airports. It is barely enough.

January 1968

New Year's Day, Monday 1st January

Staff Nurse Victoria Igbokwe invited May, Charlotte, Alicia and I for chop in her quarters. She is a very nice reserved & quiet person and we all like her, she is also a good nurse and is in charge of Female/Children's Ward. She had been given a chicken as a Christmas gift and wanted to share it. Her room was very fresh and clean and we had chicken and coconut-rice which was hot (peppery) but very good. We had drinks and then fruit salad. I enjoyed it very much and was pleased at being invited.

<u>8 pm</u> Uncle John, Harry, Mary, May and I had our evening meal together and a quiet evening. We talked, Uncle John told stories and we relaxed and enjoyed one another's company.

Earlier in the evening I had told Alicia & Charlotte about my feelings over Hogmanay but made it clear that they would be welcome in the evening. I did not invite them for a meal because I felt it would make a division – us and the Reijnierses. I don't think they wanted any company but it was not a very happy New Year's Day.

The mission field is fraught with many dangers and difficulties yet we seem to make things even more difficult for ourselves. Many people warned me that personal relationships would be a problem, I did not altogether believe them, but it seems they were right. I still believe that we can be united and work in harmony and enjoy one another if we keep Christ in our midst. Regular Bible Study and prayer together would solve this unhappy situation.

Tuesday 2nd January

Kees, Hillie and the two children set off today for a week's holiday at Norcap. They were not reconciled to Charlotte and Alicia. I had a busy Out Patient clinic and then an afternoon of emergencies. I finished the outpatients at 2.55 pm and then took an emergency strangulated hernia to theatre. It was difficult and required a resection. Before I had finished I had arranged to do a laparotomy on a woman with abdominal pain and obstruction who had been admitted earlier. When I finished the hernia I had to go to Maternity, do an internal version and breech extraction on a 28 wk – placenta praevia. I did the laparotomy – found a severe case of intussusception which was reduced with difficulty, and about six inches of necrotic bowel had to be resected. I finished at 7.15 pm. Quite a good day's work but I'm happy to say a successful one. The patients were all in reasonably good condition.

We played Canasta in the evening.

Wednesday 3rd January

We received word today that all bank notes must be deposited and that they will be worthless after 7th January. What a carry on! The Federal Government are recalling all the Nigerian notes and issuing new currency – date line 21st Jan. Now Biafra recalls but there is no word of exchange currency and there are not enough shillings available. Crisis upon crisis!

Sunday 7th January

May, Bill Cluness & I set out early on Sunday for Umuahia, then on to Itu with the Colony car. We went to Murray's house for coffee having brought our own sandwiches. Janet Brown had come to meet us and it was good to see her again. The money situation is in everyone's thoughts. On Friday we refused to take notes at the clinics, everything had to be paid in cash. We had fewer patients. Many people were rushing to their villages to collect their money to deposit it in banks and govt. treasury offices. Hospital staff were allowed to go home & collect theirs and all the money was collected at the hospital. In the evening Bill, Harry, Alicia and I sat counting the notes collected, from 8-10.30pm – £1, 10 shilling, 5 shilling notes which amounted to over £3,000. A fantastic sum! With many surprises!

Labourers who seemed to have very little money appeared with wads of notes. The driver brought £190. Since the Enugu banks fell I think people have been unwilling to deposit so they have hidden it away. They can certainly save. At Umuahia we learned that they had collected £28,000 from hospital staff. They, of course, have the staff from the Enugu teaching hospital.

We have heard so many stories.

An Ibo trader from Abiriba deposited 100,000 in notes.

Mr Eme had a pauper in his parish who was assessed and asked to pay 12 shillings and six pence per year in Church contributions. The villagers claimed that even this was too much. This same man appeared with £750 in notes and

Bought in Umuahia
15th Oct. 1968.
Ann W Jackson.
QEH.

Biafra functioned as a
sovereign state during its brief
history, issuing its own currency and stamps

£250 in shillings. He has been told that he is expected to make a considerable contribution to a new church once the money is redeemed. Some pauper!

At Onicha on Saturday, a man had a basin full of shillings for sale – 10 shillings for £1. He was arrested.

Many villages will not have heard the news in time, though it is said the time will be extended for some days. So many will lose – they are afraid to receive only a piece of paper (receipt) for all their notes. Very few received shillings in exchange, the others will have to wait.

This is probably the first time in history that money has been recalled and no new currency issued in exchange. Markets are at a standstill, shops are closed. Villagers have their farms and food but the poor souls who live in the towns must be hit very hard. Petrol is scarce, in fact not obtainable and in the few places it is available the price is 8/- and 10/- per gallon. It seems that storage tanks at Port Harcourt were bombed. Queen Elizabeth Hospital is very busy – as usual – but many of the govt. doctors who were working there have been sent to the war front. Only 4 or 5 remain so it means much hard work for Sjouka, Edgar and John. Murray gave us a warm welcome and it was good to hear the banter of these two friends, Sjouka and Murray. Everyone was in good spirits but we realise that the situation is serious.

Tuesday 9th January

Mary Slessor Joint Hospital

Morning prayers at 7am. Evening prayers 7.30pm.

I have now been several days here at the Mary Slessor Joint Hospital – much is the same yet there are many changes. We have a total of 15 inpatients, two children, three females, two maternity and eight male patients – we actually have more nurses than patients. Not a good situation! At Okopedi the clinic is still on Mondays, Wednesdays and Fridays but few civilians attend. The army, navy and militia are our main patients.

On Monday I saw about 60 outpatients – 50 military and 10 civilians, only one or two children. On Wednesday there were 50, again about 6-8 civilians. The other outside clinics at Ono and Ikpa may have to be stopped, few attend and petrol is now scarce and very dear. There must be many reasons for this poor attendance – shortage of money, fear of the soldiers, decreased numbers of people in the area. The Ibo traders have nearly all left Okopedi and gone to their own villages. Edet tells me that because of the air raids all the villagers from the Itu Hill have deserted their homes and hide all day in the plantations across the river. People are not allowed to use the river these days – the navy patrols it in engine boats.

The theatre list on Tuesday consisted of a haemorrhoidectomy and a circumcision. There is not enough work for me here yet a doctor needs to be in attendance. Soldiers arrive at any hour in the day and we are obliged to see them. They are at Mbiafor and trek 8 miles to come to hospital – many of them come from the 'war front' or are on special task duties. They are a pathetic discouraged bunch. About 8-10 come each day, uniforms sweat-soaked, dirty, just hanging on them, many with tattered gym shoes on their feet, many with nothing on their feet – all tired and very wearied looking. They complain of fever, chest pain, general weakness, dysentery of some weeks or months duration. Many do need medical attention but most of them need sympathy and a rest. I spend the afternoons resting and reading but it is difficult to fill my day with work. I should content myself and do some Bible Study. God knows best and He knows that I should spend more time with Him. I feel He is giving me this opportunity to learn of Him, to give my time to Christ and His teaching. I am reading the book by Geoffrey T. Bull "God holds the key" and this is just what God is saying – let Christ be all in all, think on Him, meditate on His life and deeds. This book tells of the author's 3 years' confinement in a prison in Red China in 1951. Solitary confinement for 1 year, nothing to read, nothing to do so he meditates on God and His Word. Atheism and Marxist doctrine make no impression him, he does not recant or capitulate to his captors and their ideals, he remains sane and true to God, true to his task of serving Christ.

O God, forgive me for letting time hang heavy on my hands, forgive me for wasting time, for feeling frustration at my reduced activity. Help me, O God, to use this precious gift aright, to use this time of quiet to rest on Thee, to meditate on Thy Word and to go forward strengthened and convicted anew to do Thy Will. Amen.

Friday 12th January

Today we received an unexpected but most welcome visitor. Dr Ted Johnstone from the Canadian Presbyterian Church came to see Ron McGraw, and Ron invited us all for coffee to meet him. What a surprise! This quiet-spoken friendly Canadian is head of the Foreign Missions of the Canadian Church and he travelled from London -> Geneva -> Lisbon -> St Isabella at

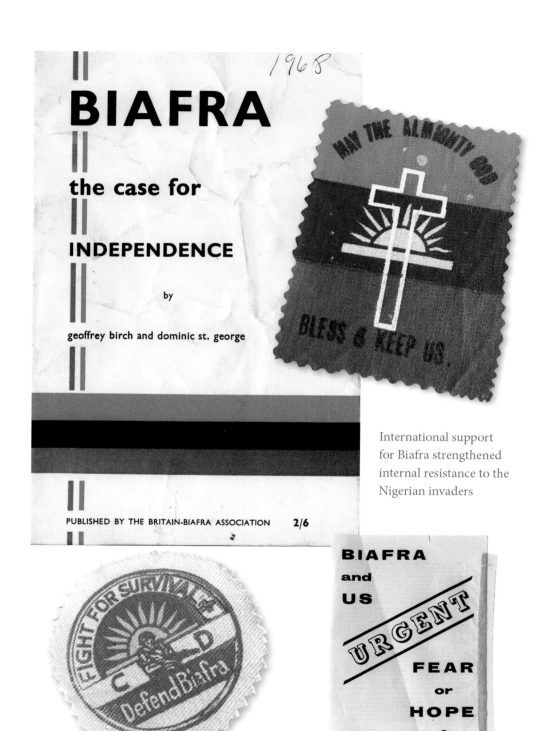

1968

BIAFRA

the case for

INDEPENDENCE

by

geoffrey birch and dominic st. george

PUBLISHED BY THE BRITAIN-BIAFRA ASSOCIATION   2/6

MAY THE ALMIGHTY GOD

BLESS & KEEP US.

International support
for Biafra strengthened
internal resistance to the
Nigerian invaders

FIGHT FOR SURVIVAL
C D
Defend Biafra

BIAFRA
and
US

URGENT

FEAR
or
HOPE
?

the invitation of the Biafran Government. As far as I understand, he is viewing the situation, collecting data and hopes to present Biafra's case to the outside world. He has connections in Geneva and with the Commonwealth Secretary in London as well as the other Churches interested in Biafran/Nigerian conflict.

He feels himself that the war has now come to the stage when both sides must be prepared to talk and make concessions. Biafra has shown herself able to withstand the Nigerian assault, able to survive on her own. Independence was declared on 30th May 1967, and she is still independent, no country has recognized her sovereignty, no country has openly supported her, she is cut off by sea and air and land, yet she has survived. This is due to the ability, determination, and faith of this Ibo people. They believe that they are fighting to survive, and I think this is true. They have certainly fought long and hard, they have clever and able leaders, and there is an excitement, an awakening in this new nation. They want to stand alone, prove themselves, make a contribution to African and world affairs. I certainly support them. Dr Johnstone seems to feel that the countries outside are realizing that Biafra exists and that a settlement must be made. He feels that Biafrans still want Britain as a friend, though they feel hurt and disappointed at her supporting the Federal Government. If only Britain would change her policy and realize that the Federation is broken up. The Ibos and Hausas could never live together, work together in harmony. Atrocities have been perpetrated on both sides, as happens in war, innocents have suffered, hatred and resentment goes deep, barriers which will last for centuries to come have been set up.

In this Ibibio area which stretches to Ikot Ekpene there is less support for Biafra than I had realised. This is a minority area and the people loathe the Ibo – many say that they would rather be dominated by the Nigerians than by the Ibos. They want to be Nigerian and not Biafran. The Ibibios and Efiks will always be minority groups, they have no guarantee that the Nigerians will give them a fair deal, they seem to want their own state. They say the Ibos want to dominate, to possess their land, to possess their exit at Calabar, their palm oil groves and fruit plantations which are scarce in Iboland. The Ibos are certainly populous and need more land, yet I think the Ibibios will be treated fairly as Biafrans. No one knows what the next days, weeks or months will bring.

The Ibibios and Calabar people fear reprisals if Calabar once more becomes Biafran. The Nigerians were welcomed there, infiltrations were supported by the local people and some Ibos speak of revenge. Ibos were molested by the local people and Ibo soldiers molested the locals, so both sides have much to answer. The situation is fraught with problems, difficulties and side issues, and no real solutions or answers are evident.

Mr Johnstone certainly gave us information about the outside world and I must say I felt encouraged and hopeful about his visit. Inter-church Aid in Geneva has a sum of money available to supply some of our needs – probably medical supplies and maybe free milk and wheat for the people. An American Catholic organisation hopes to start aeroplane trips with freight to Santa Isabella so this would open things up for us. Clyne Shepherd may be coming in with a Red Cross team, working for 3/12 with the Red Cross, then would be free to work in our own hospitals.

Listening to the discussion I realized just how 'Biafran' I felt. The others here have, to some extent, reservations because they feel for the minority groups and want a fair deal for them. I want a fair deal for them also, but I feel that the Ibos have strived hard and done well and they deserve their freedom as an independent nation. They certainly have my fullest support. They will survive and I am pleased and privileged to be in this fight with them. I set out from Scotland for Biafra believing in their fight, and I thought their cause was just. I still believe this and want Biafra to come out of this conflict victorious. There is so much ill feeling and resentment in this area against the Ibos, a long history of inter-tribal hatred and suspicion. I hope a just and peaceful settlement will be arranged. I hope that when peace does come it will be complete, that the Rivers, Ibos, Efiks and Ibibios will all rejoice and strive to rebuild their areas and the country.

O God, into Thy hands we commit our hopes and our fears. In Jesus' Name. Amen.

Saturday 13th January

A fairly quiet day again. Many soldiers were seen at the clinic but none of them very serious. We see so many with fever & headache, cough, dysentery and the usual soldiers' complaint – gonorrhea. At the beginning I tried to lecture, threatened to withhold treatment and went into detail about what will happen in later years if no treatment is given. Some were worried but I don't suppose it will last or help them to change their ways. They need treatment and we can't withhold it but I do grudge giving out our precious Penicillin supplies. At least they know I am not pleased, and I warn them not to come back with the same complaint. One young soldier complained of eyestrain, said the sun was too strong; he had been at the war front for 3 months now and felt that I should give him a paper recommending that he be given office work at Umuahia. Poor lad he asked in all seriousness. These soldiers do have a hard time, living in the bush, in this mosquito infested area and being so poorly clad and normally no medical attention for months at a time. One soldier told me that they were camped down the river from the Leper Colony. Could I give him some disinfectant so he could have his daily bath in the river? I reassured him sorrowfully but gently.

Today, Mr Wamilsa, the District Officer (D.O.), came to speak to us at Murray's house and on his invitation. This man is Ibo and his wife is in the UK, doing nurse's training at Stobhill and has been to Law Hospital. He is a young man, attractive and very nice. He is obviously very much in command of the situation here and seems to be aware of his responsibilities to all the peoples in his charge. I must say I was impressed by his modesty, honesty and the intelligent & firm way he dealt with all our questions. No sign of any cash being given out. Petrol will soon be available but at a price (7-8/- per gallon) probably because the Government needs funds. He did not think there was any chance of the Nigerians breaking through so had no plans for the evacuation of Ibos. Murray was concerned because he is responsible for the Leper Colony patients and they are very mixed – Ibo, Ibibio, Efik, Cameroon, Calabar – many of them are cripples who could not make their own escape. Ibos will definitely be victimized. The D.O. pointed out, what we had already been told, that if Murray stays with his patients then his action will be suspect by both sides. Yet how can he run away and leave them? A doctor's duty is to his patients. The D.O. is confident that nothing will happen. The situation will not arise, but he assured us that we would be given 24 hrs notice at least, and he would help with any evacuation. I think he is sincere. We can only trust and hope that he is right in his judgement.

Some planes were heard flying overhead last night again. Everyone is still very jumpy and apprehensive. Maybe I would be too if I had lived here through the bombing of the past few weeks. Janet Brown, Matron, is very nervous and she has certainly lost a lot of weight. Most folk here just want the war to finish.

The Lord's Day, Sunday 14th January

This is indeed the Lord's Day and for the first time in months I have consciously spent this day in meditating and studying God's Word.

I went to the Leper Colony Service and was urged to put on the whole armour of God, to be equipped to fight and be victorious over the devil, over principalities and powers. No matter how often we are told, no matter how much we know it to be true, we try to fight in our own strength, with our own puny weapons. Good intentions are no good, determination is no good, halfhearted prayer is no good, only the grace of God can win for us. We seem to hold on to our sins, I sometimes feel I am only half-hearted in my desire to be free from my sins. I sometimes only half-admit that they are sins. Deep down I am unmoved, unrepentant and only half-convinced. This can only mean that I am not looking Jesus full in the face, I half see His beauty and His light. I am obscure, therefore He is obscured by my own doing. We cannot have any sinful thought or feeling in our heart if we come before Christ, His beauty should make us confess our sin & unworthiness and we should seek only His face, His forgiveness and feel the warmth of His love. How can He smile on us if we are impure, if our heart's longing is not laid bare for Him to see and smile upon. I am indeed proud, I love to be loved or liked, my motives for being good and doing good are so often purely selfish. It seems I want to influence people, for me, not for Christ I want people to love me – and Christ – but I seem to put "me" first. Fine I know that it is the Christ in me shining forth in spite of myself or me that people love.

O God, forgive my foolish ways and reclothe me in a rightful mind, purify my longings and fit me for thy Service and thy Kingdom. In Jesus' name. Amen.

Thursday 18th January

Everyone has been feeling the cold this morning. Arms folded hugging ourselves, scarves and sweaters in evidence – the temperature in the Consulting Room was 73° F!!! Many of the nurses complain of cough and catarrh. The hospital is very quiet. I saw only 3 soldiers who had trekked from at least 8 miles away and who claimed they had been three months in the trenches. Poor souls! They certainly looked very forlorn and dejected with their malaria and dysentery and general weakness.

There are no patients in Maternity at the moment and I read through the Report Book for this month. Usual entry is – "Admissions nil. Patients 2. Babies 2." And the last entry says, "Admissions nil. Patients nil. Babies nil. Patient was discharged today with her baby. Wishing the night nurse good luck in admitting patients."

It's laughable if it wasn't so tragic. This Joint Hospital has about 16 patients, 25 assistant nurses, 2 midwives and 8 staff nurses and 3 sisters & 2 lab men & 2 dispensers and quite a number of labourers. I am indeed concerned, no money is coming in, there is very little work yet we are responsible for all these salaries. I must see Murray if it would not be wise to suspend some of the staff. True we do not know what the next day will bring but this situation could go on for months and the hospital estimates have not been approved by the Government so they may not give our full allowance. The situation here is serious. What is the answer?

I have been here at Itu for almost 2 weeks now, relieving Dr Murray Philip. The work here has cut down drastically so I have had a lot of free time. As already stated, I have been doing a lot of worthwhile reading and in my reading been stimulated to read more. I started reading about the life of Michelangelo and the history of the Renaissance at Uburu and I brought it with me to finish. I enjoyed it very much. I read Andrew Bonar's book about Robert Murray McCheyne, of his life and work, of his close walk with God and the results that were seen by all men. He gave a shining witness and he left a good example. Bonar also gives us extracts from his journal and it is obvious that McCheyne consciously cultivated Christ & sought to be like him. This brought home to me my own puny efforts, my lack of self-discipline and lack of zeal. I want to be holy, I want to be like Christ, I want to do Christ's work and all that God has in mind for me. I must therefore spend more time with Christ before God's throne, before the Mercy Seat. The Holy Spirit will lead me if I will only respond to His guidance and teaching.

I have also been reading Moody's Anecdotes and have enjoyed these illustrations and have already noted some of them in this journal. Geoffrey T. Bull's book "God holds the Key" has influenced me quite a bit in my resolve. This book is said to be a record of his meditations and reflections centring on the period of his imprisonment in China October 1950 to Dec 1953.

Friday 19th January

God is indeed good, and loving and patient. He waits for us though we are often so hesitant in our steps towards him. Yet He receives us into His waiting loving arms and folds us to His breast. I thank God for the many times He has waited for me and I thank Him for the definite leading and prodding He gave me. I thank Him for His Holy Word and for the guidance of the Holy Spirit who makes God's words alive and real and meaningful to me. I thank God also for His many servants who have gone before and who still bear witness to His saving grace and faithfulness. I am thinking again of these books, of Michelangelo Buonarroti who lived in the 16th century, of R. Murray McCheyne who lived in the 19th century, of Geoffrey Bull who is still living and of Paul who wrote so long ago. How can people deny God and His Son when there are countless men and women through the ages, who lived and died looking unto Jesus, proving in their very lives that God is true, and just and faithful. I hope and pray that my testimony for Christ will be a positive one, that I will give a good witness and do my share to further God's Kingdom here on earth. I have started my daily Bible Study (at long last) with Professor Barclay's notes on Corinthians. I am enjoying it and have been doing 2 chapters per day. I have also looked out the [Church of Scotland's daily prayer guide] Holy Tryst so will try to be more faithful to my dear friends and colleagues. I hope to have a definite time of prayer and schedule each evening and a definite Quiet time each morning to contemplate Christ over and above my Bible Study.

Please God help me in my endeavours.

Saturday 20th January

A very quiet day with very few at the Out Patients Clinic at the hospital. I have packed my case and am waiting now for the Uburu people to arrive to collect me. I hope that the petrol shortage will not be too big a problem. No petrol supplies have come to this area at all and there is no news of any new currency. The hospital received £50 in shillings from the Treasury to keep things going. It won't last long and the staff will soon be due their salaries and they will need cash to buy their food or to travel home to collect some. We are all dependent on local markets, we have no farms or home grown produce. Yam is very scarce and rice is dear.

I have spoken to Murray about the staff. I walked today to the Colony Market but there was not much to buy and very few stalls open – I saw crayfish, peppers, coco yam, a few yam, rice, okras, greens, beans, plantain and bananas, palm oil and palm wine. I bought 2 bundles of 3 big bananas for 2 pence. I came home and gave one to Clyne Shepherd's monkey, which is called Wendy and which lives outside my house (in an alcove). It's most entertaining. On my way home I met Murray Philip so went for tea with him and told him about the patients in the ward. I have two ill ones and the others are routine and mainly soldiers. We also have one who came in just before Christmas and who was injured at the Okopedi bomb raid. He had his back and arm severely torn with shrapnel and he will be in for a long time. A wee girl – 15 years – was also admitted as a result of that raid, she fell in the rush and has a fractured femur and is again a long-term case.

I spoke to Murray about the staffing situation here and suggested that we should reduce our numbers possibly to a skeleton staff. He says he will discuss it with Janet. I certainly feel that the decision and action should be carried out by the end of the month. Janet says we could close the Maternity Ward and combine children and female, close Okopedi clinic (we see mainly soldiers anyway and they have transport, we have no petrol) and see all the outpatients at the hospital. Janet & I counted the nurses we would need – 6 for male ward, 6 for female ward, 2 for theatre, and 4 for night duty, one lab man, one dispenser and then also cut down on labourers and possibly staff nurses. It will be a difficult decision but an inevitable one. There is also the problem of the lab men – Jacob and Ben. Jacob has been here for years and is a wily kind, he does not come on duty until 8 am because he says there is nothing to do, he does as little as possible. Ben has only been here for about 1-1½ years and he is in every way the best. He is polite & cooperative, does his work well and is always looking for work to do. He is far more reliable and would be of more benefit to the hospital. Yet it will be difficult to suspend Ben instead of him, yet I think I would do it. Murray is not keen on taking the initiative but I'm sure God will show him what is best for the hospital. I only hope the staff will not take it too badly but will realise that it is necessary to take this seemingly drastic step. Many of them may be glad to go home out of this military area – they are so afraid – yet it will be a thought to lose their job. At least their families, with their farms, should be able to feed them.

Sunday 21st January

Had my breakfast with Janet, finished packing, and the car from Uburu arrived at 11 am to collect me. We loaded the car to its fullest capacity, taking Tim Faro's fridge in its packing case, pouffe, and odds & ends in cartons. I was very pleased indeed to have Edet going with me. He seemed keen and I only hope & pray that he will enjoy his stay with me in Uburu. His wife came to see us off. Aze the driver had brought yams (£15 worth) and rice from Uburu and it was arranged that John Isey from the Colony go back with us to collect more. The Colony is responsible for feeding most of its patients, and this is a difficult time. There is still no cash but Uburu Hospital have sources they can pay by check. Bill Cluness has offered to send the Uburu car back down to Itu with loads, supplying the petrol. This is really good – what it should be – cooperation and real Christian fellowship in action. The Colony have said they will supply palm oil & help with engine oil which is scarce up Uburu way.

We left Itu at 2 pm, crossed the Cross River by pontoon at Okopedi and then travelled up the banks of the great Cross River. I enjoyed the trip, was thankful that my stay at Itu had been quiet. We had about 17 road checks and we sailed through each one – at some I was recognized but others accepted me without even my identity card. We were all surprised but very pleased. "We are travelling from Mary Slessor Hospital Itu to Uburu Hospital." "Yes, madam". No questions, only one person asked to see my loads but did not look when I had explained. We arrived at Uburu at 5.30 pm and everyone was in Chapel at the first English Sunday service. I was given a terrific welcome from all the nurses, handshakes, hugs all round. I had my evening meal with Charlotte, Alicia & Bill & John.

Uburu seems to be a place that thrives on trouble. Bill had bought new English hymn books and stamped them with a hospital stamp – Presb. Hospital, Uburu, E. Nigeria. I am sure absent-mindedly, only a fool would intentionally put E. Nigeria at this time when we are a new nation. Biafra and people are very touchy. Anyway the nurses were up in arms and they marched to Bill's office and demanded that he change them. As far as I can gather Bill lost his temper and ordered them out & told them to change it themselves. Someone reported the incident to the War Committee and the situation became serious. For the past week there have been anti-British demonstrations in various towns, Port Harcourt, Owerri, Abba, and it seemed this was going to develop into another one. (There was a rumour going round that Britain was sending 1,000 troops to help the Federal government.) The War Committee had seemingly written several letters, one to Bill, one to Kees, one to a Central Committee demanding that all expatriates be removed from this area. It was a tense situation.

Kees, Chita, Juliana & Bill went to Afikpo to see Mr Eme the Synod Clerk & get his advice on the situation. It's amazing how things can develop from a simple mistake when people are distrustful of one another. It seems that the war committee (and they have admitted it) have several people in the compound who report on our activities and conversations. Ah well, as far as I know we are innocent.

Saturday 27th January

An eventful week.

<u>Monday</u>. Clinic as usual but I was allowed to stay at home and unpack. Edet & I cleaned the house and got settled in. It's good to have him with me. The deputation to Afikpo brought back good news. Mr Eme said he would attend to things and Bill should write a letter of apology to the War Committee. It seems that the nurses are sorry that the matter snowballed into such a serious affair. Wish they would trust us a wee bit more.

<u>Tuesday.</u> Went to Onitsha Clinic and was happy to see that it is just as busy as ever in spite of the money shortage. Here in the hospital we are given a weekly sum – married & single rates – I am allowed 28 shillings, so this is good. It also keeps the money circulating and lets the nurses buy their food.

<u>Wednesday.</u> We had terrible news today. The Federal planes attacked the Mary Slessor Hospital, Itu on Tuesday evening. This seems to be a very deliberate attack. There were Red Crosses on the roofs and a flag. I think 2 bombs were dropped, then the planes re-circled and machine gunned everything. Half the hospital has been destroyed, theatre, part of male ward, offices have been demolished, windows blown out, Archibongs house ruined & bullets, a hole in the roof of the house I was staying. Terrible damage and the hospital has been forced to close and the nurses have been transferred. Murray, Janet & Wendy Ema were in the hospital at the time. Mrs Ema received a bullet wound in the arm, Murray was lying under a bed which collapsed on top of him but he received only innumerable small cuts on his face and arms & legs. God did indeed protect our people. Three people were killed when they ran outside. It was really heartbreaking and frightening. The planes even flew over the next day to assess their damage so there can be no mistake. We think this may be a definite act of revenge because Clyne Shepherd wrote an article proclaiming Biafra and his name & the address of the hospital was given over the radio. A cruel and senseless attack.

<u>Thursday.</u> Kees, Bill, Sandy Sommerville & John Isey went down to Itu. John would of course be worried about his wife and 3 children who were at the Colony. Janet was brought back for a week's rest. She had sprained her ankle while trying to rush for a trench. It was the day after the attack, the planes came back about 2 pm, and Janet was on her way up the hill, she saw the plane swooping down, raced for the trench and actually saw the pilot looking down at her. Poor Janet, feeling very conspicuous in her white coat

but he did not fire. Thanks be to God. We are all feeling very dazed and shocked by this news. Murray Philip & David Duncan have both to come up here for a week's rest sometime next month. They both need a break as well.

February 1968

Monday 5th February

Mary Slessor Hospital again shelled and bombed. This seems to be reprisal for Dr Shepherd's outspoken support of Biafra. The Mulchinsing family evacuated to Uburu.

Tuesday 6th February

Janet Brown & Henry Smith travelled to Itu to sort out drugs & to evacuate the hospital. Several folk went down from Umuahia to salvage equipment etc. – most of it was taken to Queen Elizabeth Hospital and will be used there.

March 1968

Monday 4th March

Janet started work in Uburu.

Tuesday 5th March

Bill, Kees & I travelled to Afikpo to have a meeting with Mr Eme, Sandy Sommerville & Dr Middlecoop. Queen Elizabeth Hospital are short staffed because Robin Burnett left in such a hurry. John Phillips is home on leave and there is no one to take charge of the children's ward. I am not keen at all. I don't want to leave Victoria, I don't want to leave Uburu, I don't want to work in Queen Elizabeth Hospital. However, Herman Middlecoop was looking tired and drawn – he is now living at Norcap with his family since Itigidi Hospital has been bombed. He does not want to be parted from his two children. I volunteered to go to Umuahia for 3 months or so, until John Phillips gets back. While we were at the meeting, Alicia was at Okposi

Clinic and Janet & Chita were in the hospital, Awgu Market was bombed. The nurses ran into the brush, scared stiff, leaving their patients to fend for themselves. They have refused to work in their white uniforms – targets! The nurses now wear the old Mary Slessor blue uniforms. The 9 yr old boy with tetanus was brought back in his father's arms with the Ryle's feeding tube still down his nose. What a day!

Sunday 10th March

Alicia & Charlotte left Uburu for Umuahia to wait for a plane home. Their leave is due.

Friday 22nd March

I left Uburu for Umuahia. Poor Victoria – I will miss her and she will miss me, we have spent many happy times in each other's company. I pray our friendship will be lasting and we will soon work together again. Arrived Umuahia & had my lunch with Murray Cochrane who always gives me such a good welcome. I will be staying in John Phillips' house next to Matron Bent.

Saturday 23rd March

Have hardly had time to settle in here with Ngene, Misses Cameron & McLaren arrived unexpectedly from Ibiaku. They were staying there with David Duncan – this is a school compound with no military nearby. Ibiaku school has been bombed 3 times, the Principal's house & the School House have been destroyed. Murray Cochrane called them "the rabbits" because they spend all the day in their trench with no comforts at all. They arrived with Mickey the hound dog who feeds better than I do. What a waste of food at this time! It's awful to think that there are thousands of starving children and this dog gets so much good food & milk etc. Had dinner in the evening with Sjouka – quite a company and we had a very nice evening. Clyne Shepherd arrived from UK with drugs (6 tons) & milk (4 tons).

Sunday 24th March

Ngene made scrambled egg & porridge for the ladies – he really tries hard. The "rabbits" certainly brought lots of stores with them and they handed them over to me. The Misses left suddenly this evening for the airport. Ron McGraw says he will take the dog.

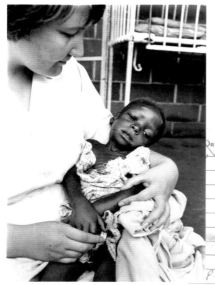

Ann caring for one among hundreds of sick children at Queen Elizabeth Hospital, Umiahia in 1968 during the food blockade

THE QUEEN ELIZABETH HOSPITAL
UMUAHIA, EASTERN NIGERIA

Monday 25th March

Started work in Queen Elizabeth Hospital. Chapel at 6.45 am was very poorly attended, yet there are scores more nurses. It was very depressing at the children's clinic today – a very large number of Kwashiorkor cases and we had only <u>YEAST</u> to prescribe for them, no milk, no multivite. Sister Chita Oje and Staff Nurse Jane came for lunch on their way back to Uburu with Bill. Wish I was going with them.

Tuesday 26th March

A very busy night – 52 children in OKPARA WARD

Wednesday 27th March

We received 15 casualties with severe burns from a petrol blast. What a mess! Six have already died. I seem to spend my evenings sorting out drugs from the Ituk Mban Hospital. The army evacuated the staff and it is all thoroughly mixed up and it will take hours & hours to sort the drugs, equipment, linen etc. There is a lot of useful stuff so at least other hospitals will benefit from the closure of one. It's terrible to realize that there are vast areas now with no hospital or medical facilities.

Saturday 30th March

I have been concerned about the refugees in Umuahia area and Edgar Ritchie advised me to see Mr Errol Roe. He is a lecturer from Nsukka University, an American who fled from Nsukka to Enugu & then to Umuahia and he is very concerned about the refugees. He has done a survey of the camps in the Umuahia Province and there seems to be very little medical work being done. I have arranged to visit the Umuahia camps with him tomorrow. I hope I can find time to help him.

Sunday 31st March

Travelled with Mr Roe to Bende/Ozuabam camps in his wee Volkswagen. It's a lovely 'bendy' road with very nice scenery, hard to believe there is a war on. Met Mr Lekiva who is in charge of the Red Cross Team at McVey High School, Ozuabam. A very nice group of young men but their Red Cross Box contained about 20 Daraprim tablets and nothing else. The refugees were miserable and in need of attention – they came from Oji River and Calabar

Provinces. 973 refugees in three camps with 700 of them children and 40 of the children orphans. They had had no visits from any medical personnel for 3 months. I agreed to hold a clinic in the camp on the Thursday, which is usually a quiet day in the hospital. Met Mrs Kalunta, a nursing sister whose husband is a psychiatrist and they are refugees from Calabar. She seems very nice & anxious for help. She is in charge of 5 camps in Bende, 491 refugees with 244 of them children. I agreed to visit them also on Thursday so let's hope Edgar agrees to release me from my hospital duties.

April 1968

Thursday 4th April

Mr Roe developed a severe tonsillitis a few days ago and was unable to go to the clinic with me. Ron McGraw, Chrissie Denholm & I set out with drugs and milk. A Red Cross team of young men from Ohafia were there and they were very very helpful. It was pandemonium, one doctor trying to see everyone and many were very very sick. 5 patients could not leave their dormitory because they were so weak from anaemia & severe dysentery. Ron gave out the drugs and Chrissie examined children, she sat in the middle of the room, I was on the platform so could watch her & pick out the more serious cases. I wrote down the doses of thalazole & ferrous sulphate etc for her to prescribe. Dr Denholm ! – she was very pleased to be helping in this way. We saw over 200 patients – a long hard day's work!

Friday 5th April

Saw Mrs Obiamarray to try to get nurses to help with the Refugee Clinics. She is very efficient yet friendly and seems to know all that's going on there. There are many displaced nurses now from various hospitals so it should not be too difficult to find helpers. My week-end off and I travelled to Uburu to see my old friends – I surprised Victoria bending over her fire cooking her food. Dear Vicky – she was so pleased to see me and gave me a great welcome. I'm happy we are such good friends!

Friday 19th April

AFIKPO CAPTURED.

There was a surprise attack on Afikpo from the River, much shelling and fighting. Terrible stories told about the fate of patients in the Mater Hospital, and the whereabouts of the Sisters and Senior Nursing staff not known.

Bill Cluness heard by chance as he passed through Amassieri that Afikpo had fallen. He tried to reach the Synod Clerk, Mr Eme and Mr Sommerville but the military prevented him. On the advice of the police and military the Uburu staff were advised to evacuate – bombing & shelling was expected. Drugs & some hospital necessities were evacuated by lorry to Umuahia but kept separate in the Maternity Classroom. Patients & nursing staff were also evacuated. The Senior Staff stayed behind with local Uburu nurses to carry out a skeleton medical service. They also cleared out the wards, dismantled beds & equipment and stored everything away in a safe place. Bill, Kees, Chita, Egwu Obasi and Janet all decided to stay. Uncle John Paterson was sent to Umuahia and he stayed with Graham Brown at Trinity College.

The first I knew of all this was when Sister Juliana arrived before me in the clinic consulting room. What a surprise on a Saturday morning! I then went to the front of the hospital and there were two great muckle lorries loaded with nurses and all their belongings. Real refugees! Blankets, mattresses, radios, cases etc. all piled up and the girls looking wearied and forlorn! Victoria and Phoebe were being taken to Owerri but I arranged a meal for them first. Poor wee souls!

Saturday 20th April

Kees started doing clinics – outpatients again during this week. Bill Cluness & Janet went to Awgu to meet the R. C. Sisters & see if they could take over Refugee Clinics near the hospital – Okpanku and 2 Mpu school camps.

In Umuahia I was going to Refugee Clinics at Ozuabam and Bende. I persuaded the Dutch Sister Brechte to stay and help me. She was originally in Itigidi Hospital but it was bombed so they travelled to Norcap with the Norwegians and did clinics for some time. Mrs Middlecoop & the children were going home but when I explained the Refugee problem to Brechte she decided to stay and help. Victoria decided to go home & visit her people in Owerri then came to Umuahia and join our clinic team. Phoebe was posted by Mrs Obiamavery to one of Mrs Kalunta's camps in Bende. I'm glad I will have Victoria's company again. She will stay with her cousin in the Village.

Sunday 28th April

Letter home to Ann's close friend Sarah Watson in Carluke

Queen Elizabeth Hospital, Umuahia, BIAFRA

My dear Sarah,

This is Sunday so thought I would sit down and give you some more news of this poor country. Yesterday I received several letters from home, from my mother and Church of Scotland but I think yours must still be to come. We receive mail irregularly these days but we hope to receive by a new route soon. At present we are dependent on people going out but for the past 3 weeks there has been a ban on Europeans going out. Some fool infringed the security laws so everyone must suffer. We hope it will be lifted soon because we still have two families waiting to go.

I am well and enjoying my work. I now do two days a week in Refugee camps with a good medical team we have got together. I do clinics and children's ward on the other days. I do thank you dear Sarah for all you and Mr Reid and others are doing for us here. Mum says that my last circular has gone out to many people and I am so glad that people are responding to this urgent need.

Already people are responding – the World Council of Churches have sent in lots & lots of milk and medicines, also the Red Cross so we can really get on with the work. We are busy distributing the stuff to hospitals and camps. We can now count the hospitals in action on one hand almost. Uburu has temporarily closed but the enemy have since been pushed back so it may open again soon. We never know from day to day what is going to happen.

By this time you will have heard that Umuahia was bombed last Thursday – 4 days ago and we are still operating on the injured. Over 100 were killed, hundreds injured and on Friday we had still a theatre list of 60 – major operations, so you can imagine how much sleep the poor surgeons have had. They are still operating today. I did minor surgery and carried on routine outpatient clinics. We had 16 children admitted and on Friday we had altogether 60 in the children's ward. 3-4 on one mattress on the floor – poor wee souls they all wondered what was going on with all these other injured all around them.

Well, thank you again dear Sarah. Please give my greetings and sincere thanks to all the others. God bless us and our work for Him.

Much love,
Ann xxx

Monday 29th April

Uburu Hospital started doing more Refugee Clinics in the area. Okpanku 300 treated: Mpu 180. Outpatients & odd emergencies were done in the wee Septic Theatre. A few patients were admitted for 1 or 2 days only. The staff were always at the ready, waiting for news of any Federal advance but things seemed to settle down.

May 1968

Wednesday 1st May

Village women arrived from miles around to attend their usual antenatal clinic but they had to be sent home because there was no staff available – all trained staff were away and only untrained local nurses were left holding 'the fort'.

Friday 3rd May

Akaeze Clinic was started. Nurses arrived back at the hospital from their homes enquiring about the Senior Staff and eager to be back at work. Nearby nurses were then recalled and gradually most of the staff were back working in the hospital. During this time I continued my work in Queen Elizabeth Hospital and it was hard and heartbreaking. Umuahia was full of refugees, ragged, hungry and sick and they were dispersed in camps all around and in Umuahia. The local villagers were also showing signs of Kwashiorkor and the death rate was really terrible. I saw terrific numbers of orphans and motherless in a state of neglect and crying out for loving care and attention. We had local refugee committee meetings on a Saturday afternoon and we tried to organize relief work – W.C.C. (World Council of Churches) in action!

Herman Middlecoop was in charge of World Council of Churches work, and he was busy with the organisation but he did not do any clinics at that time. Brechte went out daily with Grace, Victoria and an Itu nurse and Uncle John seeing almost 1,000 patients daily. Chrissie Denholm and I sat each evening wrapping papers into 'wee sweetie pokes' and filling them with tablets. It was a long day then I found it difficult to sleep at night – children running through my mind – yet not the real happy lively children I used to know. Poor wee mites with their discoloured fair or rusty straight hair, discoloured fair skin covered with running sores & ulcers, wee swollen pot bellies, ribs sticking out, swollen legs and arms and wee pathetic sad faces. No tears, no smiles just the big appealing sad eyes!

"Suffer the little children to come unto Me."

"And forbid them not, for of such is the Kingdom of Heaven!"

During these months of caring for the sick, starving and dying, Ann recounts an experience of Christ's presence with her that gave her the strength to go on. She shared it with the editors in an interview. This is holy ground. With Ann's permission, we include it here.

Ann's friend Sarah Watson led the fundraising
efforts in St John's Carluke to raise funds for
Ann's medical work in Biafra

66

DONATIONS TO BIAFRA

THOUSANDS FROM ST. JOHNS CHURCH 1967-70

✗	Miss B. WATSON. Carluke	300	
	Mr. A. Glen Perth	171	10
	Miss J. Stewart / Miss H. Barclay	30	
	Rev. W. Lillie / Miss M.K. Nibb A'deen	55	
✗	Rev. A.A.K Reid Carluke	400	
	St Ninians Aberdeen	5	
	Miss M. Craig		5
	Miss A. S. Paton	5	
	Mr. J. L. Grant	1	
	Mr. Monteith	30	
	Mr. Kinghorn	50	
	N. W. Mitcheson	24	
	Corstorphine Round Table	100	
	Miss C. Deuber	41	1
✗	Carluke St. John	400	
	Anonymous	21	
	Cambuslang Old Parish	16	7	6
✗	Carluke St. John	400	
		2010	3	6

Editors: *Ann, you've talked about something very special, which is that there was a moment of utter despair at the deaths you were seeing, and then you had a sense of Christ with you.*

Ann: *Yes. Yes. I didn't talk about that for a long, long time. It was like a mountaintop experience. Now that I talk about it, that's what I say. I was again in the Queen Elizabeth Hospital. And at that time, I was in charge of the children's ward. We didn't have, before the relief planes were coming in, we didn't have the medicines. So, it was very limited what we were able to do in the ward. So, these people would be, again because it was a built-up area, a big city, really, Umuahia, people flocked to Queen Elizabeth. I was doing a clinic from prayers at 7am in the chapel, then from half past seven, a ward-round, and then I was in a clinic from what, half past seven through to about 5 o'clock, seeing nothing but sick, sick children. People would be queuing for hours, walking to the clinic. There would be nurses selecting them out. If they weren't too bad, the sisters would send them to the food clinic. They would get milk and vitamins. The ones that were worse were sent to me, the doctor at the end of the line. And at one stage, it was my job to be selective. No point in putting people in hospital if they were too far gone. So, I had to say, "Sorry Ma. She's too sick". And they'd to take them home because they were too far gone for us to do anything. Or I had to say "OK. We'll admit the child. We can do something with this one." They had to be not in extremis.*

In that time, I had been doing that for hours with Caroline, my interpreter. Well, I used to have to stop and have a good cry. I couldn't handle it. That's the time when I was doing "Where are you [Lord]? What are you doing? You must be here, but what are you doing?" And I had one woman had come, I don't know if it's in the journal or not. One woman had trekked and been in the clinic for hours and was brought to see me with a 12 year old boy on her back and a cloth over him. And we helped her lift the boy off her back onto the examination couch. And he had just died. And he was 12. Goodness. [silence, tears] So, I had to say "I'm sorry Ma. But the boy has gone." She said "Thank you. Could you just put him on my back again and tie him up to look as if he's still alive? Because I won't get any transport if he's dead." So, we'd to put the cloth over, tie it, and… that was the worst day. [silence] I had a good cry.

And that's the time when I'm saying, "Well, where are you [Lord]? What are you doing?" And I had the experience, I just felt somebody standing beside me. I just felt if I'd looked round that I'd have seen the Lord just standing there, saying "I'm here." And that was a great affirmation. But it was like a mountaintop.

So real. And He was so near. And for me that was my answer. "I'm here. I'm standing here. I'm in it with you."

So that was quite a big thing. But if you think about doing that day after day [whispered] day after day. And all these patients. "I'm sorry Ma. I can't do anything for you." And the ward, the wee ward, all the beds were full. Patients were lying under the beds on mats. You couldn't move for patients. [All we had was] *the Carluke Fund* [money raised by the churches and community of Carluke to help Ann feed her patients and pay for their medical care].

Tuesday 21st May

Dr John Phillips arrived back from his leave in Scotland. He was looking fit and well. He helped in the Children's Clinic but did mainly Anaesthetics. I had hoped he would take over all the Children's work but he was too busy doing other things so I was left to get on with it.

The children continued to cause me much disquiet and heartbreak. Chrissie & I toured the town looking for suitable accommodation for an orphanage or a sick bay. Okpara ward had 50-60 patients and many many more needed admission. Money was scarce, protein foodstuffs were scarce and dear and the suffering was just too much. I wrote a Partner Plan letter asking for help – a real cry for help because I felt I could not go on, watching yet being able to do so little. My clinic days increased – Tuesdays and Thursdays I managed to go out and I was on call every 4th night. Clyne Shepherd was doing Medical calls and acting Medical Superintendent at this time. John P. then did my calls on a Thursday so that made things a bit easier for me. I was working very hard at this time – the children's ward and daily clinics, Medical night calls and Refugee work. I was very tired when I reached home at night. Chrissie was still staying with me and we did get on well. She really looked after me, organized meals, made sure I got some rest etc. and we had good evenings but usually I went to bed early. Victoria stayed with us for a week or so at the beginning, sleeping in the wee single bed in my room; then she only came at the weekend or an occasional night. I really enjoyed having her around and she was so quiet and unobtrusive.

MAY 30th 1968.   **1st. INDEPENDENCE ANNIVERSARY.**

His Excellency, Lt. Col. Ojukwu visited QEH, Umuahia on this day. He took the salute in the hospital grounds just above the hospital wards, the soldiers were smartly dressed and the band (military) played well. It was a very moving occasion. H.E. then toured the hospital and all Senior Medical and nursing staff were presented to him. He is a very impressive figure of a man, one who draws your respect and loyalty. He smiles kindly and gently yet one gets a feeling of that there is strength and goodness in this man. He is indeed a great leader and his people love, trust and respect him and they will follow him, expecting him to lead them to a just and honourable settlement with Nigeria. He will not betray their trust and we hope and pray that our 2nd. Independence Anniversary will be a more joyful one.

In the evening there was a special service in QEH Chapel and it was well attended — packed in fact. The National Anthem was played quietly on the organ and we all stood gravely to attention. Again very moving and we give God thanks that He has blessed and helped us all to survive our first year as an independent state. So many have suffered and died, so many more will not see our 2nd Anniversary yet we believe our cause to be just; we have a right to live as an independent people.
HAIL BIAFRA!

Ann was a proud supporter of Biafra's independence

"BE STILL, MY SOUL : THE LORD IS ON THY SIDE :
BEAR PATIENTLY THE CROSS OF GRIEF OR PAIN :
LEAVE TO THY GOD TO ORDER AND PROVIDE :
IN EVERY CHANGE HE FAITHFUL WILL REMAIN.
BE STILL, MY SOUL : THY BEST, THY HEAVENLY FRIEND
THROUGH THORNY WAYS LEADS TO A JOYFUL END.

BE STILL, MY SOUL : THY GOD DOTH UNDERTAKE
TO GUIDE THE FUTURE AS HE HAS THE PAST.
THY HOPE, THY CONFIDENCE LET NOTHING SHAKE ;
ALL NOW MYSTERIOUS SHALL BE BRIGHT AT LAST.
BE STILL, MY SOUL : THE WAVES AND WINDS SHALL KNOW
HIS VOICE WHO RULED THEM WHILE HE DWELT BELOW.

BE STILL, MY SOUL : WHEN DEAREST FRIENDS DEPART,
AND ALL IS DARKENED IN THE VALE OF TEARS,
THEN SHALT THOU BETTER KNOW HIS LOVE, HIS HEART,
WHO COMES TO SOOTHE THY SORROW AND THY FEARS.
BE STILL, MY SOUL : THY JESUS CAN REPAY,
FROM HIS OWN FULNESS, ALL HE TAKES AWAY.
        BE STILL, MY SOUL : THE HOUR IS HASTENING ON
        WHEN WE SHALL BE FOREVER WITH THE LORD,
        WHEN DISAPPOINTMENT, GRIEF AND FEAR ARE GONE,
        SORROW FORGOT, LOVE'S PUREST JOYS RESTORED.
        BE STILL, MY SOUL : WHEN CHANGE AND TEARS ARE PAST,
        ALL SAFE AND BLESSED WE SHALL MEET AT LAST."

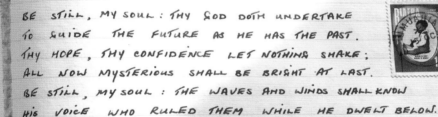

This hymn was one of Biafra's national anthems, sung to the tune *Finlandia*

Thursday May 30th

1st Independence Anniversary, 1967-1968

His Excellency, Lt. Col. Ojukwu visited Queen Elizabeth Hospital, Umuahia on this day. He took the salute in the hospital grounds just above the hospital wards, the soldiers were smartly dressed and the band (military) played well. It was a very moving occasion. His Excellency then toured the hospital and all Senior Medical and Nursing Staff were presented to him. He is a very impressive figure of a man, one who draws your respect and loyalty. He smiles kindly and gently yet one gets a feeling that there is strength and goodness in this man. He is indeed a great leader and his people love, trust and respect him and they will follow him, expecting him to lead them to a just and honourable settlement with Nigeria. He will not betray their trust and we hope and pray that our 2nd Independence Anniversary will be a more joyful one.

In the evening there was a special service in Queen Elizabeth Hospital Chapel and it was well attended – packed in fact. The National Anthem was played quietly on the organ and we all stood gravely to attention. Again very moving and we give God thanks that He has blessed and helped us all to survive our first year as an independent state. So many have suffered and died, so many more will not see our 2nd Anniversary yet we believe our course to be just; we have a right to live as an independent people.

HAIL BIAFRA!

Christians sang this hymn as their anthem for Biafra

"BE STILL, MY SOUL: THE LORD IS ON THY SIDE;
BEAR PATIENTLY THE CROSS OF GRIEF OR PAIN;
LEAVE TO THY GOD TO ORDER AND PROVIDE;
IN EVERY CHANGE HE FAITHFUL WILL REMAIN.
BE STILL, MY SOUL; THY BEST, THY HEAVENLY FRIEND
THROUGH THORNY WAYS LEADS TO A JOYFUL END.

BE STILL, MY SOUL: THY GOD DOTH UNDERTAKE
TO GUIDE THE FUTURE AS HE HAS THE PAST
THY HOPE, THY CONFIDENCE LET NOTHING SHAKE;
ALL NOW MYSTERIOUS SHALL BE BRIGHT AT LAST
BE STILL, MY SOUL: THE WAVES AND WINDS SHALL KNOW
HIS VOICE WHO RULED THEM WHILE HE DWELT BELOW.

BE STILL, MY SOUL: WHEN DEAREST FRIENDS DEPART,
AND ALL IS DARKENED IN THE VALE OF TEARS,
THEN SHALT THOU BETTER KNOW HIS LOVE, HIS HEART,
WHO COMES TO SOOTHE THY SORROW AND THY FEARS.
BE STILL, MY SOUL: THY JESUS CAN REPAY,
FROM HIS OWN FULNESS, ALL HE TAKES AWAY.

BE STILL, MY SOUL: THE HOUR IS HASTENING ON
WHEN WE SHALL BE FOREVER WITH THE LORD,
WHEN DISAPPOINTMENT, GRIEF AND FEAR ARE GONE,
SORROW FORGOT, LOVE'S PUREST JOYS RESTORED.
BE STILL, MY SOUL: WHEN CHANGE AND TEARS ARE PAST,
ALL SAFE AND BLESSÈD WE SHALL MEET AT LAST"

June 1968

Saturday 1st June

Victoria invited me to go home with her to the village near Owerri. Transport was difficult but Ann Travis & Diane were going to a meeting in Emekuku Hospital on the Saturday so we decided to go. We had the lift to Emekuku, 4 miles from Owerri then we carried our bags a short distance & hitched a lift. A mad woman started asking me for a dash [money] while we were waiting, she danced round me, speaking English well and then started to touch me. Poor Vicky was getting quite excited and when the woman put her hand over to touch me she was real annoyed. The woman meant no harm but she was certainly crazy and Vicky was afraid. Shortly after this an R.C. priest gave us a lift to Owerri. We reached the Cross Roads and then walked along the Aba road. Air-raid!! So we had to run off the road into a compound with a lot of cover from the air. No bombs were dropped so we then walked about a mile to the checkpoint. People turned to look at us – it's not usual to see a European woman walking & carrying her travelling bag especially, on a hot afternoon & especially these days when nearly all expatriate women had been evacuated home. At the checkpoint we waited 15-20 minutes then a heavily loaded van arrived – crammed in the back with people. Victoria bargained and we were given a lift for a few shillings with the two of us sitting in the front. We travelled several miles then got off at a village where Victoria had friends. We went into a shop to greet the trader and he gave us a cold drink of lemonade then we set out walking for the village 4-5 miles away.

It was hot, the bags were fortunately not very heavy, but it was a long walk! Everyone we met greeted us and then each one scolded Victoria for making this European lady walk – she should have hired a bicycle for me. I enjoyed meeting the village women and I loved to see the surprise & pleasure on their faces when they realized I was walking on. A woman was going to market with her three children and she had a basin load of things on her head – she walked with us for some miles and she made her eldest son carry my bag. He spoke quite good English so we conversed as we travelled.

Victoria's mother was working on the farm when we arrived so we did not see her until later. I met Godson her brother and her cousin and a small cousin Sam that the mother looks after. They have a nice cement house in the compound and Victoria had paid for the building of this. It was not quite finished, no bathroom inside yet. Vicky prepared a very nice palm oil chop and we had a rest – I was pretty badly sunburned.

Her mother arrived, washed & changed into her good cloth before she would greet me properly but she was so pleased to see me and gave me a very warm welcome to her house. I visited nearby relatives; then we heard that Phoebe, the older sister was ill and lived 4-5 miles away in a nearby village. Vicky had to see her and she was keen for me to meet her only sister, so I said I would go, but I was feeling tired. The rain started to pour so her cousin & her brother took us on the bicycles – with myself sitting side saddle for the first time. I did manage it all right and it was good to meet Phoebe and her family. She was looking quite well so we waited only a short time then returned to Ibebe. Phoebe was trained in Britain & is married to a lawyer and she has two lovely children.

Vicky gave me her bed and she slept in a small one in the same room. I was very comfortable and I slept really well. Washing was a laugh – no bathroom so we stood outside in the well-enclosed back-yard which unfortunately faced the village road. I was very self-conscious and did not like to strip & wash properly yet I was sweaty & sticky. So I persuaded Victoria to strip too and we washed and talked in the back yard, near the road yet very private. We went to the Anglican service on the Sunday morning and then spent the morning visiting relatives and greeting villagers. I met the village head who is a 'big man' with 40 wives. Quite an experience! He said I should have had some of my meals at his house – he would have provided European food, suggesting that Victoria's mother, a widow could not feed me properly. I said I was feeding well and very much enjoying my short visit. Dear Victoria she was so proud, and she kept telling me so and thanking me for visiting her home.

We travelled 2 miles by bicycle to another village and a relative, the Umuahia Provincial Engineer, gave us a lift back to Umuahia. When we reached home a letter was waiting for Victoria asking her to report back for work at Uburu Hospital. We had a really good weekend and I'm sure it strengthened our friendship.

Ann grew up in the O.S. (Original Secession) Church in Carluke, which traced its roots back to the first secession of Presbyterians from the established Church of Scotland in 1733. They were protesting at the appointment of ministers through patronage by landowners rather than election by church members. By the 1960s the O.S. Church, as it was fondly known, had rejoined the Church of Scotland. Ann loved the O.S. tradition of psalm singing and was proud to have been sent out to Nigeria from her spiritual home in Carluke. When this local O.S. congregation disbanded, Ann became a member of St John's Church, Carluke, along with the O.S. denomination's senior elder, Forrest Anderson. Ann's minister in St John's was the Rev. Alan S. Reid. With his congregation, Mr Reid was supportive of her missionary service as a doctor in Biafra and deeply concerned for the Biafran people's welfare.

Sunday 2nd June

We were receiving letters irregularly at this time via Father Doran and Pastor Kühl. Rev. A.S. Reid wrote me a very nice letter at this time and Chrissie & I shared it and really enjoyed its contents – a great help to us, a source of joy and blessing.

Psalm 124: "If it had not been the Lord who was on our side, then Israel may say . . ."

Sunday 2nd June, Pentecost   *St John's Manse, Carluke*

Dear Ann,

Thank you for your wonderful and yet pitiable letter to me, telling me of all your untiring and magnificent work in the refugee camps and in the Hospital. Your mother and Sarah keep me continually supplied with news – and you are always in our prayers, both personal and congregational. I want to tell you what a wonderful joy your letters are to all who know you – your mother especially. It is so fine that you can find the energy to write after such very exhausting and harrowing days on your feet, and the news does so much to sustain your parents and friends here.

The picture you paint is a terrible one. Like you we feel a fearful dismay that an Enlightened nation like our own can perpetrate such willful folly. The Conscience of Britain has at last been deeply shocked – but is it too late? The British Weekly appealed this week for an air-lift on the Berlin pattern; the 'Spectator' denounced the Government's policy as "the wickedest and most disgraceful act in the history of British government", and the General Assembly of the Church of Scotland was outraged at the harrowing news from two of your missionary colleagues who addressed them. But all this must seem a little remote from your exposed position of work and witness. We were so appalled to hear of the breakdown of the Kampala talks. Such news as we get in our papers is not good.

Meanwhile you will be throwing yourself into your compassionate work in a joyful spirit. To be used daily as the very hands of God himself is a wonderful experience known to a very few people. You pay a grim price for it but the price is the price Jesus paid, and therein lies the joy of discipleship that no man, and certainly not General Gowon can take from you. We have been terribly proud of you. The stories of the children with such malnutrition, such fear, such undeserved suffering among the aged and the widowed and the infants/infirm are moving beyond all words.

The people of Carluke want to help you – you know that. On Saturday we sent off through Neil Bernard in Edinburgh (121) a cheque for £400. He is writing to explain how you can make immediate use of it. If you want twice as much, again and immediately, we will raise it immediately and send it. I have no doubt of that. And when we read in your letter some of the prices you are having to pay for the basic necessities - rice, petrol, salt, etc, to say nothing of your drugs & medicines – it must seem that you need thousands of pounds to do anything at all. And how terribly exhausted and worn out you must become! There is a point (I discovered it in military action) where despite the adrenalin of excitement the brain and body just refuse to do more. I suppose that is where you have to try to win a daily victory.

One can only pray that outraged public opinion will force the government to halt their evil selling of arms to the Federal troops. Their reasons have never been made public, but have been hidden behind a smokescreen of evasion and hypocrisy. But do understand, Ann, that there is the most tremendous pressure on them now from the horrified organs of Society here, and from intelligent and caring people who see the folly of it all. Good must surely come. Talks <u>must</u> resume.

I write this on the Day of Pentecost, remembered with joy by all Christians. We have resources of divine strength that will bring us through. "Not by might, nor by power, but by my Spirit, saith the Lord of Hosts." To discover what that means afresh, every day, is the authentic thrill of the Life in Christ. I hope you will be sustained by it Ann, in all your wonderful work. God bless you and keep you safe, and all your colleagues. Remember your friends are upholding you. Keep Psalm 124 before you continually.

Yours ever,
Alan Reid

July 1968

Saturday 13th July

I moved back to Uburu but left my three trunks packed and labeled for home in case of any emergency. Chrissie went home on leave to Scotland so things worked out well for us. Chrissie was tired and a bit tense and she really was needing a break. She did a great job with clothing & odd jobs in refugee relief work. She was also there when everyone needed someone to talk to; Errol Roe visited us often in Umuahia and we enjoyed his company. Many Church sisters and refugee ministers of the Church came to see Chrissie as they passed through Umuahia. Chrissie did much to help them and to help many of us at this time. I was sorry to lose her company but I was very happy to be going back to Uburu.

August 1968

I went back to stay in my old house in Uburu and received a warm welcome from all the nurses and staff. I took charge of Female and Children's ward and the Refugee Sick Bay which had just started. We soon had 120 patients mainly children but some mothers as well. Patients came from our various clinics in villages all around – Mpu, Okpanku, Akaeze, Afikpo Road. The clinic car went out each day with Sister Oshi or Sister Brown, a dispenser, a midwife, 2 nurses, Red Cross Volunteers and an extra leprosy inspector or nurse at times. We were loaded with powdered milk and egg and later stockfish. Kees and I took turns to go depending on hospital work. During this time we tried to take it in turns to go to Umuahia for the week-end, to keep in touch with the rest of Biafra and our colleagues and also to get a break ourselves. We were all working hard, a full day and refugees increased in numbers daily. The clinics also increased, villagers walked for miles to the hospital for by this time we did no outside ante-natal or Infant Welfare clinics. It was great to see village women walking for up to 10-15 miles to bring their child to the Baby Welfare Clinic and the pregnant women coming for their check-up. Before the war Uburu had built up a very good Rural Health programme, and attendances to the various clinics had been good. Our campaign for better health, our talks and exhortations had been worthwhile – the villagers realized the importance of taking care of their health and they were determined to carry on in spite of the war and decreased medical services.

This was a great encouragement to Uburu staff. Alicia Bandeen had been very involved in the organisation of these early clinics and she would have been very pleased with all her women, keen to bring up healthy well nourished children. War interrupted our programme. Uburu people were still well off – the salt lake was well filled so everyone was busy producing salt. Prices were high and Uburu & Okposi natives had lots of money. The unfortunate thing was that they did not save this money for post war education & reconstruction, they spent it having feasts and buying titles for their sons. The poor nurses felt the pinch because the locals tried to outbid and outbuy them at the local market. They seemed to say, "We have the money now, let's see what you high & mighty nurses can do – we can pay more for anything you want." Firewood, yams, rice was very expensive at this time, not because of shortage as in other parts of Biafra, but because the villagers had too much money to throw around.

Salt was priceless almost and Uburu was supplying the rest of the country, almost holding them up to ransom. There should have been fixed prices or some form of price control but it would be difficult to enforce and we were told that the traders would just go to ground and there would be more "black market" trading. We needed salt for our refugees so Kees decided to make hernia patients pay in salt. A big cone of salt was required, worth £16-18 for a herniorrhaphy. "Win the war surgery". "Win the war chop." We put up with everything in order to win this awful war.

HAIL BIAFRA!

Friday 2nd August

On Friday morning I left with Janet and the clinic car to go to Akaeze clinic and then Afikpo Road. Amasserie Junction was quiet, deserted of locals but teeming with soldiers – very much war front. We passed through in the morning, saw our patients and we must have seen about 1,000 – Akaeze is terrible. We saw so many women and children who needed admission yet we had no beds for them. Janet & I carried our lunch and we always stopped for a break of 30-45 minutes but we could never eat. The refugees were all around us, many had not eaten a decent meal for months, many were hungry, waiting for their cupful of dried milk to stave off the hunger. We drank some tea but I could not eat my fried yam and plantain in front of these hungry sad eyes and empty bellies.

On the way back home after our long day we passed through Amasserie Junction – again all was quiet, but there were fewer soldiers around and 100 yds up the Afikpo section of the road we saw a group of men, soldiers busy with something on the road. They looked round at our approach & gave us queer looks but made no move to stop us. We reached home safely but sure that something was going on at Amasserie. On Sunday we learned that the bridge at Okposi had been blown, Uburu was cut off and the Biafran soldiers had withdrawn a bit. The Federals shelled Amasserie and made some advance. On Friday night we should not have been allowed to pass, it was restricted area and the soldiers were laying mines. I don't think we could get much nearer to this notorious war front.

Ann's letters home to her parents in August follow

Friday 9th August

Presbyterian Joint Hosp.
Uburu

Dear Mum, Dad & family,

This is just a hurried note to let you know that I am still here at Uburu, safe & well. Work goes on here as usual and I enjoy it. The hospital is very busy and we do many refugee clinics all over the Province.

Dr Reijnierse is going to Umuahia this weekend so I will be on my own. We have started a Sick Bay about 25 miles from here in a Roman Catholic school – the Fathers actually started it but we are responsible for medical attention. There are 15,000 refugees in that area alone so there is much work to do. Janet Brown will be moving down there to take charge of the clinic work. It will save petrol & time and give us more control over the nurses & other medical workers.

I will be staying here with Kees and Bill. The war drags on and at times comes a bit nearer our way but we are ready to move at any time. There is no need to worry. All is quiet at present and the hospital is carrying on normal duties.

We are anxiously waiting for news of a settlement but are not too hopeful. The Biafrans have suffered much and they will never agree to renounce secession. They – the ordinary people – are prepared to suffer more and die first. It's an impossible situation because Nigeria is out to crush them. Anyway we still have God and we pray that He will answer our prayers and put an end to all this misery and suffering.

Friday 16th August

Presbyterian Joint Hospital
Uburu
Via Afikpo

Dear Mum, dad & family,

I hope you are all well & behaving yourselves. It is 7.45am. and I am going at 8am to do a Refugee Clinic at a place 2 miles away and then another one at Ishiagu 3 miles in the other direction.

I have come down to Ishiagu – St John's Bosco R.C. (School) or College where we have a Sick Bay. It's about 30 miles from Uburu and the Roman Fathers started the Sick Bay in their College and we supply the nurses and supervise. We travel down on Thursday, do a Clinic at Akaeze 10 mls from here then come here and do a Ward round. Kees & I go alternate weeks and Janet Brown was transferred here last week. We stay the night & then go to the two clinics on the Friday then travel back to Uburu. It really is a good idea Janet staying here because of the poor condition of the roads in this rainy season and also because of the lack of petrol. Janet does Refugee Clinics every day in this area and supervises the Sick Bay. She is, of course, in a house on the compound and the Fathers are nearby but it is a bit lonely. However, it's a full time job and I'm sure she won't have much time to worry.

Bill Cluness came down with me yesterday and a driver. The roads are very muddy and from time to time we have to dig our way out but not yesterday. The Fathers always give us a good welcome and we ate with them last night. What a feed! They get foodstuffs flour in for themselves so we had chicken, peas, tomatoes, yam then custard, cream & fruit. And soup to start with. It was great and we had a very nice evening – Janet, Bill & I and 3 Irish men.

I may as well tell you because you will no doubt hear from other sources or guess from the news that we are quite near the battlefront. We are the only hospital functioning in this province and there are 70,000 refugees alone. We must carry on until the last minute but we are kept well informed of the news or progress of fighting by the Commanding Officer in our area. We are always ready to move out and we will be given ample warning. From this place Ishiagu we heard a lot of heavy shelling last night and even saw enemy searchlights but this is because there is only miles of brush between us. However, no road that way so we are quite safe.

The war news is not so good these days and peace talks do not go well. However, our men still fight on. Dear knows how it will all end now but our area decreases steadily and our refugees increase daily. At the hospital we have 105 in the Sickbay and about the same number in this area so it means a lot of work. However, we are at least helping some poor souls.

I must go & do the clinics but will finish later.

Sunday 18th August

I arrived back here safely on Friday evening and have been busy ever since. I had a long lie to 8.15am this morning and so far all is quiet.

Uburu is very peaceful, you look out your window & see for miles – bush, trees and wonder if there really is a war going on. We seldom hear any shelling these days from here. It seems that the hardest fighting is near Abo, not so very far from Umuahia. We always thought we would need to run to Umuahia but it may now be that they will run to Uburu. It's a 'funny' war!

But war just the same and many are dying daily. On our way back on Friday a man stopped at Akaeze – a big market place and asked if we could help two boys. They were found the day before lying beside the mother's corpse – she had died & they were too weak to move. One aged 10 yrs and another about 6 but so thin & curled up I thought he was about 3 yrs. We brought them to hospital but the small one died in the morning. A whole family almost wiped out and there are thousands like them in Biafra today – waiting for the merciful release from all this suffering.

Please keep well & don't be worrying about me. I hope to go to Umuahia for the weekend – 31st August, so will write from there. Dr Bakker my Dutch pal has gone home with hepatitis but he may come back with the Red Cross.

Give my love to all my wee nephews & wee Grace. Is Liam pleased with her? I can hardly believe a year has almost gone since I saw everyone. Anyway this time next year I will be ready for home.

Love to all & God bless & keep you.
Ann xxx

Wednesday 21st August

Presbyterian Joint Hospital
Uburu
Via Afikpo

My dear Mum, dad & family,

This is Wednesday, 6 pm and I have just finished work and had a cold shower. I was down at the Colony Sick Bay doing a ward round and I got caught in a heavy downpour of rain. Soaked to the skin so I needed a wash. I'm sitting here now eating coconut & waiting for Ngene to come & prepare my supper.

Dr Reijnierse – Kees – is going to Umuahia tomorrow so I thought I had better write you. We are really very busy here and have discovered another batch of refugees. We do a clinic at Mpu and we thought there were 6,000 people there. We learned 2 days ago that there are 36,000 refugees in that area and we have been asked to give them medical attention. We are covering a wide area and dealing with large numbers of refugees. People walk for miles to the clinics. On Monday we treated 600 outpatients at the hospital – Baby Welfare Clinic and General Outpatients.

I am keeping well and everything is quiet here at Uburu. We do still have shelling now & again but it is far away and life goes on here as usual. The Roman fathers gave us some milk & sugar and a tin of chocolate spread each so I had a "piece" in chocolate this afternoon. We are doing alright. Money from Carluke has arrived at Queen Elizabeth Hospital and £200 was sent on to here for the children in the Sick Bay. Most of the money sent will be used to feed the children from Umuahia in Queen Elizabeth Hospital. They are still the worst off because there is much overcrowding and food shortage in Umuahia.

I hope to go down for the weekend next week and I will get my hair cut then. It's a mess. Long and straight as a poker as normal. A real sight!

I hope the family are all well. Please thank John & Mgt. Gilchrist for their letter. How's Anne & Grace getting on? Have you had news of Morene Quigley? Please try to get some news of her for me. Give everyone my love & good wishes.

Much love, Ann xxx

Sunday 25th August

Letter to sister Jenny, started in August and completed in September

Presbyterian Joint Hospital
Uburu
Via Afikpo

My dear Jenny,

Thought I would start a letter to you today although it will not be posted until next week when I hope to go to Umuahia. I have been at Uburu here for almost 6 weeks and although I have had time off, I am ready for a break. Uburu is a bit isolated, but quiet at present. The road out is in poor condition because this is the rainy season and we have real thunderstorms. It is a mud road, no tar yet.

We are very busy with refugees and with civilian outpatients. This hospital is the only one functioning in this whole province and we give medical care to 80,000 refugees alone, excluding all the villages near & far. We continue to see pitiful sick destitute people and our hands are still tied. We do have milk & stock fish but not nearly enough. Daily people in rags come & ask for help, usually dragging two or three ill or dying children with them. God sees it all, surely peace must come soon.

I have just been to the service in our small Chapel. This has been a quiet Sunday I'm glad to say. We are all a wee bit on edge today and are waiting for news of the war situation. Uburu is off the main road and near the war front. We have the enemy all around us yet not too near us. However, the shelling we usually hear has become much closer. The army here removed all their patients from the hospital and we take this as a sign that the Federals are much closer. Dr McGuire & Bill Cluness left this morning to get news from the Brigade Commander and if possible get a truck to evacuate the patients & staff. We are all impatiently waiting for news. I think everyone has seriously packed ready to go but it is difficult to know where best to go. Times are very difficult. Poor Biafra is suffering much. We can only hope and pray that God will deliver her people and bind the wounds.

I never imagined I would ever be in the middle of a war, or that I would get used to shelling and enemy planes overhead. Fortunately we have had no bombings here and the shelling has not reached us. I will finish this letter in Umuahia or wherever I go to let you know that I am safe and well.

[continued on 18th September]

My dear Jenny,

Sorry I did not finish the first part of the letter – I have re-read it and it sounds very uncertain and pessimistic. Anyway I am still here and well and working as hard as ever. I did move to Ishiagu some 35 miles from here to help in the Sick Bay there but I have since come back to Uburu. The war situation is still quiet up this way but serious down South. Umuahia is now the only big town left in Biafra and it is crowded with people.

No matter what happens I will be at Uburu but I have already written you a more recent letter with up to date news. You will receive two letters at once this time. I think our letters will be late or mixed up these days because the Owerri airstrip is not working well – sometimes flights [are grounded] because the enemy is near there and within shelling range.

Keep well and be good. My mother will keep you informed of any new developments if I do not get time to write myself.

Much love & prayers.
Ann xxx.

COMITÉ INTERNATIONAL

DE LA

CROIX-ROUGE

O F F I C I A L   P A S S

By this I authorise Father Dr. J A C K S O N of W.C.C.
to use this International Red Cross Airport
at any time.

John Krille

ICRC— Delegate
in charge of this
Airport.

Before the war,
Ann travelled with
her driving licence.
During the war,
travel became more
fraught, even for
Father Jackson!

September 1968

Working with the Red Cross, Ann's first entry is hopeful:

Dr Wallace and sister and two young folk arrived at Ishiagu Sick Bay as the Red Cross team. They seem very friendly and they are certainly keen so I hope we can work together and do more for Biafra.

But it did not prove a happy experience:

As the [following] letters indicate I worked at Ishiagu for a few weeks but I was not happy there. Dr Wallace, English GP, senior partner in a group practice was friendly and keen but he had very little idea about the situation, the difficulties, the drugs available and the people he was working with. On our first days he spoke of our defeat, yet he seemed to be sympathetic but he spoke thoughtlessly in front of our Biafran colleagues. He tried to organize things but spent too much time running around and too little time doing the actual work. He listened to me yet did everything in his own way and my own experience told me he was wrong. He had a great respect for Queen Elizabeth Hospital and the work being done there among the children – I don't think he believed I had been in charge of the children in Queen Elizabeth Hospital for three months!

The Fathers seemed to persuade him to try to do Medical clinics in the village. This is good but he was not doing the refugee work and there were about 10,000 refugees and 10,000 villagers. He would not listen to Janet & I advising him to get on top of the refugee work first before he tackled the villagers. There was so much need among the refugees and we felt a concentrated effort at this time would help the situation immensely. However, he went ahead & started the clinic in the village without even asking our help on how to go about it. From grim experience we knew the difficulties and we could have saved him unnecessary troubles. However, we must learn from our own experiences I suppose.

The Fathers, Sister & Dr Wallace were always keen for Janet & I to join them for meals but we were not happy eating with them, yet feeling unhappy and uneasy in our work with them. They were friendly and generous and tried hard but we were not at ease with them. Dr Wallace was very very good to Uburu Hospital and he gave us many drugs and extras for the work there. I was most anxious for the people at Uburu and worried in case they would be cut-off. I thought often about Victoria and how scared she was but she was committed to God and He would take care of her and the others. Dr Wallace had plans made in case of an emergency but we did not agree with these at all. Patients had to be graded 1), 2) & 3) according to whether they could walk out or would need to be carried but were "worth" saving or 3) the ones who were very ill and unlikely to live so they had to go to the bush and 1) & 2) would escape in army commandeered trucks. The nurses were supposed to hide in the bush with these sick patients but they were our Uburu nurses and we had transferred them to Ishiagu and we were responsible for them. We intended to evacuate them with ourselves.

Saturday 7th September

Letter to Dr Reijnierse and Bill Cluness, hospital administrator, at Uburu, just after Ann left to work at St John's Bosco School, Ishiagu with the Red Cross.

Please let this be reply to both your letters. Ann.

Queen Elizabeth Hospital Saturday a.m.

Dear Kees & Bill,

Thank you for your letters – I decided to go straight to Umuahia so left Ishiagu at 3:30pm and arrived just after 6pm. I have been doing the usual running around but feel we have been quite successful.

Clyne has given us 80 gals. petrol and the diesel will be coming from Amuwara I did not tell him that 2 drums were at Ishiagu but he says to contact the central store as it is coming in okay from outside. Alicia Bandeen is due to come in next week and Clyne says he will come to Uburu to discuss her location with you. Anne Bent has been asking for her to go to AWKA side to help an Anglican lay girl who is doing Refugee work on her own. Beatrice Waddington goes home soon and they really need a nursing sister to help them.

Jaggi did not have time to write, he opened Dr Sjouka's letter also and he says they hope to put a team (2-4 people) at Akaeze, and Edda, Abiriba and I think Mpu area – he says Oji River Province. He will also try to get a team for Uburu – he likes the idea. The policy will be for these teams to stay put if the Federals over-run these areas and he hopes that their presence – International Red Cross – will afford protection for all personnel in the work. Teams will be available in the near future and he may not be able to give you warning – the team will just arrive. Alicia will be coming under the World Council of Churches I think.

Clyne hopes to get a landrover and come to Uburu on Tuesday – or maybe nearer the end of the week if Alicia arrives. He will call in at Ishiagu and I will travel with him to Uburu. I want to be in on this discussion and also I hope you will agree to take me back at Uburu. Dr Wallace can manage Ishiagu all right and there is not enough work for the two of us. I would have done more clinic work but I feel the Red Cross will cover that area. Janet is doing a great job at present and I should think will carry on until they take over some of her clinics. She could, of course, continue to work with them but I suppose it will depend on their numbers and on their experience. I'm giving you all these details so you will be prepared for Clyne and have your own ideas on how you want the work to be done.

Queen Elizabeth Hospital is having acute water problems because of lack of diesel. The Federals have taken Ikot Ekpene and are on the Owerri side of Abba. There is talk here of evacuation of troops (patients) but personnel (missionary etc) will remain. They seem to feel that they will be in Umuahia in a week or two – this is, of course, speculation. I feel if we are staying put then I want to be cut off at Uburu and not Ishiagu. I hope we will discuss all this next week.

I have collected some drugs and will enclose the slip – I had a good look round and asked for various things. I did not tell them that Chita has brought in lots of drugs – including Triple Sulphas, etc. I will sort out the Ishiagu drugs and send you a list.

Jaggi has promised supplies for Uburu and there is now a new arrangement. Uturu will be a sub-store and Uburu will be supplied from there – personnel are coming to staff these stores – drugs, food, transport so you will make your requests to them. He has given me a letter to get fuel from them today so I will see what I can get. A Swedish mechanic has arrived and when he heard our old car he offered to work on it. He has been busy all morning and has done a good job on it – no more pushing for a wee while. He has also promised to get us spares for it. I think he will be stationed in Umuahia meantime but his location is not definite. He is very willing to help. I will finish this letter in Ishiagu after I have seen the airstrip people.

Evening

I was well received by the Uturu folk and they are very willing to help. A Mr RASK is in charge of transport and he has promised 35 gals. petrol, 50 gals. diesel if you supply the drums. He will load a lorry with ¾ stockfish, ¼ milk and salt at a later date. I have said our lorry will go to Uburu on Sunday & return Monday & go to Uturu to be loaded for Uburu. Please Bill, write to him & tell him the mileage & how much diesel needed for the journey. I told him 60 mls but Agwu says it is only about 35 mls. You would need to send someone with the lorry.

Thursday 12*th* September

Letter home to close friend Sarah Watson, Carluke

St John Bosco's School
Ishiagu

My dear Sarah,

Many thanks for your letter received last week – I do thank God for your faithfulness to me and to Biafra. This is Saturday night and Sister Janet Brown and I are sitting here waiting and wondering. The war news continues to grow worse and our work here is a bit uncertain.

Red Cross teams have come in and they are needed and necessary and welcome but they arrive and "take over" with complete disregard to the work already being done. Maybe we are "too touchy" but we feel they think we have been doing nothing. They seem to expect everything to have come to a standstill, not knowing that the Government and the Voluntary Agencies (Missions) have the Refugee work in hand and in many areas well covered.

We feel we have a good system and we have good teams with Govt, local dispensers, nurses from all over and local Red Cross people all working together. It has taken us months but we do the Medical work and the Fathers in this area have organized Soup Kitchens and Milk Clinics with the Refugee Camp wardens. We select the patients and send them for special feeding or admission to the Sick Bay. All this set-up seems to be ignored and they have arrived with their own ideas. As you may realize we are not too happy about the situation.

We want to leave but feel the teams will not be able to cope with the numbers because they are new to the country and not used to the set-up. Yet we don't feel wanted! Uburu is very busy and Dr Reijnierse is having too much to do so I am going back. I don't see why I should stay here to help someone who doesn't much care if I stay or not, to make things easier for him while my own colleague is having a hard time. Janet is waiting to offer to stay & help the new teams but she doesn't know if they want a clean sheet or expert help. What a situation!! War brings us many many problems – even where help ("so-called") is concerned.

Uburu is quiet at present but we feel that nowhere in Biafra is quiet or safe these days. The Federals are slowly closing in on us – they now have our main airstrip and this Ishiagu is only about 5 miles from the other airstrip at OKIGWE. The road to Uburu is a quagmire and almost impassable so there is every possibility that we may be cut off. Please read my mother's letter for details of my journey to Uburu – I am a real missionary now that I have trekked!! Another experience of war – I was tired & burned with the sun but I enjoyed it all. Anyway I am going back to Uburu to help with the work there, to be with the people I know, and if trouble comes then we are, at least, all together. Trouble must come Sarah and it seems to be only a matter of time. We still pray for the miracle that will save us and Biafra, but it is long in coming. I think we will be sent home if the Federals catch us – we will be "unacceptable" as Relief workers because of our association with Biafra in these past months. It is unbearable to think of leaving this poor country and this courageous people. It will certainly be by force – I will not be coming home for another year yet of my own accord. I do thank God for all His goodness to me – for my work, for the many good friends He has given me and for the sure knowledge that He is with me strengthening and upholding me. It's a great life Sarah although it can be so difficult at times but it is also very enjoyable. I have a cold just now – in all this sunshine but rain, heavy thunderstorms at times. Anyway no doubt I will soon throw it off.

Well, the doctor (Red Cross) has been to see us and he says he does not need us so we will both be going to Uburu. Hurrah!! Janet is still worried about the Refugees in this area but it will be his concern and responsibility. We're afraid they will get less attention now that we are going – this sounds awful but this is our fear and we are not happy. No doubt God will take a Hand in all this and things will work out. We can only pray so.

Well, Sarah, I must go and I hope you will not worry about me. God will guide & protect us both as we do our work for His glory. I am still as fat as ever – in fact I look healthy with my sun tan (from my motor cycle expedition). Please give my love to your mother, Jane & Janet & family & Frances. Tell her I received her letter and will reply sometime. Tell Mr Reid I do thank him again for his prayers and work for Biafra. Surely our Lord Jesus is weeping for this people – it's heartbreaking Sarah to see so much suffering and pain.

Much love & my prayers.
Ann

By September 1968 the Nigerian government forces were threatening to capture the town of Uburu where the Presbyterian Joint Hospital was located. This is clear from the letters written by Dr Kees Reijnierse to the Presbyterian Church, Red Cross, and Biafran Government leaders on the evacuation of Uburu at the request of the local Biafran military leader. Before going on leave to the Netherlands, he handed over his responsibilities for the work of the Uburu hospital medical services to Dr Ann Jackson, who replaced him as the Medical Superintendent.

The trained hospital staff working under the auspices of the Presbyterian Church in Uburu were relocated to the Queen Elizabeth Hospital in Umuahia. This hospital in turn would be evacuated as the Nigerian troops advanced on Umuahia in April 1969. Ann continued to lead a mobile medical team of Queen Elizabeth Hospital staff in running clinics behind the warfront until Biafra collapsed in January 1970.

Friday 20th September

> *Rev. N. Eme,*
> *Presbyterian Church,*
> <u>*Igbere*</u>*.*

Dear Nwachuku,

On Wednesday evening 18th September 1968 we received a notification from the Divisional Commander at Akaeze that the military situation at Akaeze was not satisfactory and he requested us to evacuate from Uburu.

Later in the evening the staff was informed and the patients were discharged with medicines as much as possible. All staff who are not from Ohaozara-area and our files were evacuated in two of our own cars and two army lorries. With the help of an army bulldozer we reached Akaeze with these vehicles at 3 p.m. on the 19th after having left Uburu at 6 a.m. It was our intention to evacuate to the sickbay at Ishiagu, but on arrival at Afikpo Road we were informed that our Ishiagu staff evacuated earlier that morning because of a direct attack. On arrival at Umuahia we met Sister Brown, who had safely evacuated with the Red Cross team to Uturu, Okigwe.

The following arrangements have been made:

<u>*Uburu Presbyterian Hospital*</u>*: Mr Egwu Obasi, Assistant Nursing Superintendent, who is a native of Uburu, took over all keys, all drugs and all equipment of the Hospital. He is going to live in the Hospital. With him are a team*

of 1 midwife, 15 nurses and our full labour staff. They will try to keep a restricted medical service for civilians and refugees going. Mr Obasi was also given £1,000 for salaries, etc.

Uburu Presbyterian Rural Health Services: Mr D.O. Ekuma, headnurse who is a refugee from Afikpo, took over all keys, all drugs and all equipment. Together with the local staff from the general hospital he will look after the resident leprosy-patients and the sickbay for refugees, which can probably be maintained as the local branch of the Biafran Red Cross has promised cooperation. Mr Ekuma has been given £500 for the maintenance of the work.

Evacuated Personnel: The trained staff will report on 30th September to the Matron of Q.E.H. (Queen Elizabeth Hospital). By that time, it will have been possible to decide who can be absorbed in the Q.E.H. or in the relief-work of the W.C.C. (World Council of Churches). If no such employment can be found, they will be seconded to the Ministry of Health. The untrained staff has been asked to report to the W.C.C. relief worker nearest to their homes. If satisfactory work can be found the Hospital will continue their salaries. Most of the evacuated male staff will be engaged in relief work. Mr Daniel Umoh, clerk, will work with the W.C.C. in Umuahia and be responsible for the administration of Hospital affairs.

Sister Oje and Sister Brown will stay in first instances in the Q.E.H. and work in W.C.C. relief-work is being arranged for them. Mr Cluness will proceed on leave, though some days earlier than had been planned. Dr Jackson has offered herself temporary as Presbyterian doctor at the Q.E.H. with the intention that she returns to Uburu as soon as conditions permit. This understanding will be made in all secondments to other organisations or institutions. As I was due for leave in July, I felt that I should now return to the Netherlands and therefore arrangements for my departure from Biafra are being made. Both Mr Clunes and I hope to leave therefore on 21st September 1968. I have asked Dr Jackson to take over the responsibilities of the Medical Superintendent of Uburu Hospitals, to which she agreed.

With these arrangements I am of the opinion that our medical institutions at Uburu can continue to remain, administratively in Umuahia and effectively in Uburu though at a much smaller scale than before. It is hoped that after some time the staff and administration can return to Uburu to extend the work again to its level of before this evacuation.

The files of our two institutions are now in Umuahia, but I wonder if they could be transferred to your station. Could you please inform Dr Jackson about this?

I regret very much that I have to hand over the affairs of the medical work at Uburu in this way, as we had hoped so much that we could continue our work. I feel also very unhappy that I leave the country in such an unsatisfactory way, after the 8½ years in which I worked for the Church in its medical work sharing with Biafrans and expatriates all joys and troubles. As you well know I have been very happy in my work in this country, and it is my sincere wish that the circumstances will soon permit that the work can be fully continued. I am very grateful for the cooperation which I always found from government and local people, but especially from the Church. I wish to thank the Church and you in particular for all what you have done for my family and myself.

May God give that soon a brighter future appears for this our country. With kind regards, also to your wife,

Yours sincerely,

K. Reijnierse
Medical Superintendent.

Friday 20th September

The Chief Representative,
International Red Cross,
Umuahia.

Dear Sir,

Because of a threatened enclosure of our area by federal troops, the Military Commander of the Biafran Army in our sector advised us on 18th September 1968 to evacuate the Presbyterian Joint Hospital, Uburu, even though there was no danger for war activities in the immediate vicinity of Uburu. We acted on his advice and our non-local staff evacuated the next day. Our Assistant Nursing Superintendent, Mr E. Obasi, who is a local man took charge of all keys, drugs, and equipment. He is assisted by a midwife and 15 nursing orderlies and hopes to continue medical services at a small scale in the area until the staff can be increased again.

As it might be possible that a Red Cross team can be stationed at Uburu at an earlier stage than senior medical staff from our Church, I would like to ask you to consider that a Red Cross Medical team be sent to Uburu as soon as conditions permit. The hospital is fully equipped and has a stock of drugs. Houses for staff are available and a number of junior medical and non-medical staff are at the spot. Transport facilities are very difficult, and the team would have to be equipped with two Landrovers or equivalents.

As from 21st September 1968, Dr A. W. Jackson, c/o Queen Elizabeth Hospital, Umuahia is Medical Superintendent of the Hospital and correspondence about this matter should be directed to her.

I should appreciate if you give this request your considerations.

Yours faithfully,

K. Reijnierse
Medical Superintendent.

The Permanent Secretary,
Ministry of Health,
Enugu.

Dear Sir,

I wish to inform you that on advice of the Military Commander of the area, the non-local staff from the Presbyterian Joint Hospital, Uburu has been withdrawn from that area and has been evacuated to Umuahia.

Mr E. Obasi, assistant nursing superintendent, who is a local man, has taken charge of the Hospital and is continuing the work, with a midwife, nursing orderlies and labouring staff on a partial basis.

The evacuated staff will be seconded to other medical work but remain employed by our Hospital until further notice. Those for whom no work can be found within the medical work of our Church will be referred to the Chief Nursing Officer for secondment to other instiutions.

The Medical Superintendent of the Presbyterian Joint Hospital and of the Presbyterian Rural Health Services, Uburu, Afikpo is now Dr A. W. Jackson, c/o Queen Elizabeth Hospital, Umuahia and all correspondence should be directed to her.

Yours faithfully,

K. Reijnierse
Medical Superintendent

c.c.
Chief Nursing Officer

Saturday 21st September

This correspondence was followed up with a reply to Dr Kees Reijnierse from Rev. Sandy Sommerville, a Church of Scotland minister working with the Presbyterian Church in Biafra. Sommerville had received Kees' letter of 20th September, addressed to the Rev. Nwachuku Eme of the Presbyterian Church in Igbere.

Ohafia

Dear Kees,

Thank you for your letter, which I am passing on to Nwachuku to read. It was good of you to report so quickly. We are thankful to God that you are all out safely. It has been worrying to know the situation up there, with transport out so difficult, and it is a great relief that when you had to leave you were able to get through. We are grateful to the authorities also for their cooperation.

You have all done very well, keeping things going despite all odds and I am sure I speak for Nwachuku and the whole church in expressing our appreciation of your efforts.

I note that Bill should be away by now and that you hope to follow shortly. I think that is wise – this is a very difficult time for you to be separated from your wives and families. Please tell Janet that I think she has earned her leave also. She has had a very tough time, beginning with the Mary Slessor Hospital experience and I know how hard she has worked with the vast numbers of refugees. I think a rest would now be a good idea for her, and I suggest that she ask Murray Cochrane to arrange her exit papers without delay.

Ann hasn't been here so long as Janet and may feel she can carry on a bit longer, but she also has been very hard worked and is certainly entitled to take leave now if she wants. I think you have all been under considerable strain at Uburu ….

Agwu Oji is waiting to go off in the lorry and I must end this without further waste of time.

Our thanks and good wishes to you all,

Yours sincerely, Sandy

ps   Dear Janet & Ann,

I've written the above copy in case Kees is away. Our regards to you both,

Yours aye, Sandy

October 1968

Sunday 6th October

Letter to close friend Sarah Watson in Carluke, written after attending a memorial service for the Savourys, two Anglican missionaries with the Church Missionary Society (CMS) in Biafra who had been murdered by Nigerian Federal soldiers.

Queen Elizabeth Hospital
Umuahia

My dear Sarah,

This is Sunday and I am on call but I am hoping to have a quiet day. I went to Communion this morning at 6:30 am – a Methodist Service in the hospital chapel. It was good to go and I feel much the better for the early rising & long morning as well.

Yesterday we attended a Memorial Service for the Savourys in the chapel and it was well attended. The service was for the two CMS missionaries, and the Archbishop had arrived back only the day before so he took part. It was short and simple. It was moving and uplifting and an inspiration to all of us. So often we sing hymns and do not realize the depth of meaning in the words we sing.

1) "Jesus lives!" Hymn 121

Verse 4. "Jesus lives! Our hearts know well
Nought from us His love shall sever;
Life, nor death, nor powers of hell
Part us from His keeping ever."

2) "Let saints on earth in concert sing." Hymn 227

3) "For all the saints who from their labours rest",
I like all the verses of this one.

We have all been quite stunned by the news, Sarah, and it is difficult to put it out of one's mind. We heard the International Red Cross officials report on the incident – it's really awful. The soldiers knew it was International Red Cross and Missionaries and they were abused as Biafran sympathisers, stripped of their personal possessions and then soldiers fired on them. A few tried to run back into the bunker, the others threw themselves on the ground, 4 died. The survivors & bodies were driven to Awgu & then Enugu and they were abused & threatened all the way by the Nigerian soldiers they met at the roadside, denouncing missionaries and Red Cross people. Sarah, if they are so hostile to us and can murder an old couple what do you think they will do to the Ibo themselves?

BBC have reported that no educated Ibos have gone back to the Federal occupied territories. We know that all the top men in Benin were gathered together & shot. I really feel so sick and ashamed of the British Government – they said arms would be stopped if they were ill-used & the soldiers uncontrolled. Surely this incident will show them. The Savourys & Red Cross had discussed death on Sunday night & were killed on Tuesday morning. Because it was their wish they were not flown home to Britain but were buried in Enugu. British bullets killed them and the British Government is partly, if not wholly, responsible for their deaths. It was God's will and I pray that good will come out of it. At the service yesterday the Archbishop said it was to remember them & the African Bishop took the other part of the "sermon" and he said to give praise & thanks to God for their work, their lives & their witness. There was no trace of bitterness from the Igbos though they are feeling this so much & feel responsible themselves. The theme for the service was "I know that my Redeemer liveth."

Some criticized us for having a special memorial service at this time when there is so much death around us. I think it was good to have the service to make us realize that no matter how much death Jesus still reigns & we are victors because of Him. Also the service was really for all Christians who have died during these long months – we still are one and Christ unites us; also it was a witness to all non-believers, demonstrating our faith in God & our belief in the Resurrection and for each one of us it gave new strength & new hope. It was a meaningful service, I think everyone there knew that it could have been for them and that it may be their fate. The singing was good & strong and there was a feeling of victory & of rejoicing as well as tears for the families & tears because of the wickedness of men.

Sarah, I am not especially brave & I must confess I got a big shock that this could happen – we could be killed – I had not really thought about it seriously. I got a fright & I was scared. However, I have since faced it and since this service I really feel calm about it. I wrote to you a few days ago explaining any feeling. But even at that time I felt not quite sure if I wanted to run the risk. I knew God's will – to work here with the people I love and there is work for me – I felt somehow sure, yet unsure – if you know what I mean. Anyway, God has shown me to wait for Him, to live a day at a time and to trust Him. He has a plan for my life and I must be content to place my life in His hands, knowing that He knows best. The reading & prayers in my wee book for today, October 6th, says,

"*Almighty God, Father of our Lord Jesus Christ, I commit all my ways unto Thee. I make over my soul to Thy keeping. I pledge my life to Thy service. May this day be for me a day of obedience and of charity, a day of happiness and of peace. May all my walk and conversation be such as becometh the gospel of Christ, Amen.*"

Dear Sarah, be patient with me and please don't let my letters upset you. I really feel that the above prayer will be answered. I feel at peace and ready to give my all for Christ's sake. I know you are doing all you can for Biafra, please ask Mrs Leitch & all others politically minded & concerned to agitate the Government again.

I hope you are well, yourself, these days Sarah and that you too are strong at this time. It's even harder for you & all who love me to be away from here, worrying, wondering what is happening to me. I am <u>quite</u> well. Anyway, I told you I had some trouble with my chest but I am much better these days. I am taking Ephedrine tabs and have no trouble these past few days. I think it will all settle down. It's certainly nothing serious so please don't worry.

I hope my mother is well at this time. Please, Sarah, write & tell me honestly how she is – I am very much worried about Mum & Dad & their reaction to all this. Please strengthen them and help them to be brave.

I will close now and go & have a wee lie down on the bed – it's now afternoon & I have had a busy morning – 3 new admissions and 3 deaths. We have 80 children in the ward.

Thank you, dearest Sarah, for listening to me – I hope you will write soon – a nice big letter.

Give my love to your mother, Jane, Janet, & Frances, Mrs Reid, and all who know me. May God bless you and all who care about the suffering here.

Much love and my prayers
Ann

Sunday 6th October

Ann's letter to her sister Jenny, reflecting again on the murder of the two elderly Anglican missionaries.

Queen Elizabeth Hospital

My dear Jenny,

I hope you are well and happy. I know you must be worried about me in this Biafran situation but please try not to worry. I am well and still working here in Queen Elizabeth Hospital.

We have all been quite stunned here in Biafra over the news of the death of the two CMS missionaries. They were an older couple and I met them here at Queen Elizabeth Hospital when they came for a weekend or to attend meetings. They were experienced missionaries and they were prepared to die for Christ & the people. It seems they discussed death on the Sunday and were killed on the Tuesday morning. It was their wish to be buried in Biafra & <u>not</u> in Britain. The worst thing about this whole business is that when the survivors & the bodies of the 4 dead were being taken by car to Enugu all the Federal troops they met abused them & threatened them. International Red Cross & missionaries abused for giving aid & sympathy to Biafra. If the Federals are so hostile & murderous to us you can guess what is going to happen to the Ibos themselves. We can't understand why the British Government and the world do not realise how uncontrollable and blood thirsty the Federals are. Poor poor Biafra – and the world looks on – I am sick of the British Govt. who are sending so much armoury & ammunition to Nigeria.

Sorry to go on so but it's awful to watch the suffering, see the bomb & rocket casualties and know that they come from Britain. We have had quite a week of indecision and worry, wondering if we should be sent home or not. There is still much work here in Umuahia and I will be staying meantime. Some have gone home but most of us here in the hospital feel we have too much to do.

I was afraid & shocked when I heard about the missionaries' death but I have faced it & been given the choice and I believe I am staying to do Christ's work and I know that whatever happens will be God's will. I do trust Him & I will wait till He tells me to go. Before this incident I had not considered death at all – I know there is danger in a war but I thought I was exempt (so to speak). Now I know I may not be but I can only live a day at a time & know that God is with me during the day & the night.

Please don't be afraid for me – I am very sure that I must stay meantime. Maybe the time will come when it will be advisable to go. I will not be foolish – now is <u>NOT</u> the time to desert our Ibo friends. I am more worried for them, and especially for the many close friends we have here. Victoria is in the bush hiding with her people, she is cut off and has no way of coming here at present. There is fighting in her village area and I am very worried about her. I can only commit her to God's care & keeping.

Keep well & don't worry! Maybe I will be home. The World Council of Churches think the next 2 weeks may be critical for us, we will go home if there is any danger of Umuahia being cut off. Maybe I'll see you sometime soon.

God bless & keep you.

Much love & prayers.
Ann xxx

Monday 14th October

Ann's letter home to her parents.

My dear Mum, dad & family,

Just a quick note to say that I am well and that there is not much change in the situation here. It's amazing how quickly each week goes and each month as well. Work continues at the same high pitch, casualties still come in, the wards continue to expand.

On Saturday we had another air-raid outside Umuahia – a good number of people were killed and about 100 injured. It was a deliberate attack on a village – the plane circled 3 times before the attack and there were no military targets anywhere near. The Red Cross have investigated it – and so the killing goes on.

There is somehow a new feeling of optimism & hope among the people. More arms are coming in and the army seems to be holding its own. Guerilla warfare has already started and the Biafrans have started night attacks. Relief still keeps coming in but this is not the answer – there must be a cease-fire and an end to the blockade.

I am still staying with Anne Bent and Alicia has moved in with the Dutch Dr. She was supposed to be going home & I was to get her house but she has shown no sign of moving so it looks like I've lost that house. I was looking forward to sharing with Alicia. Anyway, Anne Bent & I get on fine and she keeps saying she'll be lonely if I move out. I would be more free with Alicia but I will need to wait and see.

I have still had no news of Victoria, there is no way she can come out and already she has been 3 weeks in the bush. Anne Bent says she can give her a job and accommodation if she manages to come. I'll bet she's very scared these days hiding in the bush.

I have a new address for you to try – c/o World Council of Churches

P. O. Box 201
São Tomé.
West Africa.

I have had no letters for 10 days or so but it depends on aircraft from Lisbon. I hope everyone is well and working hard. Chrissie Denholm will be visiting you all sometime this month. I know she will get a good welcome in Carluke. I think she will have a lot of deputation work to do in these coming months. Maybe I'll stay here a while longer & miss all the winter meetings! Ha! Ha! I'd rather face bombs & hard work than all these meetings!

Please give everyone my love and good wishes & tell them to keep on with the good work. Biafrans need everyone's help and prayers at this time.

Much love to all,
Ann xxx - I hope wee William is okay now.

From October 1968 to January 1969 Ann was back in Scotland on leave with her family, recovering from living and working through the worst period of the blockade of Biafra. In these terrible months of 1968, before international aid arrived to break the blockade through night time airlifts, Ann witnessed at first hand and personally recorded in her medical notes the deaths of thousands of women and children from malnutrition and disease. When she reported this scale of suffering to the Church of Scotland, she was not believed.

Carluke Missionary Returns From Biafra

15/11/68

15/11/68

CARLUKE missionary Dr. Ann Jackson got a special welcome home when she returned at the end of last week after working for more than a year amid the civil war chaos in Biafra.

Dr. Jackson (left) is pictured with her mother in the garden of their home at Chapel Street, Carluke.

So far, Dr Jackson has been taking things easy at home, but on Wednesday she will give an address at a special service of thanksgiving for her return, which is to be held in Kirkstyle Church at 7.30 p.m.

In an interview on page 3, Dr. Jackson talks of the conditions in Biafra, where eggs are 30s a dozen and thousands are dying of starvation.

from Victoria 1969 Dec.

OIKOUMENE

World Council of Churches
Refugee Relief in Biafra

Mr & Mrs Wm Jackson
49 Chapel Street
Carluke
Lanarkshire
Scotland.

Ann's beloved family and friends in Carluke were her anchor of support in Biafra

Ann on veranda of Okpara Ward, Queen Elizabeth Hospital, Umuahia

Ann with colleague Ann Travis
in São Tomé, returning from leave
to Biafra, January 1969

Ann at home on furlough, 1968

The Journal 1969

Jesus Weeps for Biafra

"Surely our Lord Jesus is weeping for this people – it's heartbreaking Sarah to see so much suffering and pain."

Ann's letter home to Sarah Watson, her friend and fundraiser in Carluke

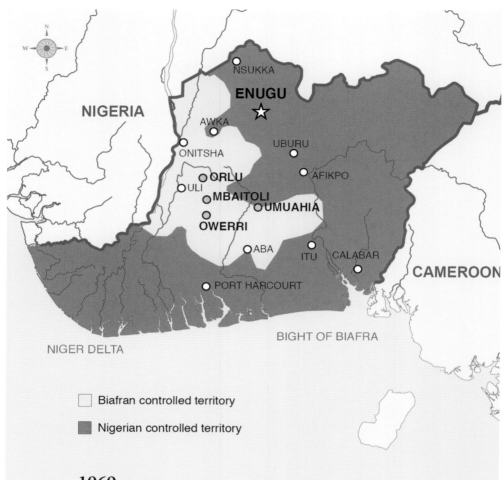

NSUKKA

ENUGU ☆

NIGERIA

AWKA

UBURU

ONITSHA

AFIKPO

ULI

ORLU

MBAITOLI

UMUAHIA

OWERRI

ABA

ITU CALABAR

CAMEROON

PORT HARCOURT

BIGHT OF BIAFRA

NIGER DELTA

☐ Biafran controlled territory

■ Nigerian controlled territory

1969

In the first months of 1969, Ann was working at the Queen
Elizabeth Hospital in Umuahia, which suffered regular air
raids and bombing by Nigerian forces. In April 1969 the Queen
Elizabeth Hospital was evacuated; the administrative and
nursing staff were moved to Orlu. Ann went to Mbaitoli, a few
miles from Owerri, where she led the hospital's mobile medical
teams close to the war frontline.

Timeline 1969

1969	Key Events
January	Ann returns to Biafra via São Tomé in a dangerous night flight breaking the blockade by Nigerian forces
February	Ann working in Queen Elizabeth Hospital, Umuahia, facing daily air raids and bombing by Nigerian military planes; many casualties
March	Nigerian forces advancing towards Umuahia; intense bombing around hospital; the local market bombed
April	Queen Elizabeth Hospital evacuated Hospital administrative and nursing staff move to Orlu, near Owerri. Ann leads medical team in setting up mobile clinics in nearby Mbaitoli
May	From Mbaitoli, Ann travels to clinics along booby-trapped roads. Medical teams at clinics see 500 patients daily, including many sick children Ann is ill with fever
June	Ann diagnosed with atypical pneumonia; sent to São Tomé on a night flight and then home to Carluke to recover
October	Ann returns to Biafra via São Tomé on a dangerous night flight breaking the Nigerian blockade. She continues to run clinics with her medical team from Mbaitoli
December	Preparations for Christmas and New Year at Mbaitoli

January 1969

Saturday 31st January

Ann is back in Biafra at the Queen Elizabeth Hospital in Umuahia. In these first months of 1969, we rely on her letters home to her parents in Carluke for her story.

Queen Elizabeth Hospital
Umuahia

My dear Mum & dad & family,

Just a hurried note to say that I arrived here safely on Thursday morning. I reached Brussels okay and had to wait until 10.30 pm according to the desk clerk so I had a nice entrecote steak meal (30/). The plane did not leave at 10.30 pm so we had to wait and wait, expecting to go at any hour and eventually we did leave at 8.30 am on Tuesday morning.

There were 15 passengers – 8 priests, 3 reporters and one of the World Council of Churches (WCC) pilots, an American lad and another chap. It was quite a good flight and the priests & reporters were very nice and friendly, treated me to coffee and a cold drink during the flight so I was well looked after. The WCC people were not expecting me in São Tomé but I was soon collected and taken to the Restaurante Yong for a meal and I stayed the night with a German girl. Elsie Taylor, a Canadian sister who was at Uburu for years is now the organizer for WCC so she was very helpful but very busy rushing around about her own business.

It was very hot there and I soon had some feet with blisters but I bought a pair of flip flops (sandals) so they are not too bad now. Actually yesterday I could hardly walk and I was glad I don't start work until tomorrow Sunday. I had a good flight to Biafra and for the first time in many days there was no bombing. I was taken straight through customs & immigration with no trouble at all and was really given a good welcome by the Biafran officials. I missed the WCC man at the airport so had to wait all night, sleeping on a couch but I was given coffee in the morning and when no one arrived for me I waited until 8 am. Then the Major took me to Umuahia in his big posh State House car – "For carrying important people like Ann Jackson" – he said, laughing. I enjoyed the drive in style, straight through all the military check points to Queen Elizabeth Hospital. I was given a good welcome here too.

I have been staying with Anne Bent but will move into my own house tonight and I have a wee Volks car to do my work so I am okay. It's very hot & dry & dusty these days …. I will have – I hope an easy first week to get used to the heat.

I will write later & give you more news. Edgar Ritchie goes on leave for a month or so and he will take the letter. Tell everyone I am well and very happy to be back again. There have been no air raids for some time now so maybe it will be quite quiet for a while.

Tell Sarah I will write soon.

Love to all. <u>Ann xxx</u>

February 1969

Sunday 2nd February

Queen Elizabeth Hospital
Umuahia

My dear Mum & dad & family,

Sorry I did not manage to write last week but the time just seemed to slip past. Alicia Bandeen had been transferred to Alor so she came down for the weekend. It was good to see her and we had a good old blether. I hope to go to her place for the weekend sometime next month but I will need to wait & see how things go.

Today is now Saturday and I am going to Bende with the Dutch doctor to do a clinic and have that section of refugee work handed over to me. I worked there before so I am looking forward to meeting some old friends. I have started work in a nearby Sick Bay and I think I will enjoy it there with 22 orphans and 50 sick children. I have only just started this week but already the children give me a good welcome every time they see me. They are all very friendly and affectionate.

I have started to learn Ibo in earnest and Victoria & Caroline are both teaching me so I hope to master it this time. I hope the enthusiasm does not wear off before I can say something sensible. Ann Travis the sister from Liverpool has arrived and settled in with me and I think we will get on well together. We have our own rooms so we can always escape to there but we are both quite busy so, in fact, do not see much of each other.

We have had several aeroplanes over in the past week and two actual raids but there were only a few casualties and very little damage done. We always get the fright, of course, but work has to go on and the Biafrans themselves seem to accept these raids as part of their way of life. There is definitely <u>not</u> the panic there used to be when a plane came over and people run & take cover but as soon as the plane is out of earshot they get up & get on with their work. I did get a fright one day because a plane came in quick & low over the hospital but it passed over and did not drop anything. So far the hospital has not actually been bombed but the town has taken some bad beatings.

Well, at least I am safe and well and enjoying being back to work. I hope you are all well and that there is work for the garage.

Give my love to all. I will be writing again next week.

With love & prayers.

<u>Ann xxx</u>

PS. *I hope you are remembering Eleanor's wedding present, Mum. Wedding is in March.*

Wednesday 26th February

Queen Elizabeth Hospital
Umuahia

My dear Mum, dad & family,

Sorry to be so long in writing this time – I always try to write at the weekend but I was on call on Sat. and was kept very busy. Alicia Bandeen arrived unexpectedly from Alor so Sunday was taken up with her and I was invited out to Anne Bent's for supper. Time passes quickly for us here but I know you must be anxious.

I received letters on Saturday so I was very pleased with myself – my first from Sarah and one from Alex & from Mum. Poor Alicia did not receive any letters this time and she was terribly disappointed – there must be a hold up of letters somewhere because Sarah's was marked (2) so the first one must be lying around somewhere. We have had quite a few bombing raids with varying numbers of casualties and damage done but the hospital compound itself remains safe. There was a terrible raid on a village some days ago with 25 killed and 50-60 injured, no military target anywhere nearby.

There have also been a lot of raids on the airstrip and quite a number of our pilots have refused to fly because of the risks involved so our flights have decreased and so too, our relief supplies. Otherwise everything here is much the same. I am working but not too hard at present so I get time for wee sleeps in the heat of the day. It really is terribly hot just now and everyone is complaining.

Sjouka Bakker now works for the Red Cross and last night he gave me a dozen cakes of soap and a lovely red blanket - a gift from the International Red Cross. I was quite delighted with myself! He and Murray Cochrane are very good to us all and they give us extra foodstuffs from the Red Cross supply for their own European workers. So we have plenty of food and we have a good store now also, so there is no chance of us starving for many months yet!

Tell Alex I really enjoyed receiving & reading his letter and also the wee drawing from John & Wm. I'm sorry Hazel's Papa died but it was probably the best thing although I know her mother must be missing him. I know Hazel's birthday is about now so "Many happy returns"! I hope Diane is keeping well these days and that Walter has not too many nights away from home. I wonder if Liam is still shoveling coal or if his daddy decided to get someone to help the wee man to move it? I can hardly believe that I have been here one month yet at times it seems like months. I am certainly feeling grand and only complain about the heat but, fortunately, I can go to bed these afternoons.

Friday 28th February

Sorry, but I did not manage to finish this letter. I have been kept fairly busy all week but I much prefer it this way.

We are supposed to have had a two days truce for the Nigerian Festival but this has been a terrible farce. We have been having many casualties in from the war fronts so the fighting has gone on without a break and we had some terrible raids on Tuesday. Five different places were bombed and one really bad one in an open market place – 200 people were killed and about 300 injured. A terrible carnage! Sjouka had to go as the official Red Cross Representative and he was really sickened – pieces of bodies all over the place, women and children mainly. Let's hope the [British] Government will soon believe reporters and missionaries and not the Federal Government in Lagos! The morale here is surprisingly good and everyone is determined to survive and they are always hopeful.

Victoria's mother came to stay with her for a few days and she really was needing a break. She seems to have had a really trying time in the bush with her two grandchildren and just missed being captured by the Federal troops. She has lost a lot of weight but is otherwise well and Victoria was so pleased to see her and hear news of the village and their relatives. People are really having a hard time here – prices are soaring and money is hard to get, some are hoarding the money so it is not in circulation and so, even if you have money in the bank it may be no good to you. Fortunately for us the World Council of Churches have sent plenty of food to keep us going. Oranges cost 9 for 5/- and used to be 4 or 5 a penny. Bananas cost 6/each and rice now costs 10/- for a cup. Salt today is £6 or £8 per cup. Crazy, crazy prices.

Well I must go but I look forward to hearing from you again soon. Alex should write more often & tell William & Walter & co to try it sometime.

Love to all,

Ann

March 1969

Friday 14ᵗʰ March

Queen Elizabeth Hospital
Umuahia

My dear Mum & dad & family,

Many thanks for your letter received this morning with Jenny's letter enclosed. Mail is still very irregular and so far I have only received one letter from Sarah – I hope she is still writing to me. I expect she must be using the Lisbon address because all my recent mail has come via São Tomé.

I am well and much busier these days but I can't complain at all because I moped around when I was not doing a full day's work. The clinics are very busy in spite of the recent air-raids – people seem to be less afraid although the bombing has been more intense and destructive recently. About 40 were killed last week and we had about 49 admissions, a Roman Catholic priest was among the dead - a Biafran. Again it was the market that was hit but it seems to be their way of terrorising us. I see the debate in Parliament did not do us any good so it seems as if this war will just go on & on.

Prices here are increasing & increasing. A bundle of wood that used to cost 2/- or 3/- now costs 10/- and rice and yams are fantastic prices. I really don't know how the ordinary working person is managing these days. Everyone is feeling the pinch in so many different ways and again the usual famine months will soon be upon us. The missionaries and World Council workers are lucky as far as food is concerned because the people in São Tomé send us in plenty, food, candles, matches, etc. etc. In fact sometimes we get too much of macaroni and beans but Ann Travis & I just divide it up and give to Biafrans we know. We just could not have lived without this food supply from outside.

Victoria is well and she sends her greetings. She did write to you last week but she has mislaid the letter. Last weekend we had both time off so we went on the Friday afternoon to visit Alicia. It took us just under 3 hours to travel there and we gave 3 of our nurses a lift to places along our way. Transport is very very difficult these days. Alicia was terribly excited to see us and had been very much looking forward to having some company. She lives in a big school compound with the school full of refugees so you can imagine the noise. Pandemonium! She has a wee teacher's house with two bedrooms and a sitting room. She enjoys the work but is terribly lonely and miserable at times. The Archbishop lives next door to her and Jennifer Carey, an English girl lives in the house on the other side of her, but Jennifer lives with a crowd of refugees and she is very independent. She spends all her time working in the store or with the families, so she is no company for Alicia.

We really had a good weekend together. We took a wee transistor record player and some jazzy records and some hymn singing so we really had some nice music. On Sat. morning we went to Alicia's sick bay and I did a ward round to help her with some problem cases. We went to one of the local markets and Vicky had a great time to herself. We bought bananas, coconuts, oranges and two cocks which usually cost £4-£5 each but we got the 2 for 11/- because we had cash – shillings and not notes so we were very lucky. Alor is very near the war front and traders cross behind the lines to trade and shillings must be used so that is why they are so scarce and so valuable.

On Friday evening and all through the night there was a terrible racket – the Biafrans were supposed to be launching an offensive and the guns were booming! The house shook with the bangs and we could hear the bursts of machine gun fire. Everyone in this area are packed up ready to move at a moment's notice and I don't blame them as they are only 4-5 miles away from the war front. We even passed a market place which was in Nigerian hands for a wee while and saw the bullet holes and shell damage to the houses.

We stayed with Alicia until Sunday afternoon then came on down to Umuahia. We branched to see Victoria's sister because we heard that the children had had measles and were not well. We went down bush roads to the village and what a difference in this family – everybody had lost so much weight and the eldest girl Ogochi, aged 7 yrs is a real wee Kwashiorkor – shiny pot belly & straight hair. Victoria offered to take her to Umuahia so we have her here and we will try to feed her up. She has spent some time in England so speaks English quite well but is shy to speak and she is a bright wee thing. She is sitting doing arithmetic now with me while Victoria is on duty. We are trying to get her to a local school as well.

Well, I think that is all my news meantime. I will try to write Jenny at the weekend also as Anne Bent is going home and she will take our letters with her. Give everyone my love and good wishes and say I will try to write a prayer letter sometime soon.

Much love to all.

Ann xxx

PS I hope you have some good times in the caravan now that Easter is near.

Wednesday 19th March

Queen Elizabeth Hospital

My dear Mum & dad & family,

Just a hurried note to say that all is well with me here. Anne Bent goes home today so I thought I would take the chance to write. I received a few letters today from Sarah and an explanation for the delay. It seems that the Govt is censoring some of our letters and they keep being held up in various places. I don't know yet if they are screening outgoing mail but we must be careful. I hope to write a partner letter sometime soon but I just don't seem to be able to get down to it. I think it is the heat that makes me easily tired and irritable ….

I'm expecting Alicia Bandeen down for the weekend so we should get some laughs together. I must write soon to Jenny but I seem to be very lazy to write these days. I am still struggling with the Ibo lessons but it is a slow business. We are still waiting for John Phillips and Edgar to arrive but it's a matter of patiently waiting. Anne Bent is very tired and is really needing a break from it all. Murray Cochrane has been here for nearly 2 yrs and he is very tired & worn out. The pace is hectic and we can only cope for a limited period. As I have said, though, I am enjoying my work and keeping well. In this war situation there are many wee things that annoy & irritate one. I think everyone is tired of the war and its frustrations and deprivations.

Please let Sarah read this letter & let her know about the censorship delay with her letters. I will write again sometime at the weekend and give you some details of work & life here just now. This is Wednesday and a big clinic day so I am writing this during my lunch.

Sarah – we will go to Murray Cochrane's at 4 pm for some tea & to see Anne Bent off. She will visit Scotland so may pay you a visit – it would be good if she could visit you & give you some up to date news of this old place.

Please tell everyone I am asking for them. I hope Alex has a happy birthday on the 9th.

Much love to all & my prayers,

Ann xxx

Sunday 23rd March

Queen Elizabeth Hospital
Umuahia

My dear Mum & dad & family,

I hope you are all well these days and managing to get out and about. It certainly sounds as if you have had a second winter though with really cold weather. I hope the business is picking up again. Have you heard any more about the house & the garage being sold to the County or have you got a definite site in mind yet for building?

I am well and still enjoying the work here. Edgar & John Phillips arrived back and they will start work in the morning. I hope to be able to do more Refugee work but I will need to wait and see. The Dutch doctor will be going on leave in the next few months and I may be asked to relieve her. Alicia will be coming back to Umuahia about that time too so we may team up. She came down here on Friday for the weekend so she goes back to Alor today, Sunday. Elsie Taylor who used to work at Uburu and now works in São Tomé came across last night and stayed with us also so we had a real Uburu re-union. Victoria's sister also arrived yesterday so she came up with Vicky in the evening also. We had quite a houseful but it was good company and I think everyone enjoyed the evening. Diane North came in about 9 pm and she cut Alicia's & my hair in the midst of everybody. I was on call last night but fortunately there was no trouble so the evening was not interrupted.

I received another letter yesterday but dated early February so it must have been delayed. I did not know that Marguerite had become engaged so no doubt the letter with that news has still to reach me. I must write to her sometime soon. Eleanor Clark would be married yesterday so I hope all the wedding arrangements went well. Have you had any news of Catherine More? I wonder if she is going through an operation in the near future. I had a long letter from Chrissie telling me that she has started work as a deaconess somewhere in Edinburgh so I hope you will still be able to keep in touch with her.

We heard on the news today that Haiti has recognized Biafra and there has been great jubilation here in Umuahia. Tonight there is a special World Council of Churches service and Zambian Church people will be there so we expect a packed chapel and the choir has been busy practicing their pieces and the hymns. It should be a good service.

I drove Anne Bent to the airstrip on Wednesday night and we had a good journey. It was funny really! We reached the outskirts of Umuahia & were flagged down to let the Chief of Staff & his escort pass – a big Bentley with a wee jeep in front and a big jeep with an armed escort behind him. We were in the wee Hospital mini so I just tagged on behind them and when they sailed through check-points and passed "flagged down" lorries & cars I just sailed on through as well. We did a steady 60 mph and made record time. The police & soldiers saluted us as well so we waved cheerily or I think, cheekily back.

I only took Anne to the store then left because it was 6.30 pm and about time for the Nigerian Migs to raid the air strip. I felt I would be happier in Umuahia so I beat it back. We have since heard that Anne had a good uneventful journey and there was no raid that particular night. Some nights it has been really hot and uncomfortable there. Anyway we are all still here and able to get on with the good work.

Uncle John Patterson has his birthday today so we are all going out to his birthday party. I will write to Sarah and maybe start a partner letter but I never seem to get down to it. I hope Diane is feeling much better and that wee Walter behaved himself – I'm sure he would keep you all going with his crack. Tell John & William, Liam & wee Grace, Walter & Allen that I am asking for them and that my wee Biafran weans send them greetings.

With love to all,

Ann xxx.

Sunday 30th March

Queen Elizabeth Hospital
Umuahia

My dear Mum, dad, & family,

Just a hurried note to say that I am safe and well, though a bit scared. The Federals have launched a heavy attack and are very near to Umuahia. We have been hearing a lot of shelling & noise and everyone is waiting, packed up ready to move out.

The trouble is there is nowhere to go and we have about 300-400 patients who are helpless – in plaster, legless and blind and unable to go anywhere. I don't know what the plans will be whether we go to the airstrip or stay with these patients. I know that our conscience will tell us what we must do and what God wants us to do.

At present we are only threatened and will need to wait to see how good our defences are and hope the advance will be halted. I think everyone is scared stiff yet going on about their duties, hoping & praying for some miracle. Victoria has gone on duty, very worried about me she says – I know that many Biafrans just now _are_ worried about _us_ and not just themselves and they have more need to worry for their own safety. God alone knows the true situation and what He has planned for us so we will need to trust and obey His promptings and guidance.

I know you must be very worried about me but try to have a quiet mind and to be confident with me in God. It's an awful situation to be in yet I feel God is in it with me, just as He brought me here to work and live with this people. I like the country and I like the people and I have made many friends who have my love and my loyalty. I hope I will be found faithful to my God and to them at this time of crisis. But please try _not_ to worry because I know everything will work out for the best. I hope I will be able to stay on and work here – only God can decide what work I must do and where I will do it.

Many thanks for the pound note and which I received today. I'm very pleased to hear that Diane is well and now out of hospital. Mr Fraser I know well and have always kept in touch with him – he's a very fine man and he has given a lot of money for Biafra. I think this new man will be good as well. Please tell everyone I am well and they have not to worry but have to keep on praying for Biafra and for peace. Dear knows when it will all end, so many people are involved in this tragedy and suffering.

We have been planting like mad these past few weeks too – maize, beans, onions, tomatoes, groundnuts so I hope we will be here to harvest it all but at least someone will benefit from our efforts. These past few days we have been enjoying fresh cucumber from the garden so bread & cheese & cucumber has been our mid-day snack and very good too.

I hope the weather improves so you can enjoy the caravan again. I will write again as soon as I can & let you know what is happening.

Meanwhile, much love to you all & may God be with you.
Ann xxx

April 1969

Friday 4th April

Queen Elizabeth Hospital
Umuahia

My dear Mum & dad & family,

This is Friday – Good Friday – and coffee time so I thought I would take time to write you a few lines. The situation here is much the same. The army are halted at present. I believe we can still hear the shelling and at times, small arms fire. We have been busy packing up hospital equipment for future use and transferring it to another safer area.

Everyone is still a bit tense but we are now more ready to move out and we have sent all the children away from Okpara Ward and sent our orphans to Orlu. Umuahia town is still very busy because more & more refugees come here but many others have moved out from the town. We can expect more bombs & raids, I think, so it is better that people are not congregated in this place. Refugees with their children are everywhere and it's a heartbreaking sight to see.

We have our plans made and we have transport so don't worry too much. Remember that no news is good news because we are now in direct radio contact with people in Holland so that if anything happens they will inform the Church of Scotland who will contact you. Soon, I hope. No news means that we are safe and well. There are many nurses who are our responsibility. Victoria has gone to her sister's place with the child Ogochi and I feel this is a good idea. She has been very worried about her and keen for her to be with her mother. In the event of a sudden emergency small girls can be an added burden.

This is now Sunday and I hope to send this letter off today to Europe so it should reach you sometime this week. We are all still here in Umuahia although we have evacuated many patients and some of our things. It's a strange life really but today we hear that the Nigerians have been pushed back. Anyway, when the time comes we will be ready so don't worry about us. The houseboy was . . . around to pack things – what a mess he made and left us with no plates or cutlery and then he mixed kerosene with the petrol so I was very angry about it all. Poor soul, he was really scared but I was too busy rushing around tending to casualties, helping to load a truck with equipment and packing other things. We have had a hectic few days but let's hope we can have a few days respite.

I'm glad all is well at home and that dad has work for his machines. Give everyone my love & good wishes. Thank you for the Easter Card.

With love & prayers, Ann xxx

Monday 14th April

Queen Elizabeth Hospital evacuated.

Victoria and I went to Orlu on Saturday with Office Books and equipment and we spent the night with her sister Phoebe at Oyuabia. On returning on Sunday evening we met 4 car loads and 3 or 4 lorry loads of police leaving Umuahia across the Imo River Bridge. The Federals had advanced to Umuahia and were definitely at Uzuakoli and within shelling distance of Umuahia. Many townspeople left Umuahia in the evening but were turned back at the check point to avoid panic.

We decided to transfer from Queen Elizabeth Hospital to Orlu and sent for World Council of Churches and Red Cross trucks to help us. We organized ourselves again to move and the trucks arrived in the evening and night time. 300+ patients were transferred to various hospitals and then nurses were transported to Orlu and Owerri areas. About 30 nurses were considered homeless and displaced so we kept them working in Out Patient Department seeing fresh casualties until we left about 5 pm with them.

John Phillips agreed to continue working in Out Patient Department until the Army Medical Corps moved in.

Ann Travis, Diane North, & I moved in convoy towards the Imo River Bridge but the queue of cars was 2 miles long and 3 abreast towards a single track bridge so we turned back & went via Ubakala and the other bridge.

We arrived at St Mary's Church, Orlu about 7:30-8 pm very tired and hungry. Spent the night on an airbed in the Church while the nurses slept in tents put up for refugees in transit. Paddy Hargreaves certainly has organized things in Orlu.

Tuesday 15th April

Spent the day sorting out drugs and equipment for the clinics we hope to start. Water was a problem in this place, the nurses had to carry water from a very difficult source about 1-2 miles away. Nurses organized themselves into two teams to cook and collect water for all of us in the camp.

Wednesday 16th April

Went to Atta early in the morning but Amachara Hospital had already occupied the Health Centre we were going to move to. We went to Paddy Hargreaves to find us other accommodation. The World Council of Churches folk moved to their central store but they had an uncomfortable crowded time in the store, sleeping on airbeds so they, too, were seeking accommodation.

WORLD COUNCIL OF CHURCHES

UZOAGBA SUBSTORE:

N A M E   C A M P

1. Umudi
2. C.K.S. Umuagwu
3. L. A. School Umuehihie
4. St. Andrew's Church Uzoagba
5. Aka's Farm Yard
6. St. Andrew's School, Uzoagba
7. St. James' Umueze
8. St. John's Amambaa
9. Chinedu Maternity
10. L. A. School Nduhu Obokwe
11. O.P.T.S.S. Uzoagba
12. Holy Ghost Umualumaku
13. L. A. School, Umueme
14. Market Hall, Umuomi
15. Macco Bakery
16. St. Patrik's Umuehihe
17. St. Mary's School Aboh
18. St. Michael's School Umuomi
19. St. Michael's School Akabo
20. St. Peter's School Akabo
21. St. Andrew's School Akabo
22. St. Michael's School Amatta
23. St. Joseph's School Uzoagba
24. St. Francis's School Amatta
25. St. Stephen's Amii Akabo
26. St. James, C.M.S., Obrangwu.

F E E D I N G   C E N T R E S

1. St. Andrew's School Uzoagba
2. St. Andrew's Church Uzoagba
3. St. Paul's (C.M.S.) Avuvu
4. E.C.T.S.S. Emekuku
5. Charity Maternity
6. Casita Maria
7. S.D.A. Umuorri/Umualum
8. Ukwu Orji Azarauwalla
9. L. A. School Umueme
10. St. James, Umueze
11. Okwu Emeke
12. St. Peter's Akabo
13. St. Stephen's Akabo
14. St. Michael's School Amatta
15. St. Andrew's School Akabo.
16. Umuene, Obrangwu.
17. St. Thereses, Obrangwu.

As thousands of Biafrans were displaced by the war,
the World Council of Churches ran refugee camps and feeding centres
in any available school, church, or village hall

W.C.C. Parish Store. Mbieri

NO.	NAME OF CAMP OR FEEDING CENTRE	POPULATION
1.	St. Thomas Refugee Camp, Ubakuru 'A'	214
2.	Dimorji Hall, Obokwe Refugee Camp A	273
3.	Umunnekanma Hall, Amaike I Camp A	274
4.	G.K.S. Obokwe, Camp A	151
5.	St. James' Zion, Ubakuru Camp A	177
6.	Mbieri Parish Sickbay, Ubakuru	
7.	St. Thomas, Umuagwu Refugee Camp A	553
8.	St. Jude's RCM Umuobom Camp A	174
9.	St. John's Church, Umuomumu Camp A	499
10.	St. John's RCM Umuduru Camp A	572
11.	St. John's Sch. Umuomumu Extension Camp A	315
12.	C.M.S. Amaike 1 Camp A	712
13.	St. Paul's Ubakuru, Camp A	310
14.	C.K.S. Orie Mbieri Refugee Camp A	562
15.	L.A. School/Okwoba Hall Refugee Camp A	612
16.	Baptist Mission, Awo, Camp A	127
17.	Zion Mission, Amankuta Camp A	130
18.	St. John's School, Umuomumu Camp A	260
19.	St. Peter's Church, Otura, Camp A	135
20.	Zion Mission, Umuduruorie Camp A	130
21.	Umuagwu Town Hall, Ifakala Camp A	102
22.	St. Dominic's School, Afara Camp A	157
23.	C.M.S. Ohohia Mbieri Camp A	183
24.	St. Cyprain's School, Afara Camp A	401
25.	Umuchinewe Village Hall, Ifakala Camp A	164
26.	Uba Hall, Ifakala Camp A	142
27.	St. Thomas Church, Eziama Obiata Camp A	82
28.	L.A. School, Obeakpu Umunoha Camp A	125
29.	C.M.S. Umunoha Camp A	219
30.	St. Joseph's School, Ifakala Camp A	300
31.	St. Paul's School, Umunoha Camp A	207
32.	Zion Mission, Amaike 1 Camp A	356
* 33.	Grant to Workers' Kitchen	
* 34.	Cost of one note book used for cash book	
35.	C.M.S. Ohohia Feeding Centre	3,750
36.	St. Peter's, Otura F.C.	3,132
37.	Ubakuru Feeding Centre	1,000
38.	St. John's Church, Umuomumu F.C.	1,500:
39.	St. Thomas Parsonage Eziama F.C.	4,935
40.	Umuagwu Mbieri F.C.	1,118
41.	Emmanuel Church, Eziome F.C.	
42.	Christ Church, Umunoha F.C.	5,000
43.	St. Cyprains Afara F.C.	5,000
44.	D.S. Centre Ifakala F.C.	3,000
45.	Obazu Feeding Centre	6,050
46.	St. Paul's Church Ubomiri F.C.	400
47.	St. Luke's Church Achi F.C.	1,700
48.	Ebom Feeding Centre	1,400
49.	All Saints' Ch. Awo Feeding Centre	
* 50.	Cost of making 12 pairs of dresses for camps	
51.	C.M.S. School, Umunoha B.Camp B	1,533
52.	St. James' Ubakuru Camp B	350
53.	St. John's School Umuomumu Camp B	821
54.	Umuchinewe Hall, Ifakala Camp B	300
55.	St. Cyprain's Church, Afara Camp B	429
56.	St. Dominic's School, Afara Camp B	700
57.	Dimorji Hall, Obokwe Camp B	1,122
58.	C.M.S. Amaike 1 Camp B	1,133
59.	Umunnekanma Hall Amike 1 Camp B	937
60.	St. Peter's Church, Otura Camp B	544
61.	St. Thomas Ubakuru Camp B	1,076
62.	St. Thomas' Umuagwu Camp B	571
63.	G.K.S. Obokwe Camp B	385

In the closing months of the war, Ann and her Queen Elizabeth Hospital
medical team assisted the World Council of Churches' relief work,
as well as running their own 'sick bay' clinics behind the war front

Thursday 17ᵗʰ April

John Phillips and I went with Alphonsus Akachukwu to explore the possibilities of clinic work in Ihaji area which has recently been disturbed. We went across the beautiful Oguta Lake by pontoon and visited one big Sick Bay. The road was bad with many obstacles and tank traps and evidence of the war, much destruction of buildings and overgrowth by the bush. We visited two bad refugee camps who have no nurse or medical attention. The need in this area is very great and John hopes to take a team there depending on the war situation. We reached to within 3 miles of the front.

Friday 18ᵗʰ April

I visited Bishop Nwankiti and explored down towards Owerri with Mr Anyama from Irete College who now works with World Council of Churches. We met the Secretary of the Mbaitoli County Council who agreed to let us use the Health Centre for a base and Sick Bay. Much work will need to be done on the buildings and the area will need to be re-camouflaged. We are 8 miles from Owerri and the Federals are still there so this place is still not occupied by local people although they are all moving slowly back.

Saturday 19ᵗʰ April

For the past 2-3 nights Anne Travis and myself stayed with the Rev. Sisters at Ihiama and we were well received. Lovely to have a hot bath and a proper sit-down toilet!

Wednesday 23ʳᵈ April

Left Orlu for Awo Mbieri to start clinic work – Thompson Oragown, Chinyere Ekeocha, Victoria, Rose, Godson, Murray, Elizabeth, & Carol – a very good team. Dr Bakker gave us his Red Cross truck to carry our loads and it's amazing how much stuff we actually carried. The carpenter had already started work on the house so all of us settled down in the one block meantime. We received many visitors who came to welcome us into the area.

Thursday 24ᵗʰ April

Orodo & Awo Mbieri Red Cross members came to welcome us & offer assistance. Chief Eronini came to see us.

Friday 25th April

Meeting with Mrs Ihizwe, in charge of Women's Work in Owerri diocese, very keen & helpful & pushing for Sick Bays. I visited Mbieri Sick Bay – 20 beds, much space and more of a show-piece but an efficient & keen nurse in charge.

Saturday 26th April

Left the Health Centre at 2 pm for Obibi – Owerri with Victoria and Rose. Owerri town was cleared on Friday so we tried to go through that way. Directed to Umuguma – we saw much destruction, many houses burned, many obstacles on the way, a stinking corpse and every sign that fighting had taken place very recently. We learned that the Nigerians had been there the previous day! Owerri town was deserted & bullet ridden but it definitely is Biafran.

We arranged to do a Clinic at Obibi on the following Friday with the Church Agent and Mr Ejofo. Had two punctures on the way – no spare wheel so we were lucky to get the help of one Lieut. Amadi and his men who removed the wheels, commandeered bicycles and took them to be vulcanized. Unfortunately it poured rain and they could not return so Amadi, Igbokwe & I spent the night on a bed settee in Lieut. Amadi's sitting room. Mosquitoes bothered us too much! In the morning we ate a hearty breakfast of yam & eggs & yam pottage – supplied by the army. Later in the morning we met the Sisters from Emekuku, now at Amaimo and they gave me tea and sympathy and apples.

Monday 28th April

Started our clinic at the Health Centre and there were hundreds of people clamouring for medical attention. Red Cross boys helped us to register:

Numbers: Children   195
              Adults   120

Proposed Schedule

Monday	Clinic at Health Centre
Tuesday	Orogwe & Avu areas
Wednesday	Mbieri + Children's Clinic
Thursday	Ifakala & Ogbaku
Friday	Nekede & Obike & Children's Clinic
Saturday	Morning clinic at Health Centre

Dr. Ann Jackson tends a child as nurses unload Sketch readers' supplies, watched by Dr. Clyne Shepherd.

British newspapers took up the cause of Biafra's starving children
and raised funds to support Ann's relief work

Tuesday, 29th *April*

We had hoped to do Avu & Orogwe areas together but only Orogwe was informed and it was enough. 2-3 thousand people turned up sitting under the trees and all around the church. These people are in a very bad state and have no adequate feeding centre going. We ran out of tablets & promised to give the Red Cross boys food.

May 1969

Saturday 3rd *May*

Letter on Queen Elizabeth Hospital letterhead to Ann's parents.

My dear Mum & dad & family,

Please forgive me for not writing last week but I have been very busy and did not get the time to sit down & write. I am now stationed at Mbaitoli Health Centre about 8 miles from Owerri with Victoria and Godson and nurses. John Phillips has gone with another team to a different area and Ann Travis, E. Ritchie and Murray Cochrane are now in a big house in Orlu helping nurses get settled in different hospitals.

Last week I explored the area looking for buildings to live in near this area. Owerri still had some Nigerians in it but this place seemed safe and it was deserted. The Nigerians reached to within 3-4 miles from here in December and all the people fled and they had not yet returned so we could choose the Health Centre or Court House or School. We have a big ward for a sick bay and 4 houses for our staff and the carpenter has been fixing it up for us.

We really are very comfortable and Vicky & her brother continue to look after me very well. We have two medical students Thompson & Chinyere with us and they are good company and good workers. At present we are all eating together but the boys should be getting someone to cook for them this weekend. Already we have started clinics and we see about 500 patients each day.

We travel out each day and the people here really receive us well especially since they have had no medical treatment for months. These people all ran away into the bush (jungle) when the Nigerians reached Owerri, many were killed, all of them were separated from the Biafran relief supply so we are seeing very bad Kwashiorkor cases, just as bad as in the early days and hundreds come to our clinics. We see 300-500 then send the rest away although many still need treatment but we work from 8 am – 4 pm or so then travel home before dark because there are many obstacles and booby traps on these roads – set for the Nigerians and not yet removed.

I really enjoy it here although we never get a minute's rest, because many people have been coming to welcome us & greet us & arrange meetings with us. Red Cross, Akanu Ibiam Ambulance, local councillors all come to my door in the evening when I can't be bothered with anyone. Anyway I hope we will settle down very soon but at present it is hectic, we are starting clinics and people get excited & anxious to be seen so they make a terrible noise & push & shout and we have a time to control them. Anne Bent came back some days ago so she may visit us sometime soon. I will try to go to Orlu today for the WCC meeting & to post this letter.

Please tell everyone I am safe & well & enjoying my new work and my Biafran friends are spoiling me, checking that I get time to eat & bath & get some rest so don't be worrying about me. Please thank Mr Reid & Sarah for sending another £500 to Queen Elizabeth account – it has been transferred to my account so I can use it in this area.

Much love to all.

Ann xxx

PS. Please tell Sarah I will be writing as I hope to have Sunday free to unpack properly and write letters. I hope my plans work out anyway.

I will finish this later.

Am now at Orlu but must work back. Murray Cochrane goes home on Friday and he has promised to visit you all. He has been a great help to us all but he is ready for a break – I hope he will decide to come back here.

Please give him a good welcome – I know you will!

Love to all & God bless and keep you.

Love,
Ann

World Council of Churches,
Central Stores,
UBULU - IHEJIOFOR,
BIAFRA.

14th May, 1969.

Dr. A. W. Jackson,
Queen Elizerbeth Medical Team,
Nbaitolu Health Centre,
OWERRI.

Dear Dr.

We have received your request dated 10th May, 1969
for some Drugs.

You indicated in your note that you see an average
of 400 to 500 patients a day. May we know if the drugs
requested are for a weeks supply or more.

We are also sending herewith a letter addressed to
you for your attention.

Best regards.

Yours sincerely,
for World Council of Churches

E N Isong
PHARMARCIST

ENO/GWO.

When the airlift of food and medical supplies broke the blockade,
Ann received vital supplies from the World Council of Churches

June 1969

Sunday 1st June

> Queen Elizabeth Hospital Medical Team
> c/o World Council of Churches
> BIAFRA

My dear Mum & dad & family,

It seems ages and ages since I wrote you a decent letter and I know you must be wondering why. It is 8 am on a cool pleasant morning and I am sitting on the verandah of a big white two storey building taking things nice and easy. Queen Elizabeth Hospital have been given this priest's house as headquarters in Orlu – I think no one wanted it because it's so big and conspicuous and Orlu is a possible target for bombers. Anyway, we are all enjoying its big rooms and using it as a Rest House for weekends etc and nurses are encouraged to use it, and they can always get a bed here.

Now for confessions – for the first time in about two weeks I feel really well today! I have had fever on & off, very high ones over the last 5-6 days and aches & pains. A doctor has seen me & says it is Dengue or Sand fly fever and I am now recovering and responding to treatment. I was down in Mbaitoli until Tuesday morning when my staff decided I must go to hospital but I insisted on Orlu first. Victoria has been nursing me and has been really wonderful, doing everything to help me and get me well again. She has come with me to Orlu and is continuing to nurse me, prepare meals, etc. Anne Bent is here but she is very busy rushing around about hospital business and I did not want her to be tied down with me so I brought Victoria back to Orlu with me and she & I share a bedroom.

I really am much better now but a bit weak so I will be resting here for some days before I go back to Mbaitoli to continue clinics there. Back to work on Monday or Tuesday. I will have a few more days rest first

Love Ann xxx

Wednesday 4th June

Queen Elizabeth Hospital Medical Team
c/o World Council of Churches
BIAFRA

My dear Mum, dad & family,

I hope you are all well and happy and that Dad had a good birthday. Again it is almost the weekend and Dr Reijnierse goes home to Holland tomorrow so I will ask him to post this. He has done 6 months and will be going home for good. I'm sure his wife and children will be pleased to have him with them again.

My fever has now completely gone and a definite diagnosis has been made. I have had Viral or Atypical Pneumonia as shown on a chest X Ray and I am responding to treatment. I must admit, I was getting worried because it was going on too long for Dengue. However everything is all right and I will gently ease myself into work. We have many more nurses working with us now and the team is working well so there is no great need for me to go rushing into things.

I hope to get a letter from you this weekend with some more news.

Sjouka Bakker came in to see me today and brought me chocolate and orange squash which were most welcome. He is working very hard and is really tired and worn out looking. Lucky him is due to go home in July for 6-8 weeks. I have not been working for almost a month now so may stay here until September but I will let you know. Six months seems a very short tour indeed compared to the usual 2 years and the most I have done so far is 14 months.

Sjouka had a letter from Murray Cochrane telling him that Diane North & himself visited Carluke. I hope you all got a chance to meet them but Sjouka says that Murray has been very tired and depressed. It's a complete change of life for him, of course, living in a small cottage in Freuchie, Fife. Alicia Bandeen will also be in touch with you in the near future. She was looking terribly thin when she left here. I'm sure her mother will get quite a shock when she sees her. I am a bit thinner but not too bad and I am really quite pleased about it.

Ann Travis has now moved down to Mbaitoli Health Centre so I will have her company. Anne Bent continues to keep the Queen Elizabeth Hospital house at Orlu and I will be staying there this weekend. John Phillips always comes up from Ihagi at the weekend for a break so we will all be together for a change. I'm hoping Victoria will come up as well. She sends you her greetings again and faithfully asks news of you when I get any letters. Last week Godson opened a tin of steak and I told him how to cook onion and add to it and he made a terrific job of it. I hadn't had anything so tasty in a long time. He really does try hard to please me. I don't pay him any money but I give him salt & soap etc for himself and his mother so he is quite happy. He is 14 yrs old but looks about 16 yrs and cannot go out of the compound on his own in case the army conscripts him. Anyway he moves around with us quite safely and I take him home to see his mother every two weeks. She is a widow and very good and she always gives me fruit or yam and treats me like her own daughter. I'm a very lucky somebody to have so many good faithful friends here and at home.

Last weekend I wrote many letters – to Leitch, Sarah and one or two others so I hope they arrived. I will write to the Irish this weekend and to Morene Quigley. Tell everyone I am asking for them and that I am now getting on fine. I hope the sun keeps shining for you all. You must let me know when folks plan to go on holiday and where.

Much love to all,

Ann xxxxx

Saturday 14th June

Queen Elizabeth Hospital Medical Team
c/o World Council of Churches
Biafra

My dear Mum & dad,

I hope you are all fighting fit. I was expecting some mail from you for two weeks now but no luck. This is the World Council of Churches meeting so maybe I will get something today.

Representatives came in from São Tomé for the week-end so they will take the mail out with them. I hope you receive this in time so you can give me a good homecoming. I thought of springing a surprise on you but my friends dissuaded me.

I have been resting here for the past week at Orlu and have been told not to work for a while yet so rather than do nothing here I will come home for two months. This will fit in with Edgar Ritchie who is due leave in mid-September so I will come back in the first week in September.

I will arrange my flight today and should be home in 7-10 days – end of June almost. I will leave this letter open until the meeting when I may learn the actual date the plane leaves São Tomé for Europe. Please do not let folk know at present. I want to slip home quietly and it will need to be complete rest I am really looking forward to seeing you all ….

I have lost a bit of weight – I could afford to lose another stone – and I have a good suntan with lying around so I am looking well. I am looking forward to some steak, onions and chips!!! and to lazy days in the caravan with Ma & Pa!!!

You could let Sarah & Mr Reid know but tell them I would like it kept quiet until I get home. In fact _don't_ tell them and we can surprise them.

Thursday 19th June

My dear Mum & dad & family,

Just a quick letter to let you know that I arrived here in São Tomé last night from Biafra. I had been told not to work for two more weeks so decided it would be better to rest at home. Flights are now irregular into Biafra so I was unexpectedly asked to take this one.

The next plane to Europe is on the 25th June so I will have a week's holiday here lazing around in the sunshine by the seashore. A Canadian couple are also here so I will have company. I left Victoria well but, of course, depressed that I had to leave early. It means I will be home late on the 25th or 26th June so I will be in plenty of time to see Jenny.

I had a Birthday Party on Tuesday evening and Victoria bought a chicken for my lunch. It was really nice and she made biscuits and things for the nurses on the compound so we had a very nice get-together. Let everyone know I am home to convalesce hence my early leave. All I need is a long rest.

Looking forward to seeing you all

With love & prayers

Ann xxx

THE CHURCH OF SCOTLAND

Department of Overseas Mission and Inter-Church Relations

OVERSEAS COUNCIL

121 George Street
Edinburgh 2
Tel.: 031-225 5722.   Groms: EVANGEL

.............4th..July,..1969..............

Military news is at present meagre, on the Biafra side because of technical difficulties in the communication system and on the Federal side because press correspondents are severely restricted and forbidden to approach any officer in the armed forces. Comparatively small scale, but sharp exchanges continue in the Mid-West where Biafran infiltration has reached the point at which Brig. Katsina has informed the civilian population that anyone found guilty of assisting Biafrans will be shot on sight.   In spite of quite heavy Nigerian artillery fire in the Orlu section, the Biafrans say they have held their position.   Other reports, such as that the Biafrans were being forced back near Owerri have not been confirmed.

What have been given prominence are the food relief position in Biafra and the administration of relief in Federal held territory.   The food and drug position in Biafra is deteriorating and is now at the crisis level of July, 1968. With no International Red Cross flights and few by Joint Church Aid, many feeding centres have been closed.   Dr. Bakker of I.C.R.C. on 28th June reported that his medical supplies were finished.   During the past week only 1 - 2 Joint Church Aid flights have been made per night.   Even should the airlift be restarted, it is feared it will be too late to save thousands and if there is no resumption of supplies it is thought that within a few weeks we shall have to report thousands dying daily.   It is just possible that the forthright statements by Red Cross may result in concerted action by a sufficient number of governments, acting quickly, to bring negotiations at present in deadlock over routes to some form of agreement.

Simply to read the Federal Government's statements makes evident that without intense outside pressure, neither daylight flights nor the water route will be approved.   "The total economic blockade of the rebel held areas remains in force.   The armed forces are under strict orders to enforce to total embargo, and the Federal Government will not bear responsibility for any attempt to break the blockade."   Further Chief Awolowo had denounced all relief agreements: "All is .fair in war and starvation is one of the weapons of war".   In spite of all such statements pilots at Sao Tome have stated that they are prepared to fly during daylight if assured that the World Press supports them.   Why run such risks?   Perhaps because they understand what lies behind the recent statement of a Biafran: "I see Biafra as a diseased heart ... it is very sick, but it is still beating.

In spite of official denials, there are strong rumours that the British Government is more than anxious.   Recent strong leading articles in the Financial Times and The Times asked in what way, in the present emergency, has the supply of arms from Britain moderated and mitigated the evils of this war./

Ann was sent to Biafra by the Church of Scotland,
which kept its prayer partners informed about the war situation

Between June and October 1969 Ann was home on sick leave in Scotland. By early October, she was back in Biafra for its final months as an independent country. After the Queen Elizabeth Hospital in Umuahia had to be evacuated with the advance of the Nigerian army in April 1969, Ann and the Queen Elizabeth Hospital staff formed mobile medical teams to continue running clinics just behind the frontline of the war – daily risking their lives to care for the sick, starving and dying of Biafra until its last days. Ann continued to run her medical team from Mbaitoli.

October 1969

Thursday 2nd October

49 Chapel Street
Carluke
Now São Tomé

Dear Mum & dad,

I arrived in São Tomé this morning at 11 am and I have had a good shower and my breakfast. I am writing this in the World Council of Churches office then going shopping for batteries (too heavy to carry) & cloth etc. I had a good flight to London, then with very little waiting I boarded a plane for Amsterdam and arrived there about 4.30 pm. I waited in the Tax-free lounge and looked around but everything is very expensive, but there was no harm in looking!

The flight was delayed until 10.30 pm but I met Kees Reijnierse who had heard at 9 pm that I was due to go on the São Tomé flight. I was very pleased to see him and we went for some coffee and a long blether. He is now doing some studying then doing industrial medicine with Phillips factory in Holland. When I went to the plane I then met Brother Norbert who comes from Coatbridge and I had known him before so I had his company on the journey.

We flew with Martinair, Holland, had a meal at 1 am, slept a little and then breakfast at 5.30 am and we arrived in São Tomé at 7 am. There were about 30 people on board, crew for the aeroplanes flying into Biafra, some wives & children who will be staying with them in São Tomé and the rest were mainly Sisters & Fathers & Brothers. I met a nice nurse from Denmark who is going to a Sick Bay and an American lad who works with WCC at the airstrip. We will all go into Biafra tomorrow night, Friday, and then to Queen Elizabeth Hospital Orlu for me for the week-end.

All is quiet here just now, no really bad air-raids so we should have a quiet flight. Sandy Sommerville is going to Scotland this week-end so he will post this for me and you should get it on Monday or Tuesday. I will write again as soon as I get down to Mbaitoli and see what is happening. I think John Phillips is coming out soon on leave and Murray Cochrane and Ann Travis are due back in 10 days or so.

It's difficult to adjust from cold blustery Europe to hot, lazy, sunny Africa and I am still wearing my skirt so will need to search out a dress and sandals. São Tomé is really a lovely island, full of colour, sunshine and lots of flowers and shrubs. I will have two days here so that will give me time to get orientated.

4.30 pm. Whew!! I went to bed at 1.30 pm for a wee rest and I have just woken up – sweating still tired & feeling worn out with the heat. So it will take me a wee while to get used to it all again. As you know I am quite happy to have got this far and I am looking forward very much to seeing all my old friends again. Aunt Ina I do thank you very much for all your running around after me – it's great always to have you at home and I do appreciate it all altho' sometimes I may forget to say "thank you". Happy birthday, Walter!! Happy birthday wee John on the 3rd October!! Thanks very much for everything Mum & dad and please don't be worrying too much about me. I was well taken care of last time and I am in His same Hands this time. I will write soon. Give my love to Sarah & the others.

Love,

Ann

Despite the chaos of war, Ann's medical team of staff from the evacuated Queen Elizabeth Hospital continued to work professionally to provide medical care for war victims, with supplies from the World Council of Churches (WCC)

THE QUEEN ELIZABETH  HOSPITAL, UMUAHIA
~~REPUBLIC OF~~ BIAFRA

Mr Burke,
Our ref: W.C.C
Your ref: Egbu

Dr Jackson.
Q.E.H. Medical Team 1.

Telephone: 53
Telegrams: "QUELHOSP."

11th Oct 1969

Dear Mr Burke,

I'm sorry I have not managed to meet you in person but we are very short of fuel. Recently the Medical Team have been receiving 6 bags milk from you and I am grateful but I feel I must make further requests to you.

The team has now increased in strength with myself and Sister Ojs being added this week and we are now able to see 600-700 patients each day. As you know the majority of our patients are Kwashiorkor or Protein-Calorie-Malnutrition cases and I feel that treatment must consist of drugs and protein supplements. Could you please consider the following requests and let me know as soon as possible what you will be able to supply. I must confess I consider these supplies absolutely essential for the efficient working of the medical team.

Could you please supply,

① ---10 bags milk
② ---10 bags formula 2
③ ---2 bags egg powder. } each week
④ --1 bag beans.
⑤ ---1 bag stockfish } each fortnight.
⑥ ---1 bag suet

Friday 17th October

Report 18
Mobile Clinic Team 1
17/10/69

Report for fortnight ending 18th October 1969

The Mobile Clinic Team 1 based at Mbaitoli has now increased in strength with myself and Sister Oje being added. Sister Chita Oje from Uburu, and recently Annang Province, has considerable clinic experience and I am very pleased to be working with her again.

We are now able to see approximately 600 patients each day and we have arranged to do a fortnightly clinic at AKABO, Owerri. We also hoped to start a clinic at Orodo, Owerri sometime soon. Let me just comment that since my return two weeks ago I have seen a marked improvement in the general condition and environment in the Ogbaku and Orogwe areas. I am very pleased to see villagers now more settled and crops replacing the devastated and overgrown areas. Regular medical clinics, even at fortnightly intervals, have obviously helped improve the general health of villagers.

Protein – calorie – malnutrition (PCM) continues to be widespread and I would like to state here that I feel that treatment from the team must consist of drugs and protein supplements. Recently the World Council of Churches representatives at Egbu increased the supply of relief materials for distribution by the team and I am very grateful. This clinic team is fully operational and mobile and with the assistance and cooperation of Mr & Mrs Burke & Miss Covey at Egbu we hope to provide a reasonable mobile medical relief service in Owerri Province.

Thank you.

Ann W Jackson
Medical Officer in charge of Medical Team 1

Sunday 26th October

Queen Elizabeth Hospital
Mbaitoli

Dear Mum & dad & family,

This is Sunday morning and all is quiet and peaceful. Alicia & Janet Brown have spent the weekend here and I have very much enjoyed their company and blethers. Janet has not been well for the past two weeks so I was pleased she came out for a break and I think she has enjoyed herself.

Alicia is moving from Etiti with the Dutch girl to take over John's team which is stationed about 12 miles from us so I should see more of her. John is going home on Tuesday or Wednesday so I will give him this letter to post for me and I will also give him a spool to send to Kodak. I have put Dad's name on it so it will go straight to Carluke once it is ready. I have taken several pictures at one of the clinics, then some views of the Queen Elizabeth Hospital at Mbaitoli with the new ward which is being built. The last few are of Chita or Helen Odi who visited you & is a friend of Mrs Leitch. She has since married and has a lovely big baby son so their picture was taken outside my house. His name is CHUKUDI OJE. There is also a picture of Victoria and her fiancé Uche . . .

Yesterday, Saturday, I went to the wedding of Phoebe and Cyril – a minister and a nurse, two good friends of ours. Unfortunately there was a hitch! It was held in Owerri Cathedral and the Bishop made a mistake in the time – it was supposed to start at 9 am but he had thought it was 12 mid-day. So we all had a 3 hour wait. Anyway Phoebe was lovely and it was a nice service and we had a good reception in a big hall afterwards. There was no dancing but many speeches and plenty to eat – wee sausage rolls, cake, bananas, paw paw and we really enjoyed it all. We left here at 8.30 am and arrived back about 5 pm so it was a long day.

In the evening time I had invited several folk for a meal so we had 10 at the table and six were former Uburu staff. We really had a happy time together and I'm sure Janet and Alicia enjoyed the wee change. Janet has now gone back to her base and Alicia gone with John – it's 6 pm now so I will have an early night.

Victoria's mother sent me some fruit and two eggs to welcome me back – she says in her note that she bought me a hen and it has started to lay so she will be sending me the eggs until I can collect it. She is very good to me and I hope to find the time and the petrol to spend a weekend at her place.

The clinic work continues and although it is strenuous I do enjoy it and the team are still as helpful and hardworking. Victoria sends her greetings to everyone in Carluke.

I hope everyone is well and that you had a happy birthday Mum. I wonder what you bought in London at these various fancy shows.

Much love & prayers to all, Ann

November 1969

By November 1969 Biafra was on the point of collapse as the Nigerian Federal troops closed in on its remaining territory with indiscriminate aerial bombing of civilians and fierce fighting on the shrinking war front. Ann faced the daily possibility of being killed herself in this final stage of the conflict, as she continued to run clinics with her two medical teams near the front line. The following letter from the World Council of Churches (WCC) on 22nd November, relieving Ann of her medical duties because of the danger to her life, is best read in the context of her own account of being bombed while carrying out those duties – and the Church of Scotland's contrasting response to the prospect of its missionaries being killed.

Ohaji Sick Bay

In November 1969 John Phillips was on leave. Alicia Bandeen was running Team 2. I was asked to go and check out the sick bay while John was on leave. I stayed the night with Alicia. In the morning I joined her medical team to do the clinic. The driver then took me down a small escarpment to the Ohaji sick bay, built next to an army camp and only a few miles from the war front. The driver left me and I entered a newly built ward, mats on the floor for the patients – a table over the door end. I had my stethoscope in my emergency bag (passport and extras). Two nurses came and introduced themselves.

Before I could start the ward round the Mig Fighters came over. Everyone ran outside and I was left standing at the table. I quickly got under it and waited. Then they remembered me and took me out to a large trench to wait for the other two planes to come. Bombs were dropped. Planes came over and strafed the compound in front of me. A woman was killed. I heard the rat a tat tat and the strafing in front of me. I said the Lord's Prayer, thinking I was done for. When it was over the terrified driver came to get me and take us back up the hill to where Alicia and the clinic team were. They were situated above the camp and the sick bay and so could see all the action. Everyone was crying. They thought I had been killed. The team did not do much that day. I was a bit shattered too.

Saturday 22nd November

Headquarter:

WCC/QEH/22

UBULU-IHEJIOFOR
P.O. Box 47,
Orlu.

Date: 22nd November, 1969.

Dr A.W. Jackson,
Queen Elizabeth Hospital,
Mbaitoli.

Dear Dr Jackson

You are relieved of any responsibility of supervising the Ohaji Sick Bay as long as it is in its present location. We appreciate very much your work in this Sick Bay but we must forbid your continuing to expose yourself to the dangers involved in carrying out this work.

Yours truly,

(signed)
E.T. O'Dell, M.D.,
Medical Secretary
WORLD COUNCIL OF CHURCHES REFUGEE RELIEF.

December 1969

After the World Council of Churches wrote to relieve Ann of her frontline duties in order to save her life, the Church of Scotland asked Ann to make a will relieving it of the responsibility and expense of repatriating her body. Ann's comic account of this incident reveals her gifts as a writer in describing the Kirk's parsimony.

LAST WILL AND TESTAMENT

Murray Cochrane, the Administrator of Queen Elizabeth Hospital lived near the airport, away from the war front. Queen Elizabeth Hospital had been evacuated with all the staff scattered. There were 3 teams doing clinics around the war front. It would be around early December 1969 and Murray invited the 3 Church of Scotland missionaries to his place for a special meal. Chicken with rice and all the trimmings, fresh fruit, real coffee and chocolate. A real feast! It was good to be in a safe place with fellow Scots. By this time there were few Europeans around and we were each isolated, working with African staff. We were relaxed, enjoying the time off and having a good laugh. Then Murray said "As you know the situation has deteriorated and we need to make plans to evacuate when the time comes." Made sense! Then he said that the Church of Scotland was short of money. What's new? – we all laughed. The church could not afford to send our baggage and our bodies back to Scotland when we were killed!! So we were really there to make a Will – to relieve the Church of Scotland of any responsibility for us!! In some ways it did make sense. No need to waste money on us when there was so much need around us. We spent the rest of the evening making a Will. Then we dutifully went back to the war front to get on with the work God had given us to do.

Wednesday 10th December

Queen Elizabeth Hospital, Biafra

My dear Mum, dad & family,

I hope you are all well and not too busy with Christmas preparations. I hope you all get some good presents and I'm sure the children are already excited. We will probably have a party for the children and a "feast" for the staff but it's difficult to get things these days so it will be nothing elaborate. It's so hot here that it is hard to believe that it is December and almost the New Year. I wonder what 1970 will bring? Plenty of good food and peace I hope! I am still much the same weight although I am working hard so it must be all the powdered potato I am eating. We don't have much variety but at least we have plenty to eat ourselves.

The clinics are very heavy and we are all very tired by the time our day's work is done, too tired in fact. At least I am well and I still enjoy the work. Victoria is busy these days preparing for her wedding and the date is set for January 3rd so we will have a good celebration and feast that day. Her sister's wedding dress is lovely and is in reasonably good condition although it has been buried for months in a tin trunk. All their goods were buried at their place just before the Nigerians invaded Owerri so she is very lucky that it is still serviceable. She is getting very excited and anxious that everything is ready in time.

She is busy preparing soup just now while I sit out here in the cool of the evening in the daylight writing. Bill Roberts, the Scripture Union missionary, has been quite ill and is due to go home tomorrow so I am trying to have my letters written. I am enclosing one for Sarah & one for Winnie to let her know about Victoria's wedding because she went to a lot of trouble to get me a wedding dress. The date has now been set for January 3rd as I've said but she still seems to have a lot to do before then.

I am pretty tired these days so am looking forward to having some days off at Christmas and the New Year. The clinics are heavy and the malnutrition seems to be getting worse again so each day we feel we have not done much yet we are dog tired and our drugs are finished. It's a hard struggle! We are a lot on BBC news just now but we don't seem to be anywhere nearer peace.

I hope you are all well, please write more often as letters seem to be getting through easier these days. I am receiving letters okay and feel more could be sent on. I have had no letter from Jenny since I came here two months ago. Give everyone my love and I will write again soon.

Much love as always,
Ann

PS. Victoria sends you all good wishes for Christmas & promises to write again sometime soon.

Love & prayers.
Ann

Saturday 13th December

Queen Elizabeth Hospital Medical Team 1
Mbaitoli

My dear Mum & dad & family,

I wrote a few days ago but I am now at Orlu and I have some time to spare so thought I would write another letter. Yesterday Mrs Grace Igwe, the wife of the World Council of Churches Chairman in Biafra, invited me to stay the weekend with her. She said I was looking tired and needed a rest so she would take me to her home for a couple of days. She has been a very good friend to us, has a growing family of 4 so I should enjoy myself. I will go this afternoon and return tomorrow evening.

Alicia is now at Alor and she has not come down this weekend, maybe she will come on the 27th for the next World Council of Churches team meeting. I hope she will be in Orlu with us all on Hogmanay and then she can go with us to Victoria's wedding on the Saturday. Yesterday we looked out all her things, tried on the wedding dress which fits her perfectly, the shoes, gloves, etc. She has gone home this weekend to collect some other things so I hope everything will be ready for the big day. Her fiancé has been in bed with some malaria but he is now recovering.

We have been trying to get two chickens for Christmas & the New Year and I have been keeping some tins of meat and some salt to trade for them. We gave it all to a woman trader and now we have <u>6</u> chickens and I'm hoping one will lay eggs for us. We collect them together in the evening and put them in a big box and during the daytime tie them to piles of wood so they will not stray away. There are many thieves around so we have to take many precautions. So if we can keep them safe we will have a good Christmas and New Year Dinner. I think Ann Travis and I will have Christmas at Mbaitoli and Hogmanay with Murray here at Orlu. Then I will return to Mbaitoli to help Victoria with her final wedding preparations. So we should have a busy time and I hope an enjoyable one.

It's amazing how quickly the time passes and the New Year comes. Anne Bent is expected back at the beginning of February and John P. in January and then it will be nearly time for Alicia to go home on leave and then me. And so it goes on. I was sorry to hear that Aunt Ethel has been ill and I hope she is improving. Tell Auntie Mary & Maggie I am asking for them and I hope they are well. It's good of Aunt Ina to warm the house up for you in the mornings and I'm sure you enjoy the longer lie. I hope you are keeping well and Aunt Ina too. Give everyone my love and good wishes.

Could you please start sending me the [Carluke] Gazette ... when there is something interesting in it. Also try to send me a good magazine and some paperback books. There are no restrictions at present. Tell Mrs Leitch I received her letter & hope she is taking things easy. I am keeping my last spool for Vicky's wedding – hope it is okay.

Much love & my prayers
Ann

Sunday 21st December

Queen Elizabeth Hospital Medical Team 1

Biafra

My dear Mum, dad, & family,

Christmas is fast approaching and today, Sunday, we will have our special Carol Service in the chapel. We will have Christmas and Boxing Day off and have a real rest I hope. There will be a Christmas Party for the children and Ann T is busy organising presents. The hospital staff will have a feast on the Saturday and maybe there will be some dancing. We hope the war situation will improve by next week but we seem to have lost some ground recently.

Please do not worry about us as everything is quite stable in this area and we are more or less in the centre of things. Life goes on here as usual but we get disturbed by the rumours that constantly get bandied about but which are usually groundless fears. We can only wait and see. Some Americans who have been living in Aba Province and quite near the front have had to evacuate and I'm not sure where they will be working. They are Seventh Day Adventists and doctors and nurses but we do not have the accommodation for them here. Something will no doubt be arranged for them because they have only done 3/12 and WCC wants them to stay on and complete their contract. Poor souls they must have had quite a fright and I'm sure were ready to run.

They are not real war veterans like us! They are coming down here today for the Carol Service so we will hear what they are saying now. Murray Cochrane is entertaining them at present in Orlu and Ann T says there are 7 of them and they have more or less taken over the house.

We have had a very busy time in the clinics this past week and our car broke down last Monday in Owerri. I managed to hitch a lift to the World Council of Churches provincial headquarters at Egbu [near Owerri] to borrow another vehicle so we could continue with our clinic. I left driver Isaac to take care of the repairs with the garage mechanic – the gear box was smashed up – and they said it would cost £87 for repairs. Isaac went to Egbu to borrow money but Mr Burke had no cash so he gave him an equivalent amount in Relief – salt, cornmeal, egg etc. Eventually the vehicle was repaired but we did not return here until 7.45 pm – very tired and weary but with our vehicle repaired and our clinic done. The van broke down again yesterday so it has just been towed in and I can only hope it will be ready for work tomorrow. At least we will have a short week.

Victoria went out early this morning to make arrangements for her chief bridesmaid. I hope she manages to get transport but it is all very difficult and very costly. Elsie Taylor sent us the ingredients for the wedding cake from São Tomé and she has found someone who has agreed to bake it for her and have it ready in time. There is so much to do and things are very very difficult. Poor soul, too, Uche was caught by the army who did not look at his papers but carried him off to their camp & kept him for 24 hrs. They shaved his head & beard then decided to check up on his protestations – he was released, exempt because he is teaching – but he got quite a fright although not too roughly handled. There are still some men trying to dodge conscription so the army have a hard time. I hope he will be okay for the wedding but Vicky was crying because he has lost his nice beard. He is a very quiet person and always well groomed and tidy so it is quite a blow for him . . .

I collected a wee refugee girl from one of our clinics last week – very emaciated, wrapped in a loin cloth, about 7 yrs old. She is in the ward at present but I will then keep her for 6 weeks or so and feed her up. She is a very pathetic wee thing, orphan who is being cared for by a relative who is weak and sick herself. I will let you know how she gets on. Give everyone my love and good wishes for Christmas. Hope to hear from you again soon.

Love & God bless,

Ann.

Friday 26ᵗʰ December

My dear Mum & dad & family,

Someone is going home on Saturday so I decided to get a letter posted to you. BBC is not giving much news but the situation here is not too good at present. We are in a quiet place & the work continues but there are many refugees from other areas and we can only hope & pray things will settle soon. We have had a good Christmas with services and parties and a Swedish film team did an interview with me. I hope it turns out well and maybe you will see me on the screen one of these days because there have been several teams here at Queen Elizabeth Hospital and I am in some of them.

Sandy Sommerville has returned & he has brought me some films so I took one on Christmas Day and am sending another one home so it should reach you soon. I hope it turns out this time or Dad will be shouting again . . . it will be some time yet before I know definitely when I'll be home. I hope to see Alicia this weekend & hear all her news and I will have a hectic day tomorrow. I leave the house at 6 am to attend a wedding in Owerri Province at 7 am then I must be in Orlu for 10.30 am for the World Council of Churches team meeting, then return to here for the staff Christmas Feast so I hope to fit in time to talk to Alicia. Maybe she will come down here and join us. Victoria has gone to Ogwa to see Uche and will return today – she hopes to collect her wedding cake tomorrow so I hope it will be ready for her.

I had a letter from Anne Bent saying she would be returning at the end of January, also John Phillips and maybe you could ask him to bring me a pair of nice towels which I need for wedding presents. Please buy a pair and send to him for me – I hope it won't be too heavy! I don't really need anything else just now and we are getting enough food.

I am supposed to be having two days off but I seem to have spent my time making up monthly drug lists, supervising tablet wrapping, issuing drugs & petrol, settling palavers because Dr Abergave is on leave at present (on duty overseas actually) and I am acting medical superintendent. Maybe the New Year holiday will be quieter! I hope the children all enjoyed their gifts and good feeds. I hope to get a letter sometime this weekend with your news of Christmas preparations. On Wednesday I was given presents from the community – a fowl, pineapples, paw paw, oranges and bananas and a coconut so I was very pleased. Victoria also gave us some fruit and Cor Middelkoop sent us some Dutch cake and glazed fruit and chocolate so we didn't do too badly. We enjoyed our Christmas Day but were a bit depressed by the war news. Give everyone my love & good wishes, tell them I am well and in no immediate danger so don't be worrying. I know the World Council of Churches have plans made for us in case of emergency. Anyway, maybe a miracle will happen and we will see the peace we all crave & need.

Much love to all,
Ann

These letters home complement the story Ann tells in her journal of the last days of the war in December 1969 and January 1970, when she was running sick bays with her medical teams very close to the frontline of the fighting.

Early December 1969

We set quickly to work and saw 400 patients but did not stop consulting until 4:30pm. Fortunately the committee fed us well with rice & stew & fruit so we could last out. We travelled back to Egbu, no Isaac so waited for him for 1 hour. I discussed several problems over with the Burkes.

Chima the Medical Student who wants to stay on at Egbu & help with clinics. He deceived us into believing he was a final year Medic but is really 6th year secondary, not admitted to Medical school. I feel he should be removed from Egbu altogether where he is regarded as Dr Chima & has a position of authority still, though he has now lost his responsibilities and access to drugs. He is very keen to remain so I voiced my suspicions of his refusal to join Queen Elizabeth Hospital as a medical student under Dr Abengowe. I feel he has 'an axe to grind' with World Council of Churches at Egbu and feel he has too many medical friends in need of drugs at Emekuku Hospital. The Burkes are sympathetic to him yet afraid to take chances and seem unwilling to make any decision. I will need to see O'Dell and Abengowe.

Relief supplies are a bit short and Queen Elizabeth Hospital feel they are getting short measure in comparison to the team's supply. Comparisons have been made but this approach is unreasonable as we are doing completely different work. I feel we should be given according to our needs as a hospital and as a clinic team and I have already given Mr Burke a list of what I consider to be the team's basic needs. Mr Burke asked me what I thought about the allocation of foodstuffs and asked me to advise him so Queen Elizabeth Hospital and Dr A. would not be pleased to know this. They can rest assured that I was fair in my estimates and did my best to improve their own allocation. I must admit I was annoyed when Mr B. told me Dr A. had complained that the team's allocation was way out of proportion. Anyway the Burkes and Jenny Carey are certainly sympathetic to the Medical team so there is no need to get "my hackles up."

I discussed various problems about Sick bays with Jenny Carey who is in charge of all the W.C.C. ones and is most cooperative. She has now moved into the Bishops' court across the road, moved up in the world and is definitely more comfortable than in her previous cramped quarters. She gave Chita, Vicky, Helen & I nice cold drinks which were most welcome.

We drove back to Owerri because Isaac the driver had not returned with our own vehicle. Met Isaac in Owerri with the repaired vehicle at a cost of £87. He had trekked to Egbu to ask Mr Burke for money to buy the spare parts but as World Council of Churches has not given cash to the Provincial Reps. Burke had no money but he gave him the amount in Relief. So Isaac traded for the spare parts and we owe Mr Burke £87 cash. The mechanics had worked well all day, leaving their other commitments to finish our van and Isaac had spurred them on because we need the vehicle so badly for the clinics. We gave the workers some egg powder & cornmeal which we had saved for them for the clinic so everyone was satisfied with the days work. Murray Cochrane would be pleased the vehicle was already repaired, no further headaches for him, the clinics could continue and we would not have to wait for the Uburu mechanics, even although it had cost £87 it was worth it.

We returned home at 7.45 pm because we stopped to fetch water in our containers at Owerri. We were tired but I felt quite pleased because we had made a good team effort with Isaac doing his duty well, the nurses worked hard and uncomplainingly and we had finished the clinic. On Sunday evening Ann T. and I were feeling depressed and disappointed in staff and co-workers feeling inadequate and useless in Biafra, feeling that the standards of nursing and conduct had fallen so badly, everyone was tired and not prepared to do a good days work. Today everyone tried hard, the nurses were most anxious that we did not cancel the clinic and disappoint the villagers even although our vehicle broke down and they made the effort to fulfill their obligations. The garage people, Grace Igwe, Jenny Carey, Bob Burke, Isaac, the nurses – we had all worked together and helped each other and it was good. I arrived home very tired but in a good mood – so good in fact that Ann T. remarked on it, I suppose I usually return home late, tired and grumpy and not a very good companion. It was a worthwhile inspiring long day!

Tuesday 16th December

Umuguma – We set off as usual in the morning but Staff Nurse Edeh was sick. The Church as usual was crammed full of people so we asked the organisers to put the people outside so we could do a proper selection of the worst cases. Imagine the mad wild scramble out doors and windows, shouting, crying, pushing, fighting. Eventually we managed to collect cards, I stamped while Chita took prayers. We worked hard, had ½ hours break then I went to Umuguma & Avu Sick Bays.

Umuguma Sick Bay has been opened for several months but did not contact the Mobile Team although we are both World Council of Churches (WCC). On J. Carey's request I paid them a visit one month ago and met the midwife in charge whose husband runs the sickbay and it is in his buildings.

I was not impressed at all. She had no records of drugs or patients no really ill patients in bed altho' we saw many sick & bad kwashiorkor patients at the clinic. I asked if she had any patients she wanted me to see but she said "no", so I told her that if she had no patients ill enough for a doctor to see then there should be no patients in the Sick Bay. I told her I was not pleased & asked her to have patients and records for me to see next time. I reported the visit to Jenny Carey who said that the WCC were already thinking of closing that Sickbay. On my next visit the Midwife was more organized but again had no real bad inpatients. The local Red Cross came in a deputation to me with a protest letter and complaints about the WCC Sickbay and an order that only Red Cross Personnel should run it. I told them it was a WCC Sickbay no matter how badly run, it was a matter for WCC to decide & not the business of the Red Cross. It seems the husband & wife Sickbay took only relatives & not so ill people and there were many complaints from the local people.

Today I was asked by Jenny Carey to discharge patients and send the bad ones to Avu Sickbay which was only 2 miles away. I expected opposition and the Sickbay Committee was waiting for me. I told them I would listen to their side of it, but that the decision had been made by WCC, I would do as I was asked and they would have to petition Egbu WCC if they wanted the Sickbay to remain at Umuguma. The man himself was angry but the others were reasonable and polite. I explained the situation as I saw it.

There were 2 sickbays in Avu Parish, two miles distance between and no real need for 2.

There was a food shortage and it was more economic in food & people & drugs to have one big Sickbay instead of 2 smaller ones.

My first visit to the Sickbay was not good, no records, no ill patients & no need for a doctor according to the midwife.

Many complaints from Umuguma people about the running of the Sickbay – unfairness etc.

They gave their own case, fearing that Avu people would not take care of Umuguma people well, longstanding history of feuds & ill feeling, I suspect over land. I assured them that I would admit the cases to the Sick Bay on the purely medical basis, no thought of their place of origin. I would supervise the nursing & medical care and see that there was no bad feeling. The Sickbay would be for the whole parish and if there was any discrimination I would be the first to protest to Egbu. This took a lot of time, then I told the nurse to discharge all her patients except two motherless children who were not too bad but I felt I had to take some to keep the good feeling of the committee. I also took about 10 bad cases they had collected for admission and I feel they had been chosen to impress me. I took some in the van but the parents had to carry the other children down to Avu.

AVU Sickbay run and organized by the local Red Cross had 35 patients on my first visit. Well organized but no nursing staff (qualified) so had very few drugs. However, they were organized and did have bad kwashiorkor patients, some ready for discharge, some selected for admission, awaiting my approval. I was impressed and complimented them. Jenny had said I could increase the number of patients to 50, combining the two Sickbays but she had also told the Avu Red Cross. Previously she scolded them for taking only local children so they had gone to Oforola and selected 30 bad cases for admissions. From the clinic and the Umuguma selected patients I had 20 candidates, all very bad, to admit. Quite a diplomatic game! There was, as the Umuguma people had said, some rivalry between the two places, I sensed it and felt they resented me bringing so many patients from Umuguma. I discussed the problem with them, explained the fears of the Umuguma people, asked them to do all in their power to make the Sickbay a happy, organized and parish project, to avoid friction at all costs and give the Um. people any cause to complain. The Oforola sick children had come from 5 mls away and been left by their parents so this presented a problem. The less sick (they all needed admission) I admitted for 2 wks only, the others I admitted and then had to write a note to Jenny Carey explaining the situation. I was told she would provide food for 50 but I now had 69 admitted and this would not go down well but I felt for the sake of good relations it was better to share out the relief goods over 69 for a week or two then I would sort things out. I have not seen Jenny to hear or see her reaction & comments – should be interesting! I left Umuguma & Avu friendly with Dr Jackson at least! When Isaac & I returned to the church at Umuguma – 5 pm – the nurses were all packed up, sitting on the drugs boxes, tired and wearying to go home. Another long day but a satisfying one with many problems tackled.

One boy of 10 yrs – a reasonably bad malnutrition case – had been sent home without treatment because he was not accompanied by an adult. When I arrived he had returned with his mother, poor soul, she was even more sick than himself, could hardly walk yet she had come so her son could receive treatment. And so the tragic story continues, every day more cases of misery & suffering are seen. We work hard in our clinic work but we really do so little because the suffering & sickness is so great & widespread and the problem beyond us. Wish to God this war would end!

Wednesday 17th December

Amauzari – our midweek heavy clinic day, always tiring, chaotic and full of fights. The orphans, 31 of them, came for treatment so I was greatly cheered by their smiles and enthusiastic friendly greetings. They are unsupported by Caritas or World Council of Churches and fed by the local Women's Association and they manage to get one meal a day so most of their complaints are of stomach ache – maybe worms, more likely to be hunger!

This continues to be our worst clinic, many bad adult malnutrition cases and many TB cases. We saw over 700 patients and were very tired (as usual) at the end of the day. I paid a visit to the Sick Bay which originally refused the team's medical help. I scolded them about it, said I was offended but eventually agreed to help them with drugs & supervision. I'm afraid I am a boss when it comes to supervision of medical work and things must be done my way – when I feel I am right. Anyway, I hope we work well together in the coming months.

We left Amauzari late and reached home to find our relief had arrived from Egbu so had to manhandle bags & bags of milk, formula 2, salt, oats, cartons of beef and baby milk so we were more than tired at the end of the day.

Thursday 18th December

Ogbaku – Helen Edeh is still sick so Rose Amadi went with us on the team to help. She was one of the original members, a cousin of Vicky's, a very nice person and a good worker. It was good to have her with us. We moved this clinic from the tar road (Onitsha/Owerri) into the bush and see worse malnutrition cases. It is held partly in a school (classes continue in the other classrooms) and partly in offices of a refugee camp. We collected all the cards, hoping to sort out cases & give appointments to the less severe cases in 6 wks time, instead of 1/12 (two weeks to 1st January so that clinic had to be cancelled). What a task! Again we finished late, tired, bad tempered but we saw more than 750 patients and saw, in fact, all the old cases with about 10 new very bad ones.

The man who organizes this clinic for us is a Grade 11 teacher but very good, quiet and efficient. He has his voluntary workers helping us and everything goes smoothly. This is Roman Catholic territory so I asked Chita to take prayers, stress that we were World Council of Churches and give them the real Christmas message. Usually the R.C. man takes the prayers with a few Hail Marys thrown in but I asked her to do it herself for Christmas. We still have our missionary work to do. The people are friendly and cooperative and pleased to receive us and our medical services and we can all give thanks in our own ways so long as God gets the credit.

Two weeks ago at Ogbaku I took a fancy to a wee girl of 10 or 11 yrs, slightly cross eyed, obviously a refugee, very skinny & emaciated wearing a small piece of loin cloth. She was wearily stacking firewood when we arrived and looked as if she should be in a sickbay & not working. She was very pathetic and alone. She was a refugee from Port Harcourt Province and was picked up on the road by a relative at the time of the evacuation of Port Harcourt. She was living with a small group of refugees (135) at this school. Her guardian had gone off to look for work so I could not meet her. I gave her soap, relief food and asked her to ask the guardian to allow her to follow me to Queen Elizabeth Hospital for some weeks. The other children obviously tormented her and made fun of her and I was very annoyed about this and promised to help make her strong so she could stand up to all the bullying healthier children. Her name is Omasalam (do you like me) and I liked her. Today she greeted me and said she would like to follow me so I met the guardian, an Aunt who is very sick and weak herself with no other helper so I promised to help the girl and return her in a few weeks time. I admitted her to the ward for a week for investigation & treatment & then I will feed & care for her until the end of January (D.V.)

Friday 19th December

Nekede and our swimming day. We did not leave the compound until late because Helen was still sick, Rose Amadi was due to start her leave and Sister Nwama did not have anyone else allocated to the Mobile Team. Chita & I were annoyed as we are always dealt with as the poor relation, begging for help so we said we would sit & wait for another nurse. We did not leave until 8.30am. Not a good start to the morning and I was already in a bad mood. I think partly because of sheer tiredness and frustration, also because Victoria had a long face. The night before she came back all depressed & worried from Ogwa where she had trekked to see Uche about wedding invitation cards. They were not ready and Uche had been conscripted, later released but minus his hair and beard. Poor Vicky, she was very sad and no wonder with the wedding only 3 weeks away and he looked always so neat and well groomed. At least he was released because he is a teacher and the conscriptors did not care to read his papers until he was 24 hours in their custody. He must have had a big fright himself and I'm sure was worried about what Vicky would say – she was in tears! I felt really sorry for her as she bewailed the hardships for herself and her people at this time of war. I felt depressed with her but she recovered a bit after a night's sleep (probably a restless night).

I stayed depressed and in bad humour, aggravated by our late departure for Nekede.

Chita started the nurses singing choruses and hymns, for my hearing she said, to drive away my long face and bad humour. We tried our new system – everyone out in the open, under trees, lined up so we could take all the cards but separate out the bad ones from the not so bad. The usual bickering, fighting, squabbling with the weak ones standing meekly waiting to be chosen. We again saw over 500 patients with a short break and a meal of yams & stockfish soup. Vicky's mother trekked from Amazarie, 4 miles away to give me yam & plantain which she traded with cigarettes I had given her. Actually ones which I carried from Umuahia in April, a bit dry but still trade goods. We had another long very tiring day and finished consulting at 4pm. Then we loaded up, made our way to the River, did our washing bathed and enjoyed ourselves in the fast flowing relaxing river. I really enjoyed my swim and felt really refreshed afterwards. We filled our water containers then slowly made our weary way home all singing choruses and hymns and national songs. At least we all returned in a good mood. Ann T. went to Orlu in the evening and I read "The Red Barbarians", story of Mao Tse Tung and had Victoria's company.

Saturday 20th December

Had a long lie – 7 am – listened to the news, Sierra Leone will try to make new peace moves because the latest Addis Ababa ones have again failed. Elija came early to sort out egg powder & the store, Victoria & I did the drugs, helped Matthew the Obudi Agwa driver. The team 2 arrived here last night with firewood and water and Matt. had to be housed with Godson and fed by me. He is a nice quiet obliging boy or is at present and has newly started working for World Council of Churches. Chita came late but we had already organized people to count tablets, seal bags over the candle flame and wrap egg powder. Quite a busy morning and we all worked until 1.30

pm, then Chita had lunch with Conrad & I. Had a quiet afternoon finishing my book, started writing this journal again.

One man appeared looking for Dr Jackson just as it grows dark. He explains that he is a former gate man of Queen Elizabeth Hospital, Umuahia and he fled to Ihe in April and has been working at the Seventh Day Adventist Hospital at Ihe which became disturbed by Nigerian enemy forces. The hospital has evacuated & for the past 3 days he trekked with his wife and 4 children looking for Queen Elizabeth Hospital – poor souls they looked worn out and real refugees. Christopher is not in to arrange accommodation, so I have housed them in the tent at the gate for the night. It is used as a gateman's house and is empty and will serve until tomorrow. Godson is busy preparing cornmeal & egg for the family to eat – the Christmas story repeats itself but there is room in Biafra these days for the refugee and the homeless.

Isaac the driver appeared at the door to say the bus with Sr. Travis, nurses, loads, diesel etc. has broken down just after the Umuahia bridge with jammed gears. He managed to hitch a lift so I have sent the Obudi Agwa driver to collect them and asked Isaac to arrange for a nightwatch for the vehicle until tomorrow when we will try to get a mechanic to repair it in time for Monday. I hope it will not be too big a job. Poor Ann T. It is very dark now and they have not returned. The other hospital vehicle is broken down also so we are going to have a difficult week. Ann T. arrived with the news that Northern Nigeria Hospital has evacuated & Aba Province seriously disturbed. The Seventh Day Adventist people have run to Murray in Orlu to await news of the situation.

Sunday 21st December

Carol Service – Queen Elizabeth Hospital, 5pm

A Nigerian reporter arrived in the afternoon so we had to talk to him & show him around. The Seventh Day Adventist people arrived at 4.45pm for our service in which all members of staff took part. The choir sang well and everyone read well – it was a good service and well attended. In the evening time Ann, Conrad & I had our meal then Monica & Victoria joined us for a very good hymn singing session. The fellowship was good and we had a very nice quiet time together praising God.

HERE'S A PRICELESS CHRISTMAS CARD

I T'S not much to look at.
But this Christmas card is unique. It arrived last week at the Jackson home in Chapel Street, Carluke.

It's from Dr Ann Jackson.

She's working with a Church of Scotland medical team in the battle area in Biafra.

When she decided to send her parents a Christmas card, she found there wasn't one to be bought in Biafra for love or money.

There wasn't enough food for starving children, never mind such luxuries.

She looked around the medical tent for something to make a card.

She spotted a brightly-coloured box that had held stomach pills. She cut it up and shaped it into a card.

On the plain side she wrote this message to her parents and friends:—

"From Biafra. Land of hunger. Land of war. Land of want. Land of hope and faith.

"Country striving for peace and freedom.

"To wish you a blessed Christmas, and may peace be with you and us in the New Year."

Now the home-made card has pride of place on the sideboard.

A NN'S been in Biafra three years.
At first she worked in the Queen Elizabeth Hospital, which took a beating from Nigerian bombers.

She escaped unhurt, but still risks her life daily.

She was forced to come home for a break this year because of malaria. But she insisted on going back at the beginning of October.

DR JACKSON

We are grateful for the opportunity to salute Ann and the hundreds of young people like her.

No posters or banners for them.

While others shout of all that is wrong with the world, they quietly go about the job of trying to put things right.

God bless them.

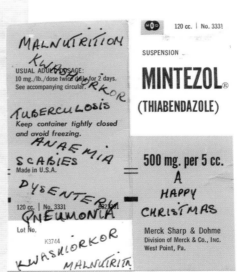

In the closing stages of the war, Ann sent a pro-Biafran Christmas card made out of a medicine box, which became famous back home in Scotland

Monday 22nd December

AKABO CLINIC We set out in the hospital pick-up but were late in leaving. Owerri was quiet & Akabo people were waiting for us. What a hectic terrible clinic – we saw only 400+ patients, finished at 2pm, made our way back to Owerri to collect water and then made our weary way home. We left presents of soap and tinned milk for the voluntary workers who assisted us.

We have decided not to see pregnant women in the Mobile Clinic here at Akabo because there are many midwives in the area and we attract (our relief attracts) them away from proper antenatal care. They were not pleased today but we have been having 90-100 at this clinic and there is no point in us duplicating the nurses' work or depriving them of full antenatal care. Monday and a wearisome clinic and the beginning of a week!

Tuesday 23rd December

Orogwe Clinic

This clinic is now held in the village, deep in the bush, way off the main road. I really enjoy this site, in our wee thatched consulting rooms, with the people all waiting patiently among the banana groves. Up to & over 1,000 old and new patients but with many voluntary workers organizing things well.

One month ago the local committee asked me about a Sickbay and there is great need for one in this area but the site they had chosen was too near the main road. Today they showed me a complete Sickbay ready to receive any patients I would admit. We decided 12 children would be a good beginning because W.C.C. has still not sent food and the locals would have to supply the food for them for a week or two. I was very pleased to see this initiative & hard work and it's a great encouragement to us in the Mobile Team. The committee had also arranged on their own initiative a place for us to rest during our break and a very nice new latrine. They are certainly looking after our welfare and the welfare of the people. It has taken the hospital 6 months and almost £3,000 to build a new children's ward and they have built a Sickbay, kitchen, latrines etc on a slightly smaller scale in less than 1 month. Granted it is not so sophisticated or as well finished but it is all that is needed to care for the sick children. We worked away quietly, I did not lose my temper once (almost a miracle) and we saw 600+ patients. I really enjoyed this clinic and we were home by 3.30pm singing hymns and choruses all the way. Victoria's birthday and she invited Monica, Chita Ann T and myself to join her in the celebration. We set up the ironing table in her room, put two boards on top, then cardboard then a nice new pink plastic tablecover. By the time we set up our candles and Christmas & Birthday cards it was very nice indeed. We had a lovely meal of yam and chicken then beautiful pineapple & paw paw. It was a very tasty meal and I was looking forward to a nice evening. Conrad & Anna (the Seventh Day Adventist girl who joined us for this week until she leaves on Saturday) had their meal together next door.

Daniel arrived suddenly to say that the water lorry loaned to us by WCC to carry much needed water from Owerri for the daily needs of the hospital had been commandeered. Stephen then arrived, Ann T had a bad back & was not feeling well so I agreed to go & look for the vehicle & beg it back. Victoria, poor soul, agreed to go with me for company so we set off in silence, reached the place (Irete) was admitted to the Divisional Headquarters and taken to see the Transport Officer. He had no knowledge of the vehicle, sympathised & advised us to go to another unit. Dan then said that he could take us to the place where they off-loaded our water drums. I was angry because he could have done this in the first instance & saved all our time, energy & more important petrol.

At the place, 3 miles from our own hospital we learned that the vehicle had been released at 5pm. We were relieved because we felt it had been sent to the war front because of some emergency. Lo! it had gone to Owerri for ½ hr to collect the army band to play at the engineers' Christmas do. Anyway, people were enjoying Christmas and we had our lorry back but we were just in time to eat our fruit, clear up the party things and so to bed.

Chita Oje had not turned up in time because she had gone to have her hair plaited and soldiers surrounded the compound and turned everyone out while they searched for missing petrol from the refinery. They would not even let them take out the lamp so she had to wait impatiently with her hair half-done until they went away, so it was anything but a quiet day for each of us. So Victoria is 29 years old and getting more excited every day at the prospect of her wedding on January 3rd. So life goes on, babies are born, young people marry but death & suffering is staring us all in the face.

Wednesday 24th December

We set off in our pickup, the nurses all perched in the back in the midst of the boxes of drugs, cornmeal, milk and stockfish with their wrappers & head ties wrapped round them to keep out the inevitable dust. We stopped at Ogwa so Vicky could off-load some things for the wedding. I had given her some rice, cornmeal, sweet milk, stockfish and meat to help in the entertainments of her family and wedding guests. Reached Amauzari and again there must have been 1800-2000 people there, with the voluntary workers all in evidence. New cards for very ill patients issued, old cards selected, no new cards for ante natal clinic and we set to work. I stamped & sorted cards while the nurses took prayers and told the Christmas story.

The voluntary workers could not keep control, at times they were shouting & making more noise than the patients. In the Okwelle Hall it was impossible for me anyway, to keep calm & work well, Chita was feeling faint & I was bad tempered, so we did not do well. Always people crowding round us begging to have new cards from the window, wanting their cards stamped and generally annoying us. We saw 440 patients, finished at 1.30pm but I was in real bad humour, feeling homesick & fed-up with all the noise & the fighting & my wee interpreter was annoying me, wanting her own treatment in the midst of all this confusion and noise. I was feeling miserable & unable to concentrate on the last of the patients when the two community leaders arrived to give us our Christmas gifts. A fowl, pineapple, oranges and bananas for the nurses, a fowl, pineapple, oranges, pawpaw for me. Fowl costs £10-12 just now so this is a great gift and I was quite floored by their generosity and ashamed at my bad temper and bad thoughts about these heady selfish Amauzari people. We thanked them & set off to see the orphans & take them the gifts we had for them. What a good reception we received – Doktor! Dokatar! Welcome! And all these wee shining faces to greet us and smile their welcome. We asked them what they would like – stockfish would do they said so they all gathered round and we off-loaded stockfish (16) meat, rice, formula 2 and salt and each time they laughed & cheered & obviously grateful. We then took photographs and my wee boyfriend, a 4 yr old cheerful faced wee boy said he would be my husband & Chita took our photograph. It was a very happy time & we gave them small pieces of soap – all 31 of them. We then went back to the market place to collect our patients – 3 bad cases who needed admission & were eligible for Gabon. In spite of all our frustrations & difficulties it was a joy to see these children and help them with Christmas.

In the evening time the staff collected outside Maternity Ward with torches, candles and lamps to sing carols. So we sang, the Christmas story was told in the wards and we all walked from ward to ward, house to house in the bright moonlight. We were happy, joyful, singing, dancing and I really felt Christmas has come. We then had a drink in the Court, sang another hymn, Ann T said a very lovely prayer and we went to bed – 11pm. Another eventful day!

P.S. 4pm. Labourers children's party – very enjoyable. Wish there had been one big children's party but social discrimination made it two.

Hospital protocols were observed to the end. Ann received this official note, typed on the Queen Elizabeth Hospital letterhead:

24ᵗʰ December, 1969

Dear Dr Jackson

This is to inform you about the Christmas party and other entertainments during which you will be at high table.

I thank you in advance for your co-operation.

Yours truly,

(signed)
Emeka Udeary

Thursday 25ᵗʰ December

Christmas Day

The morning service was at 7.15am so I went & had breakfast afterwards. No real news about Biafra, no really good Christmas music, Dick Nwoke closed the pharmacy for 2 days so no emergency service available, so Dr J had to issue drugs, no Christopher available so Dr J had to issue petrol to the Prof.

Ambrose the wee boy received a sweater at the Party last night but because I gave Abakaliki John a shirt & shorts for the party, he came whining for a shirt. I was annoyed. His brother Dan then came & said he had no shirt for Christmas, that the one I had given him 3 months ago was an old one – I was annoyed. Dick Nwoke arrived & said he thought because Outpatients Department was closed for Christmas Day & Boxing Day then he let his staff off. I told him every hospital had to have an emergency service and that I was disappointed in him. Anyway he apologized & said he would arrange for someone to be on duty for a few hours during these days. So that problem was solved. I bluntly told the Prof. I was not pleased to be running around on Christmas Day doing Christopher's duties. He was not too bad & I felt I made my point.

A team of Swedish TV people arrived unexpectedly to do interviews & take films about Christmas Day in Biafra. The ward services started at 10am

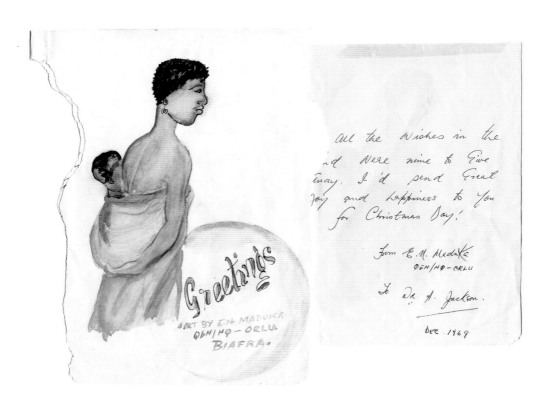

Hand-painted and patriotic cards, sent to Ann from colleagues
for what turned out to be Biafra's last Christmas, 1969

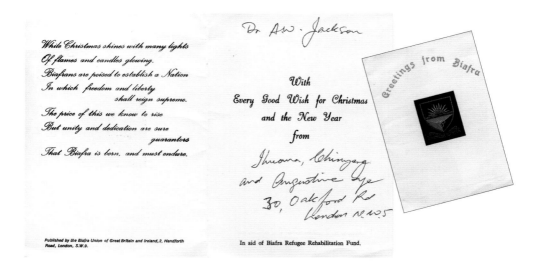

so they were just in time – the children were all gathered round the nativity scene & the fir tree to listen to the Christmas story. It was very nice in the new ward, new Red Cross blankets had been issued for Christmas and balloons were up dancing in the warm breeze. In one corner a child was quietly dying while doctors struggled to put up a drip, children were clapping & singing, crying, looking and the TV team photographed and recorded. I was able to take some photos, too, by their artificial lighting so I hope they come out. Later the children were given toys and presents, Conrad, Prof. & I did short interviews. The Swedes & a German photographer accompanying them were all very impressed & saddened & obviously sympathetic. The German said he would never forget this Christmas.

Christmas Dinner consisted of potato cakes, chicken, stuffing, carrots & peas then fruit salad and dream whip. Very enjoyable and then Anna, Ann & I all talked into the afternoon eating chocolate and nuts kindly sent to us by Cor Middlecoop. Tea time we had biscuits and Dutch cake and chocolate but the tea was stewed & too strong.

After tea our spirits were quite high, we enjoyed one another's company and Anna can sure talk and Ann was waiting to cut Conrad's hair. Prof. Ogan came at 5.30pm & asked to listen to the radio at 6pm – focus on Africa. Sommerville (Rev) had been in on Wed. & told us that the situation in Aba Prov. had deteriorated & the situation was critical. Suddenly a landrover drove into the compound and Dr Evoh from the Seventh Day Adventist hospital arrived looking very tired. He was very depressed and brought us up to date with the news from that side. The Nigerians had quietly & quickly come up from Aba by roads parallel to the main tar road, the soldiers just ran away, and the Feds. had gained 10mls each day.

He had managed to evacuate most of the equipment from the hospital, his nurses, patients & family but on his last trip with his wife he had been jammed in a road traffic jam caused by two big lorries. He says about 100 cars waiting to cross the Imo River (probably exaggerating) and the Nigerians came upon them, everyone abandoned their cars & fled into the bush. He says he saw a Nigerian Lieutenant who shouted after him & his wife to stop running & come back to 'one Nigeria' but they ran on falling & stumbling through the bush. A terrible story! Prof Ogan asked him if the Nigerians were molesting civilians and he said that a friend of his, named him, had been caught yesterday and taken to a certain place & told they would all be taken to Aba. The men were separated from the women and then the Nigerians started to rape the women, the men could not stand around watching this so he tried, and succeeded in, escaping. Evoh says they don't know what happened to these people after that. He has lost his car and all his personal belongings & was wearing his brother's trousers because the pair he was wearing was torn in the bush. He said he wished the war would end soon, the men had no heart to fight & the whole place was a shambles. He has 14 trained nurses, 12 ward maids & wants to deploy them here. W.C.C. will not at present sponsor him in a new hospital (emergency) and I think the Seventh Day Adventist hospital has not been a very happy place in recent months with various palavers and political issues involved.

We will need to wait & see but the situation is very serious – Aba & Umuahia divisions may have joined up already but His Excellency General Ojukwu is in Owerri tonight according to Prof so maybe he will put some heart into his men. Everyone in the hospital is subdued & wondering since Evoh's visit. Mrs Nwama came to talk to Ann, Conrad & I played chess & Anna read, all with our own thoughts & worries. So ends Christmas day.

Friday 26th December

<u>Boxing Day</u>

A quiet day with the Team nurses wrapping tablets after helping with the bathing of the children in the ward. I spent the morning doing the drug lists for Team 1 and Team 2, also making my report for the WCC meeting in Orlu on 27/12/69. Waited impatiently in the afternoon for Conrad to finish in the children's ward so we could all go to Orlu and I wanted to fetch water on the way. Eventually he came but we were 2 hrs later in leaving. Matthew the driver collected the water for us at Umuaka and it was a heavy task for him but he has been very good, obliging and uncomplaining. Christian the previous WCC driver arrived, his lorry had spoiled in Owerri & he was on his way to Obudi Agwa to collect his loads; I agreed to let him go with Matt to collect them, a bicycle would be conscripted, he had a raw deal being dismissed from the team without warning so I felt obliged to help him a wee bit. Godson, Chinedu, Christian & Matt all went and they brought back two containers for water. Godson says the place is too crowded & noisy & it would not be good for me to go there to work!

I went to Orlu to discuss things with Murray but only saw him briefly because he went to Shaunha's for a bath. The 69yr old doctor from the Seventh Day Adventist hospital had been offered to Queen Elizabeth Hospital so that Conrad could go out with the team but we have no good accounts for them, also dietary difficulties, also he is a senior man who would want to take charge and we are managing just now with Chi being away. Conrad is enthusiastic, keen & a good worker but he is very much involved in the ward and keen to do hospital work. Clinic work can be difficult in that non-medical problems arise & have to be dealt with on the spot, voluntary workers and local situations change so experience is needed. I feel we would continually be anxious about him and the nurses would take advantage of him being new in the country. It seems that their services are needed in Alor by Izium Hospital so there is no problem.

Murray invited me to stay for dinner & Jeremiah quietly told me we were having <u>fresh</u> meat so I should stay. A beautifully set table, very tender roast mutton and peas, carrots, potatoes then sour sop fresh, then chocolate pudding so I felt very full and satisfied. What a man! Dear knows where he gets all the "specials' but he gets them and takes great pleasure in sharing them with us all. I was late in getting back but blethered to Victoria and it's interesting to hear her say that she wishes the war would end, let it be over quickly and may God spare us all. The people are really tired, they want peace but still fear for their lives.

Saturday 27th December

Rose early this morning to attend Rose Amadi's wedding which was due to start at 7am. We did not leave until 6.45am, no breakfast and all in a rush. Three nurses, Godson, Vicky, another male guest & I all set off and reached Ihiagwa about 7.40am to find that the wedding had not started but Rose had arrived and was looking lovely in white. It was a simple Baptist ceremony but Rose's people did not arrive because they are CMS and his are Baptist. Many photos were taken so I hope they all come out. Rose persuaded us to go on to her place to take something – even a glass of water she said – so I agreed but time was short. Victoria collected her wedding cake which a relative made and it was really lovely. We carried it, as carefully as we could, home and only a little of the icing fell off. The road was bad, we were delayed but I was pleased to be at the wedding and Rose & Edwin obviously appreciated the visit from the hospital nurses.

On arrival at Queen Elizabeth Hospital we were met by Chinyere Ugochi and Vicky's sister Phoebe who brought them from Emekuku for the wedding but also to be safe and everywhere near her is in panic so she is feels happier to have them with us. They are lovely lively children and it will be a joy to have them around.

I rushed & changed & went with Victoria to Orlu for the WCC meeting which started at 10am yet arrived at 11.40am in time for the benediction. Vicky had heard that Elsie Taylor had arrived for the weekend so she wanted to greet her, thank her for all her help in the wedding preparations and to give her some grapefruit and pineapple. Grace Igwe is making a dress for her so she wanted to see her as well. Grace is alone these days because Rev. Igwe has gone overseas to recuperate and his children have all gone to London to be with Miss Green. Grace is a good friendly soul and I enjoy her company.

Elsie Taylor arrived & hopes to spend some days here seeing the countryside (what's left of it) taking photos etc before she goes out on leave on the 12th January. She is going with Ron & Hazel McGraw who have newly evacuated from Northern Ngwa & who are still living near the Imo River surrounded by refugees so there will be much for her to see down there. Someone estimated 180,000 refugees on the road from the disturbed areas, must be a frightful & depressing sight. Elsie will spend a few hours with us and then go on to Alor to be with Alicia's team. I hope all stays quiet for her.

Anne Burke did a hair dressing session although she was feeling miserable with laryngitis & no voice. Alicia is well, bouncing and seems to have enjoyed her Christmas time with the Anglicans. Elizabeth is good for her. She hopes to come to Orlu for Hogmanay & for Vicky's wedding but refused my invitation and plans to stay for the Queen Elizabeth Hospital Christmas Party.

Elizabeth, Medical Superintendent of Iyi Enu Hospital, is having a hard time with nursing staff and many problems to deal with. She is obviously working very hard and has too much to do. She hopes to take Dr & Mrs Yates to help her and will also try to take the other two Seventh Day Adventist girls, Norwegians. Problems are housing, feeding (Seventh Day Adventists are vegetarians) and also the girls are young & inexperienced so would need to work as staff nurses & not as sisters. They would need to work under more experienced Biafran staff who are touchy about Europeans walking in above them – and rightly so. So she could not stay the weekend because she has to discuss the nursing problems with the Matron at the hospital.

Beatrice Daddington, CMS senior missionary stationed at Alor also came for the weekend but has been feeling unwell with diarrhea & tiredness – Jenny Carey, CMS Missionary as well seemed in good spirits but lost no time in telling Ann T the WCC Owerri would have to cut the staff relief supply. Poor Ann T is having a hard enough job to make ends meet to supply some relief to hospital personnel, at present they get what is left after the patients have been fed. There seems to be some antagonism (felt rather than anything else) between Jenny & Queen Elizabeth Hospital, probably from Anne Bent but Jenny does seem to be unsympathetic to the problems here yet helps me a lot with the team and Sickbays.

Martha Bender was there, unperturbed as usual, yet is now refugee at Mbaise, having been almost cut off at Ohafia. Estimate of 150,000 refugees on that Anga Road.

Ann T, some nurses & myself returned to Mbaitoli in the late afternoon for the Party and Matthew the driver fetched water for us. Gallons & a very heavy container yet he managed it on his head, alone & uncomplaining. Party should have started at 7pm but we had to spend a lot of time finding lights, no lamps, no kerosene, shortage of candles. The nurses & sisters had prepared very nice chop with plenty for everyone – rice, formula, mi-mi, goat and fruit. (Goat est £90) and palm wine & squash. I was invited to sit at the top table, several other guests were squeezed in, Chief Eronini, Mr Anyanu, & Mr Ezedike who had all helped us originally to settle the hospital here. Prof. Ogan chaired the meeting & Emeka was master of ceremonies. A good meal, light entertainment in the form of dances and singing, more English schoolgirl type entertainment & we were sorry there was not more in Igbo. It was a mixed company, labourers & nurses & should have been better organized with Igbo & English songs & dances. It's amazing how English the Biafrans are!

Dick Nwoke the Pharmacist looked splendid in his native dress and he volunteered to do a native song after Prof. complained that it was all in English. He sang softly a song he had learned as a boy, he said, welcoming the 'bekies' (Europeans) and he sang it well. Then he said he would sing as if he were at the war front and he did a real rousing war like song & dance in which everyone joined in 'Biafra Quin'. He was very good and raised a great cheer. There was some dancing & Prof. & Mrs Ogan were asked to lead the dance, he agreed reluctantly but said they had not danced since the war started and they wanted to wait for peace. Anyway he did it but there were only about 2 dances then we had an item entitled 'The Christmas Story' in words & dialogue. It was fantastic and I have never attended a Christmas Party like this one.

Staff Nurse Monica Iheanacho read a story from a card, asking about Christmas, not a time of parties, & eating & drinking but a time to look to Christ & the cross. Several Scripture Union members then briefly stated what the coming of Christ meant for us – the salvation message. Iheanyi & Monica then had a dialogue – where is God? Why doesn't He save us? With the Nigerians linking up Aba & Umuahia where will we go, what about our loads, our families. To each question Monica quietly answered from her own personal experiences and from God's word. With quietness & confidence & assurance and everyone was spellbound listening to the fundamental teachings of Christ being given in answer to the present situation of crisis & fear. What a tremendous witness!

At the beginning of this session when the Scripture Union girl stood up there was some shuffling but Prof. Ogan stood up and with vehemence scolded everyone. "When the gospel message is being preached we must be compelled to listen and take heed, we are a Christian institution and our lives and work depend on these teachings." He shouted "Mechianu" (Be Quiet) to the children so silence reigned for Monica to begin but what she was saying kept everyone quiet & listening. This is life and life more abundant & this young saint gave a tremendous witness to her Lord & Saviour Jesus Christ

Can you imagine a Christmas Party like this one? A 40-minute talk on the Christian faith and everyone intently listening then Igbo chorus & dance & closing devotions in Igbo. The evening finished at 10.40pm everyone tired yet felt we had had a good evening. Mr Ekwedike, a Roman Catholic, says he was most impressed. So were we all!

Sunday 28ᵗʰ December

Prof. Ogan spoke to me during the previous evening's entertainment about emergency plans. He had been to Emekuku and Owerri and they were thinking ahead and so must we. In the morning Godson prepared bacon & egg & tomato for us, John had gone to Alor for the weekend. Then Prof., Ann T & I set off for Orlu in the landrover with Matthew to see Murray. A quiet Sunday morning meeting and I'm sure Beatrice & the Yates who were staying with Murray wondered what it was all about. Prof. knew a county council health centre similar to Mbaitoli but with a good water supply in the bush between Orlu and Ihiala. It was agreed that he should go and explore the possibilities for future use by Queen Elizabeth Hospital. Murray, Ann & I then discussed the situation.

Owerri was quiet, the people in Aba Province & Mbaise & Mbawsi had all run for fear and all that side of the country was in panic, rumours and no real grounds for the fears had sparked it all off. The Feds. could consolidate their positions across the river, bring up their heavy armoury and start shelling Owerri town. Queen Elizabeth Hospital would be caught up in the running with nowhere to go. The Church at Amefeke is not suitable because it has nothing to accommodate people, it is a good store though but we learned the hard way in April – no water & no latrines! The staff have nowhere to go, many of their homes have been disturbed, the patients are all locals so our first responsibility is to our patients. Prof. returned to tell us that there is a WCC Sickbay at the place with school rooms still vacant and Caritas have a Sickbay in the other place so Murray would see Sandy Sommerville & try to make arrangements for us to have the place in the event of any emergency. I was pleased that a Biafran was thinking ahead for us and advising us because in Umuahia no arrangements were made for us, we were left to fend for ourselves and our staff. No doubt the Prof. was taking care of his own interests as well – a set up sponsored by WCC but he was helping us as well.

We returned to the hospital, I was not feeling well with catarrh, chest pain & cough so I went to bed. Conrad was very worried about a member of staff, Samuel who had headache & fever and he thought it was yellow fever. We decided to send message to Dr Bakker to confirm or deny & to report the matter. A Pastor from Orodo had to be collected to conduct our Christmas Communion Service. The Obudi Agwa Staff Nurse Llivo Ekocha was late in arriving to go to her station and the driver was kept waiting until it became dark & she eventually arrived & set off. I instructed her to pack up everything & we would do the clinics from here 1) Because there is no senior person to supervise the clinics 2) Because it is difficult to keep check on them from here 3) Because we have no reliable vehicle here at Queen Elizabeth Hospital 4) Because the situation in the country is uncertain and it is better for us all to be in the one place & not scattered throughout the country. She should do things quietly & not cause panic among the local people. After the service Ann T. said she assured the nurses that their interests would be looked after, the hospital would make all necessary arrangements and they had not to be over anxious about the situation.

Murray Cochrane arrived about 7pm, not too pleased with Dr Yates to see Samuel. We had forgotten that Dr Bakker was out of the country at a Red Cross meeting in São Tomé – Dr Yates said he had never seen yellow fever or blackwater fever but recently he had seen many cases of fulminating infective hepatitis and a doctor & two nurses had died recently at Mbawsi. The poor boy was bleeding from an infection site, mouth, tongue and complained of chest pain. He was very weak & restless.

Monday 29ᵗʰ December

The clinic vehicle is still broken with damaged gear box and I thought the hospital pickup had to go to Amandaba for fuel because Isaac did not arrive until 7.45am. However, it was a misunderstanding and we would do the clinic this morning & cancel tomorrow's one so Christopher could use the vehicle. We were due to go to Umuewere and Sister Nkwocha came pleading for us to help her. It seems all her most precious possessions were put in a trunk and left at a relatives house at Ife for safekeeping when she ran from Umuahia. Now the relative had run & left the trunk and she was in a terrible state, desperate to recover it and she wanted us to take her to Ife, 14 miles from Umuewere. I wanted to help but felt I could not take the risks involved – the place was only 4 miles from the Imo & the Nigerians. I would have to escort the vehicle in case it was commandeered, it was the only sound vehicle the hospital had and there was much confusion in that area. Victoria said I could not go & Isaac advised against it also so I decided to offer to take the hospital bicycle to the tar & let her husband cycle the 12 miles to collect the trunk and we would transport it back at the end of the clinic. Anyway, she & her husband went off to find other means of transport and I heard later she borrowed a car and bought 4 gallons of petrol. We eventually went to the clinic & came back reasonably early.

Poor Samuel the lab boy is still very sick, & continues to bleed. Prof. Ogan took the vehicle into Owerri to try to get someone to advise us because we are still not happy about the diagnosis – fulminating infective hepatitis or yellow fever. Dr Okero arrived with Prof. Ogan but Samuel died at 7.15pm. It seems a doctor & two nurses & a driver's wife all recently died at Mbawsi Hospital of the same illness – fulminating infective hepatitis. 4 days illness – then death in spite of all our efforts. All the staff are very upset & surprised at the outcome. Christopher approached the catechist & the funeral will take place in the morning. The boy's mother is in a terrible state – screaming & moaning & wailing. Samuel was the breadwinner and she has one younger son and they only the day before ran from Umuahia to seek refuge with Samuel. So now she has nothing & no-one to care for her & her boy. It's a tragic business. The service is to be in Mbawsi Church but there is much discussion as to whether he is baptized a full communicant member of the church. If not baptized then he will be buried in any place outside the church grounds but if so then in the church burial ground.

Tuesday 30th December

Samuel's funeral

We have no vehicle available because of the need to go for fuel and the unexpected funeral arrangements. The Church is 2 miles away so many of us trekked while others were taken in the pick-up. All the hospital staff attended (one or 2 on duty in the ward) and it was a very quiet moving service in Igbo. The young men in the lab. were openly and unashamedly weeping, the mother was almost prostrate with grief and there was a respectful silence over all. I suppose each one was thinking it could have been his or her self, it was all so sudden & unexpected, thousands were dying on the war front, of hunger & starvation yet this one healthy young life was taken away in the midst of the quietness of the hospital routine. After the service the white sheet decked coffin with the home-made wreath was carried by his work mates to the grave yard with everyone in slow procession behind singing 'When I survey the wondrous cross'.

This was my first funeral in Biafra. The first time I had been involved in the treatment & management of a patient, seen him die and be buried. Usually we leave all the grieving & arrangements to the relatives but somehow we were all part of this tragedy. The words were read, several mournful Igbo chants were sung by the relatives then the coffin was lowered and the soft red earth thudded in. Staff Nurse Iheanacho and Carol quietly slipped away & returned after quickly making two fresh green wreaths to lay on the grave. Many were weeping then we all quietly & reverently walked the two miles back to the hospital. There must have been almost 200 of us walking in silence each with our own thoughts that early morning. Christmas had been such a hustle & bustle, many grumbled about off-duty & presents yet this incident suddenly brought us all to our senses cut in on our selfishness & waywardness, seemed to tie in with Monica's party piece and there was a feeling of a group united. God was indeed in the midst of us that day, asking each one of us, "are *you* ready to meet me?"

Samuel's mother was taken care of by some of the other lab. staff and the maids. Mr Cochran sent down £15 to help the mother and for the time being the hospital would be responsible for her & her son. The rest of the day was spent wrapping tablets and getting the clinic drug store in order. Victoria's mother, cousins Ada & Irene, Sam, Uche's sisters all arrived with us on Monday evening – we picked them up on our way home from the clinic so the back door was crowded & noisy but it was good to see them all. They all managed to find a place to sleep anyway – in bed & floor.

Wednesday 31st December

Obendi Agwa team arrived late last night and did not bring all the loads one time as requested. I was angry with them & scolded them & decided to go with them this morning to check up on their doings. Matthew & one Staff Nurse and I set off, forgot the key to the store, returned & set off again. Obendi Agwa – a very very big market there, almost like pre-war market. We had to ease our way slowly through the crowds. Saw the landlord Kevin & apologized for the suddenness of our departure & decision to go but promised to continue the clinics for as long as possible. I gave him 2 stockfish, 2 tins meat, cigs, and soap as a New Year gift & in appreciation for all his help & cooperation. He has certainly been very good – a Catholic compound. We loaded the car with an empty drum, a bicycle, a bed and masses of firewood which the nurses had collected. Each TB patient had to bring a small bundle (2 or 3 pieces) of firewood from time to time for their injection so this saved the team having to look for it and it was no hardship for the patients. Each villager is free to collect firewood from the village common ground but the team would have to pay someone to get it for them. At Mbaitoli here we pay 5/- for about 10-12 pieces.

Originally Murray, Alicia, Ann T & I were going to be at Orlu for Hogmanay & a Scots New Year but because of the uncertainty of things we decided not to leave the compound but stay with the staff. Murray was going to Sjouka's away for the evening meal so I don't think he was keen to put himself out for us. Beatrice Waddington had gone back at the weekend & told Alicia that we were all in a stew and that Murray was not having any celebration so Alicia wrote to say she would not be coming. She had a clinic on the Friday and no one had offered to lend her a small car. I was very disappointed because I was very much looking forward to having at least one Scot with me on the last day of the year. This was in fact, the first year in my life with no Scot near me at Hogmanay. I felt it a bit but Victoria was very good & said she would be a Scot for that day & would sing & dance for me. I played What then chess then had a quiet think by myself on the step listening to the quietness and watching the stars with shiny eyes.

We arranged to have a Watchnight Service and I was asked to read the Old Testament lesson from Joshua 1, 5-9. Monica led it, Sister Nwama did the New Testament reading from Revelation 1 and Ann T did the preaching with various nurses taking prayers. Quite a number of people turned up for the service and it was very good finishing at a few minutes past 12 so Monica was able to announce in the New Year. Later she said she was very worried in case they would not finish in time. One of the nurses Ngozi Ugundu prayed on & on & Monica said she opened her eyes and peeped at the clock in front of her. She said she was glad it was 1969 so she would be sinning in the New Year. Later again she discovered the clock was 5 minutes fast so she finished exactly on time so again she said she was glad the girl had prayed for so long, that God must have known the exact time. What a girl! After the service we all came to the house, had a piece of shortbread then opened a bottle of champagne Murray had given us. We all had a taste then Conrad went to bed, Ann T, Vicky & I sat out on the step waiting for Monica so we could sing a hymn before going to bed. When she came she told us this story about prayers & the time & had us in stitches laughing. She kept us waiting because she was busy in the kitchen. She said she had just reached home when her chicken greeted her with "Happy New Year" then "putter putter" it gave up the ghost. So she had immediately plucked it, cleaned it and put it on the fire all in the early hours of New Year's morning as we waited for her. She is a very funny girl at times. We had a good laugh over her antics anyway. This was the sixth chicken to have died in the past 7 or 8 days. Already all 5 of ours died and all Sister Nwama's so there must be a bug going round. An expensive business with chickens costing £12-£14 each but we managed to sell one for £5-10. Monica invited us to have supper with her. We eventually went to bed about 1.30am, tired but in good spirits. At that time silence reigned with all the compound asleep. Not really like Glasgow or Carluke at all!

Despite the war, Ann's journal
records the careful planning
for her friend Victoria Igbokwe's
wedding on 3rd January 1970

NEW YEAR WEDDING
—o.o.—o.o.—

The families of Igbokwe of Amaorie - Obibi Owerri and
Nwokeforo of Idem - Ogwa Owerri
request the pleasure of

Rev. Chief, Mr & Mrs Mr. *Wm. Jackson*

at the Wedding Ceremony of their Daughter and Son
VICTORIA UGWOADUNACHI IGBOKWE
and
FRANCIS UCHECHUKWU NWOKEFORO
on Saturday 3rd Jan 1970
Service begins at 11 a.m at St. Mark's Church Idem - Ogwa.
Light refreshments follow immediately after Service at C.M.S.
School Hall Idem - Ogwa.

Telegrams:
Uche Nwokeforo
C.M.S. Idem - Ogwa
Owerri

R. S. V. P.
F. O. Nwokeforo
Iyi-Enu Hospital
c/o Okija Gram. Sch.
Okija.

Ann and missionary colleagues after
they had been airlifted out of Biafra
on 10th January 1970, en route home

The Journal 1970

Biafra's Last Days

"What a tragic war this is and no-one knows where it will all end."

One of Ann's last journal entries, 2nd January 1970

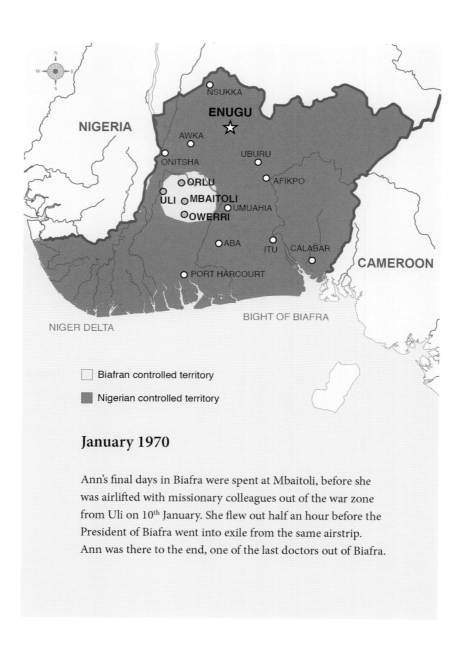

Biafran controlled territory

Nigerian controlled territory

January 1970

Ann's final days in Biafra were spent at Mbaitoli, before she
was airlifted with missionary colleagues out of the war zone
from Uli on 10th January. She flew out half an hour before the
President of Biafra went into exile from the same airstrip.
Ann was there to the end, one of the last doctors out of Biafra.

Timeline 1970

1970	Key Events
Early January	Ann visits clinics, covering large distances by Land Rover, at times only 3 miles from the war front. World Council of Churches sends tents for Ann and her staff in case they have to flee into the bush.
3rd January	Ann attends wedding of nursing colleague and friend, Victoria Igbokwe
4th January	Final journal entry
Second week of January	Southern front of Biafran line of defence breaks, and Nigerian forces advance into heart of Biafran enclave, heading for the airstrip at Uli
8th January	Shelling around Mbaitoli; staff awakened during the night and told to flee
9th January	Ann and colleagues leave Mbaitoli and drive to Orlu; thousands of refugees on the road. World Council of Churches staff and missionaries under its care instructed to wait for a plane. Ann has to make a detour to find a Canadian nurse working at a camp for wounded soldiers and get her to join the departing missionaries.
10th January	Ann drives in convoy to Biafra's only remaining airstrip at Uli. She is on the second to last plane out, flying to São Tomé. General Ojukwu, President of Biafra, flies into exile on the last plane, half an hour after Ann and her missionary colleagues
11th January	Biafra's Acting Head of State, Brigadier-General Effiong, formally surrenders to the Nigerian Government
14th January	Ann arrives at Heathrow Airport, avoiding reporters
15th January	Ann arrives in Glasgow, where her family awaits her
Later in 1970	Four months after return, the Church of Scotland sends Ann as a medical missionary to Malawi, running a hospital

With the New Year, Biafra's symbol of half a yellow sun took on a more fateful meaning. Once the proud emblem of a new and rising nation, emblazoned on its red, black, and green flag, it was now the setting sun of a beleaguered people. As the Nigerian Federal forces closed in around the shrinking territory still under Biafran control, the southern flank of Biafra's defences suddenly collapsed in the second week of January. By the Saturday of that week, its leader had fled the field.

The long feared defeat of an independent Biafran state was finally upon it, after two and a half years of resistance to attack, blockade, bombing, and starvation. The longing for an end to war and civilian suffering was finally met, not through peace talks, as Biafrans hoped, but through military conquest, as Nigeria determined, armed by Britain and the Soviet Union.

Reading the final entries in Ann's journal against this backdrop of looming military and political defeat, we are struck by her singleminded focus on continuing her medical work with her team, even if they are overrun. Ann's last journal entry is about one of her patients. She was there for them to the end, a doctor dedicated to healing and a disciple dedicated to the Healer.

January 1970

Thursday 1ˢᵗ January

<u>New Years Day</u>

A very quiet day for me and a real day off. I rose late – 7.30am, had breakfast and then went back to bed to lie & listen to the news and a BBC programme with Kenneth McKellar introducing Scottish Songs. It was very good. Victoria then came to join me as her room was full of people and many children so she could not have any peace to rest. She had tidied her room, changed her bedding for the New Year so she badgered me into doing the same and she helped me. For weeks now the rubbish has been piling up and there was much sorting needing to be done so at long last, and several hours later, we managed to have a nice tidy clean bedroom. I was very pleased.

Yesterday evening I went to Umuaka Sick Bay to attend patients and Matthew went on to the river to collect water for us in the two big containers. I suggested I take Victoria to Ogwa to check up on the wedding arrangements and to help her to transport her loads. And what a load! On Monday she asked me to pick up her mother on our way home from the clinic and I agreed but when we reached Naze there were about 6 people waiting laden with garri and yams and assorted baggage. I was a bit annoyed but we managed to squeeze everyone onto the pickup. They were bringing the extra food to help with the feeding at the weekend so all these people had to squeeze in to Victoria's room until Friday. Anyway, we took the cartons of yams etc. and her wedding dress etc. and her suitcases to Ogwa for her so she was very pleased. Her sister arrived on New Year's day and she is now several months pregnant and her husband had carried her on the bicycle from Obibi (14-15 miles away). The children are very lively but good fun to have around. Chita Oji moved to her new house today – two rooms near the hospital, part of a building called "Honolulu Bar" and the other 3 sisters are also living there. In the early evening I strolled over with her to see the place and she is very comfortable. She has built a small outhouse for her hens and the two young Army boys assigned to her by her husband, Col. Oje.

In the evening, Conrad, Ann & I & Victoria went to Monica's for a meal and it was very nice yam & beans & pumpkin but a bit peppery. She said that even after all her hard work in the early morning hours the chicken did not taste good so she decided to give us meat instead. We were all very pleased about it and thoroughly enjoyed the meal with no qualms. She gave us a very nice fruit salad with milk afterwards. We were very pleased to be having a meal out because Godson & John had washed all morning and had neglected to leave water for the evening so we could not wash or cook anything. These boys don't seem to think ahead at all. Some scolding done.

We enjoyed our time with Monica playing one or two games amidst much laughter and then we had a short time of fellowship together. In the afternoon Monica had asked each one of us to think about a promise Jesus had made and to say something about it so we each took our turn – Vicky – Everlasting life if we believe on Him. (John's gospel). May God help us to believe, to claim the promise and help us to give others the opportunity to know Him and claim it for themselves. Monica gave the text from II Corinth. "My grace is sufficient for Thee". We are to accept the thorn in the flesh, to overcome & give a good witness in spite of it and to remember always that God's grace is available for each one of us. Ann J. – the communion promise – "come unto me all ye who labour & are heavy laden & I will give you rest". We struggle on, we try by ourselves, we feel tired & wearied & sometimes are too wearied to say our prayers, to attend worship. Yet it is only when we do go to God with our problems & weaknesses that we can find rest and strength. Come unto me and don't struggle by yourselves.

Conrad was not sure of what we meant but he enjoyed listening and we all felt refreshed and happy. We sang a hymn 603 then had a reading from Daily Light and I finished with prayer. It was a very good evening of fun and fellowship together. Vicky moved in to my room & slept on the camp-bed so her sister could have her bed.

Friday 2nd January

The Obendi Agwa team went to Awa to do a clinic and Sister Oje went with them but they were very late in leaving the compound. It seems they do not hurry themselves in the morning and are not organized so I have said that come Monday both teams will report at 7a.m. and we will attend prayers at 7.15am and leave the compound at 7.30 sharp. I do hope it works out because we will need to return home about 2pm each day in case of any eventuality and with both vehicles in use each day.

Eliza and nurse Onyechi did tablets for a time with Victoria who was becoming excited & anxious about her wedding preparations. I suppose I was too because I was bickering at her all the time. I insisted she wear her uniform and help with the tablets for a time but I fully intended letting her off to prepare her clothes and hair. Poor soul I did not tell her this so she thought I was going to make her work all morning and she was not pleased. Maybe I bend over backwards not to give her favours yet other nurses would expect to be off duty that morning. I did not want to give anyone the chance to criticize but I should have explained my actions to her. Onyechi and Eliza were later sent to Out Patients Department to help there because of the shortage of staff – many nurses (pupil midwives especially) have left to be married and many are off sick. Resistance is so low these days that the least thing puts a person on their back & off duty for days. We have 3 nurses in the Sickbay and one is in the Gynae Ward and is quite serious with abdominal pains & fever but no definite diagnosis has been made.

Victoria had her hair stretched then put in curlers, then she ironed her clothes & packed her bags – a sad sight and I will miss her even altho' she will only be away for one week. I'm sure we will all miss her here – Monica, Ann T, Godson & I because she is always in & out this house and is always bright and smiling.

During the day the Norwegian girl Clara who works with Brechté Tolkuts at Etiti arrived in the Queen Elizabeth Hospital with Earnest the driver and a note from Murray. It seems there was a push from across the Imo and at 9pm the past evening they had received a note from Wendy Ijema telling them to evacuate at once. Wendy & Sam had received word from a senior army man so they spent the night evacuating their big WCC store and had previously found a new site to go to. Brechté sent all her nurses to relatives or to a refugee camp, Clara went to Orlu & Murray went down with Brechté to help evacuate the Terre des Hommes Sickbay which had 350-400 children. It's uncertain whether the bridge has been blown or not.

Poor Brechté – it seems this is her 5th evacuation and she is now determined to carry on & do Sickbays with herself and the driver Sam – faithful Sam. Clara was tired & a bit excited but was keen to see over the famous Queen Elizabeth Hospital hospital. In the note Murray asked Ann T. to go up to discuss the situation and go to see the proposed evacuation site for the hospital. Needless to say, this depressed us all very much but we did not discuss it much for fear of starting a panic among our own staff. There was hurry scurry as Ann collected her things & left for Orlu but the hospital here was very quiet except for the normal crying of the children nearby in the ward.

Before she left Ann cycled to the place where Samuel's mother was staying. Poor woman, since the funeral she has been distraught and half crazy with grief and no-one has been able to communicate with her. She paced round & round the small room in the village, crying, screaming, moaning, refusing to eat or drink and everyone has been concerned about her. Thanks be to God she recovered, became sensible, apologised to Ann for her poor behavior & said she would try to live for her other son. Poor woman she is only one of many unable to comprehend the awfulness of this situation. What a tragic war this is and no-one knows where it will all end.

Saturday 3rd January

<u>Victoria's wedding day.</u>

At 10.15am we all set off in the landrover for Idem Ogwa – packed in like sardines about 15 of us plus the bicycle & the two big water containers because Ogwa has tap water and enough to spare. Monica took the bicycle because she was on duty at 1pm but did not want to miss the wedding. Sister Oje, Ebelimi, Nwama, Pepple all came with the nurses. Driver Matthew took us and he is happier this morning because he now has a room. These past weekends when he visited us he slept in the sitting room next door and we fed him but now we are operating both clinics from Mbaitoli he needed a place to sleep permanently. John, Koppert's cook, said he had 5 people sleeping in his room so there was no place for Matthew. Mind you many of these people are not hospital workers but hangers-on who followed us from Umuahia. Dear knows who is feeding them even. Anyway, Matthew came to me yesterday & said John did not welcome him & he would rather stay on my compound & begged me to let him sleep in the small cubby hole where we keep the firewood. Poor soul he is willing to go anywhere. Ann T. gave John a long lecture about being non Biafran & non Christian rejecting a stranger like this and it really was too bad. Ann & I were going to give him a tent but he wanted to erect it in our backyard. However, Paul the cook to Dr Abengowe agreed to let him share his room so he is happy.

We all arrived at Ogwa in time and Victoria was in the small room surrounded by her sister & attendants, all fluttering around her. She really looked lovely and was quite calm and composed. The bridesmaids were lovely in their deep pink dresses with white lace trimmings. Ugochi and Chinyere were all excited. We greeted her then went to the [Anglican] Church, St Mark's Church Missionary Society Church Idem-Ogwa, which is a fairly new building & not quite completed. A Canon & Rev. Okue conducted the service in Ibo and it was quiet and fairly short. I took photos and I hope they will come out good. A very English service really, signing the register & the usual group photographs. Uche asked me to join the family group photograph so I was very pleased. They made a lovely couple and wedding group so I was thankful to see this happy event come to fruition. After the service we went to the school hall for the reception & had to wait a very long time. Native drums were beating & some guests were dancing but I was feeling hungry & very thirsty & was impatient. Eventually the wedding party came and I was invited to sit at the high table so I got a good view of the young couple. Uche seemed quite excited & kept frowning his face but Victoria was quite composed. We were served chin chin, formula balls, roast goat on a stick, palm wine and a piece of wedding cake. It was very good and there seemed to be a lot to eat & drink. The wine used as the toast was very strong – probably home made Brandy but it burned! Goodwill speeches were made and Rev Okere mentioned my help given to him in December 1968 when we tried to get Victoria out of Nigerian occupied territory – OBIBI. Uche thanked me for all the help & encouragement I had given them both in planning & preparing for the wedding. He did it all in Igbo so I don't really know what he was saying. After the speeches the tradition is for friends & relatives to give gifts of money & the amount is announced to the assembly. Uche's dad gave £50, his mother £20, Vicky's mother gave £85, her brother in law £42 and so on and I later learned that the sum collected was over £600. It's especially good at this time. We left the wedding before it really finished because Koppert was worried about some patients. Victoria gave me a roasted chicken to take home with me. She looked very happy there with Uche in the midst of their people. I will miss her very much though.

When we returned to the hospital compound we learned that one Staff Nurse Mercy Nwanah who was a member of Team 2 & who has been ill in the Gynae Ward, took a syncopal attack & was in a serious condition. She had to be taken to Emekuku Hospital that evening so Prof. could operate under good conditions i.e. electric light & General Anaesthesia. Matthew set off with his landrover, the nurse & a friend & the Prof.

Ann Travis & Murray arrived back later but with no real news. Murray is still very anxious about the situation yet he seems to be more in a flap than doing anything to help us. He could explore possibilities up beyond Orlu yet he seems hesitant to do anything. He seems to have given up hope & wants only for us to make for the airport but I for one do not agree with this. I feel we should have a safe place to go to, off the main road, tucked quietly away somewhere & we would take our destitute or refugee staff then try to redeploy them and continue as a medical team. Even in the event of our being over-run I would still want to wait until things quieten down and then try to continue as far as possible with medical work. The need will be even greater then and I don't think anarchy will prevail if things collapse and I'm sure there are enough drugs in the country to keep the teams going for sometime. I will try to speak to Sandy Sommerville & find out what he says about our future and emergency plans. I hope we can agree on this matter. I certainly don't want to run to the airport & abandon all my friends & my work here. I could not behave dishonourably even to save my own life. May God give us the wisdom and strength to do the right thing.

Ann T. received a note from the Professor written at Emekuku to say that the nurse had gone through an emergency operation, had 3 pints of blood and that it was an ovarian cyst and abscess that caused the trouble. She also had fibroids which could be removed at a later date. He asked Ann T. to collect him at 10.30pm & visit the nurse who was in a serious condition. Poor Ann! I had just given her a Phenergan tablet to let her have a good night's sleep so she was feeling very dopey by 10.30pm. She set off with two nurse friends to visit the girl and I went to bed. She says she returned at 1am but I did not hear her come in but she was quite quiet & anxious only to get to bed. The nurse was improving and we thank God she was spared because with the death of Samuel less than a week away, and the depressing war news and the arrival here of old labourers who were with us in Umuahia now fleeing from that area, the morale is very low. Ann said she met a UBTH [University of Benin Teaching Hospital] nurse who used to be with us in Umuahia & she said quite calmly & matter of factly that before Anne Bent could return the whole country would be run and "liberated" by the vandals.

A surprising statement & we wonder if this is the general feeling & sentiments of the UBTH staff. Emekuku is now near a disturbed area, plans have been made for their evacuation so I'm sure they are all in a state of tension & disquiet. As soon as Emekuku evacuates then Queen Elizabeth Hospital at Mbaitoli will move as well because once Emekuku & Owerri is taken then we are on a straight road from there. Emekuku Hospital is now run by the Rev Sisters in the Maternity Section and UBTH with the rest – mainly children and surgical cases. They have 200 patients in each ward and it was pathetic to see them. Young men, emaciated, lying on beds, on mats on the floor, on bamboo beds with their assorted wounds from bullets and shells. They all seemed very cheery yet it was all very strange with the shaded electric lights showing them up in funny colours – orange & green & unnatural somehow. In the children's ward we saw 19 or 20 patients some mothers with their children sitting & lying on the floor in the middle of the ward looking very desolate. They had been admitted 4 days previously with injuries sustained when their village was bombed & strafed by the Nigerian Mig fighters – Ulahwa village where we used to do our clinic. We saw Sister Ibezie who used to be at Queen Elizabeth Hospital with us in the children's ward. She now has a 6 month old son but her husband Captn (Dr) Ibezie is now cut off behind the lines and she has had no news of him so poor soul she must be very worried and there must be thousands of troops in the same position. They are a very fine young couple and I hope nothing happens to him.

We carried Victoria's sister Phoebe with us to the hospital where she works in the Intensive care Unit but she is now on nights off. She wanted to collect her suitcase & bring it to us in Mbaitoli in case anything happened in Emekuku side. Already she has brought her two children Chinyere and Ugochi to stay with Victoria and she, herself, is pregnant so feels she will now have only herself to worry about in the event of an emergency. So Uche got a wife and two nieces dumped on him on January 3rd but no doubt in true Biafran fashion he will expect & accept this responsibility of the extended family.

We had to wait a long time for Professor Ogan but eventually he arrived so we travelled back to Queen Elizabeth Hospital [medical team base]– very tired & hungry and anxious to get to bed. I have added to Saturday's notes some events & comments of Sunday.

Sunday 4th January

Prof. Ogan, Ann T, Sisters Oje & Pepple & I all went after church to visit the nurse and a boy Harrison who has been lying in Emekuku for some time. We took Phoebe with us as stated. Harrison has an infected abscess in his thigh after a chloroquine injection here in the hospital. It then progressed to a septic arthritis of his knee so was transferred for physiotherapy. He has languished there for almost 3 months but has grown in length and is not as emaciated as I would have expected. The patients are now getting two meals per day so that's not too bad. So ends Saturday and Sunday!

(Signed)
Ann W Jackson

CAMP FOR WOUNDED SOLDIERS.
DIANE, CANADIAN NURSE THERE
JAN 1970

WE FLED FROM HERE
SAT, JANUARY, 1970.
BIAFRA COLLAPSED ON THE SUNDAY

As Ann was fleeing from Mbaitoli to her airlift out of Biafra
from Uli airstrip, she made a brave detour to this camp
to rescue a stranded Canadian nurse

And so ends Biafra. The British journalist Frederick Forsyth covered the war on the Biafran side. This is what he later wrote about those last days in January 1970:

> Then in the second week of January 1970 Biafra collapsed. It came quite suddenly. A unit on the southern front, exhausted beyond caring and out of ammunition, quietly stripped off its uniforms and faded into the bush. Units on either side of the missing men took fright and followed suit. Soon a gaping hole ran along the entire defence line from Aba city to Okpuala Bridge. A Nigerian armoured-car patrol, probing north, met no opposition and rolled forward. Within a day the front was breached. Colonel Obasanjo's Third Nigerian Division rolled forward into the heart of the Biafran enclave, heading for the airstrip at Uli. There was no opposition; men who had not eaten for days had no strength left to go on fighting.
>
> In a last cabinet meeting on 10 January General Ojukwu listened to his advisors for the last time. Their advice was unanimous. To stay and die would be futile; to stay and be hunted through the bush would bring further misery to the entire population. That evening, after darkness had fallen, he drove to Uli as the Nigerian guns rumbled on the southern front. With a small group of colleagues, he boarded the Biafran Super Constellation, the Grey Ghost, and flew out into lonely exile. Brigadier-General Effiong, taking over as acting head of state, sought surrender terms twenty-four hours later. The long struggle was over.

On that same Saturday 10th January 1970 Ann also made her way to the airstrip at Uli. The World Council of Churches had arranged a small plane to airlift Ann and her fellow medical missionaries to safety. With her colleagues, Ann Jackson was the last doctor out of Biafra, just half an hour before General Ojukwu. She stood by its people to the end.

Only four months after she escaped from Biafra, Ann was sent
by the Church of Scotland to run a maternity hospital in Malawi.
This is Ann at the mission hospital in May 1972. Along with
fulfilling her responsibilities as a senior doctor in Malawi and back
in Scotland, Ann has lived with health problems from her years in
Biafra, strengthened by prayer for healing.

Afterword

Dr Ann W. Jackson MRCOG

When Dr Ann Jackson and her Scottish missionary colleagues flew back into London from Biafra on January 14th 1970, the news reporters and camera crew from the BBC were waiting for them at Heathrow airport to scoop their story. As Ann sat waiting for her connecting flight home to Glasgow and her family, the reporters scurried passed her, unnoticed. Incongruous in her summer dress for the heat of Africa, she did not fit their image of a heroic doctor fleeing a war zone.

Ann was hiding in plain sight because for her, the story was never about Ann Jackson. She respected the Church of Scotland's wish to the very end – she remained incognito as a missionary in Biafra even after she left her beloved country. She has remained incognito ever since, until now and the publication of her journal.

But how does Ann see her own story as a doctor in Biafra? After she returned to Scotland, she was asked by the Church of Scotland to go back to Africa, this time to run a maternity hospital in Malawi. Throughout all Ann's years of service as a missionary, first in Nigeria, then in Biafra, and finally in Malawi, she gave talks on her Christian faith to church audiences around Scotland. We close this book with the notes from one such talk. Like her journal, it is Ann's testimony to her Saviour.

Waiting on our LORD

ISAIAH 40: 25-31 Nigeria & Malawi

HAVE YOU NOT KNOWN? *Have you not heard that the everlasting God, the LORD, the Creator of all things, faints not, neither is weary?*

This is God's answer to His people who cry in Verse 27 "My plight is hidden from the Lord and my cause has passed out of God's notice."

God does not seem to be concerned with their problems.

Sometimes we feel that God must be weary – tired of this world of ours – with wars and rumours of war, with strife, strikes, unrest the problems and unhappiness of His people today. There are times in our own lives when we cry out "where is God in our situation?"

"Has my cause passed out of God's notice?"

Tonight, I would like to share with you some of my own experiences when I cried out to God. – and how He answered. His answer is still the same!

In 1966 I set out as a missionary of the Church of Scotland to Nigeria. I was young, enthusiastic, full of God's love for me and for His people in Africa. I wanted to show forth His love in my medical work – I was not a good speaker, I found it hard to talk of my faith but I felt my work would be my witness.

My first year in Nigeria was full of hard work and homesickness but God kept His promises to me – "My grace is sufficient for you – for my strength is made perfect in weakness".

I had a lot to learn as a doctor and as a missionary and it was a hard year. Overwork and ill health brought me home after one year for a short leave. I came home in April.

In May Biafra declared independence and plans were made for me to go to Ghana. I was so sure God wanted me in Nigeria but I did wait on Him and I was asked if I would like to return in September to Nigeria – under cover, thro' Cameroon and I went back with two male colleagues.

Most of you will remember Biafra and the pictures. No story can be as awful or as horrible as it was. Thousands did die of starvation and neglect – caught up as the war progressed and Biafra dwindled to a few square miles.

I spent 3 years in the midst of the war – in the midst of suffering and death – I came home every 6 months or so for a break. [I worked first in Mary Slessor Hospital, Itu and then] I was in charge of the children's work in Queen Elizabeth Hospital, Umuahia. I was involved in refugee camps. Each month I filled out the Report – a death Register – usually I did it after church on Sunday. 24 bed ward. 120-150 patients, 40-60 deaths each month. Anaemia, casualties from the daily air raids on Umuahia & district. Throughout the Biafran War – I heard many people here at home ask why?

Bewildered Biafrans cried out "My plight is hidden from the Lord and my cause has passed out of God's notice"

Many people seemed to think that because I was a missionary in the situation, I would have all the answers. I was asked to explain the situation, give facts and help people in Scotland to understand and accept the suffering.

As a believing Christian – who never doubted God's Word or His Promises, I could only say "God does not weary or grow faint". He is still Lord, He is still in control and He is working out His purpose. Wait on the Lord.

One day in Carluke I met an old lady, I was due to return to Biafra the following week –

"God knows why you're going back there, hen?" Irreverently said, but that was my only answer. God knows why!

Deep down in my heart, I asked why? I believed God was there in the midst of it all – giving us grace and strength to live through it. It took me years to accept it wholly as God's will, that there was purpose in it all. He has to teach us to accept His Plan for the world. He has to teach us to be obedient without knowing all the answers.

The victorious Nigerian Government would not let me back to my friends in the Eastern Region. The Church of Scotland asked me to go to Malawi, to take charge of a very busy hospital with a great reputation as a midwifery school and a hospital. Good relationships with the Malawians, 2 Doctors, 5 European sisters, 26 student midwives to cope with 2000 deliveries each year. Busier than Falkirk Royal – Your own Joy Fraser [was one of my colleagues].

It was so different from Biafra.

There was a lot of work – but constructive – a new Maternity Hospital to plan, under fives clinics, basic Maternity work and a real need for missionaries in the situation.

God was so obviously blessing the work, everyone worked as a team and the hospital was booming. There were problems, disappointments and frustration – but God was there in the midst.

When we failed it was because we were carried away with our own work – putting in the hours, doing successful operations and not taking time to wait on the Lord. We tried to do too much in our own strength – I forgot at times that it is God's work – and I only have a part to play.

Many times His Answer was to humble us – show us that it is His Work and He is in full control.

I remember the day we had a woman – near to death with a ruptured ectopic pregnancy. She was admitted, assessed, a drip set up and theatre organized in a very short time. We operated – collected 8 pints of blood from the woman's abdomen – unheard of in this country – filtered it and re-transfused 6 pints via the drip. There was prayer before operation and real teamwork. The woman lived – God really was working in the midst of us. By our own efforts she should not have lived. I considered it a real miracle and we thanked God for it. And what now?

Only God can help them. His is the answer and we need to tell them so. The message is the same – God sent His Son to save us from our sins and restore us to a right relationship with Him.

The Lord Jesus Christ, this Saviour, is in our situation – in our home, in the office, in the consulting room – He will give us all the answers we need if we acknowledge Him as Saviour and Lord.

I don't cry out the way I used to in Biafra – but I do wonder as I am faced with situations with people who seem to be abandoned by God – who don't really expect help from Him or from us. – Just like that wee boy by the roadside in Biafra. I wonder what will God do.

We can be so busy wondering and busying ourselves trying to give answers – we can be carried away by our own efforts. Be a good Christian & do what we can – a kind word, a good deed – yet in our hearts be a little despairing for the situation and for the people we are trying to help. God is in our midst, working out His Purpose. We need to wait on Him, day by day, be prepared to change our ideas and our ways, <u>to be fully obedient to Him.</u>

"Have you not known? Have you not heard that the everlasting God <u>the Lord</u>, the <u>Creator of all things,</u> faints not, neither is weary."

He is our Saviour – He is our Lord – and we are asked to wait on Him to renew our strength.

Ann's love for Africa shines through, even today

Jesus of Africa

Jesus of the desert,
wrestling with the devil,
give us your strength.

Jesus the Rock,
broken for us,
build us together.

Jesus of nail and wire,
bleeding for us,
cleanse us and wash us clean.

Jesus of Africa,
hope of the world,
lift us up to the light
and power of your resurrection.

Amen

A prayer evoked by a sculpture of the Cross in the Faculty of Theology,
University of Stellenbosch, South Africa
– made from stone and barbed wire found in the Karoo desert.

William Storrar,
Visiting Professor, University of Stellenbosch, 2009-2018

Joanna Storrar,
Fundraising Consultant to the University of Stellenbosch, 2019